FLANDERS

Landscapes of the Imagination

Landscapes

FLANDERS

A Cultural History

ANDRÉ DE VRIES

Signal Books
Oxford

First published in 2007 by
Signal Books Limited
36 Minster Road
Oxford OX4 1LY
www.signalbooks.co.uk

A catalogue record for this book is available from the British Library

ISBN 1-904955-28-2 Paper

Cover Design: Baseline Arts
Cover Images: courtesy Toerisme Brugge; Baseline Arts
Production & Design: Devdan Sen
Photographs © frontispiece, p.125, 129 Toerisme Brugge; p.xii Jeroen Peys/istockphoto; p.2
Toerisme Limburg; p.16 WWI Image Archive, gwpda.com; p.23 Josee Dens
vickysgallery.fotopic.net; p.30 Toerisme West-Vlaanderen; p.40 Wendy Skinner Smith; p.42,
188, 235 Marie-Jeanne Smets; p.47, 57 Sportimonium; p.49 Paul Ilegems; p.72 Pictures
Tourist Office of Ghent; p.98 Derek Blyth; p.102 Wim Kooyman, Duo Foto; p.115, 190,
Technifoto Van Wambeke; p.118 Charles Wade; p.149 Michael Wright/istockphoto; p.152
Tijl Capoen; p.168 Daniël de Kievith; p.172 Peter De Rycke; p.183 James & Co; p.192
Antwerpen Toerisme; p.198 Marc Vermeirsch/istockphoto; p.210 Antwerpen Toerisme; p.228
BITC O. van de Kerchove, Brussels International; p.240 Marnix Van Esbroeck; p.244
Stephan Jennart; p.249 Eddy Daniels; p.256 Nico Limmen/istockphoto; p.262 VVV Sluis;
p.266 Vincent Vanberkel; p.275 Ville de Dunkerque

Printed in India

CONTENTS

Acknowledgements

This book is informed by discussions with numerous experts in Flemish culture and support of many Flemish friends and colleagues, none of whom is in any way responsible for any opinions expressed here.

I learned much from discussions with the following: Derek Blyth, Toon Brouwers, Peter Burnett, Leo Camerlynck, Patricia Carson, Peter Flynn, Prof. Jan Kerkhofs, Stan Lauryssens, Anne-Marie Lontie, Leen Meganck, André Posman, Lucien Posman, Hugo Ryckeboer, Bart van der Herten, Geert Van Istendael, Kristof van Mierop, Erik Verdonck, Jacques Vermeulen and Marc Vuylsteke. In Antwerp, Paul Ilegems initiated me into the world of deep *frietkot* culture, as well as Flemish modern art. Jonathan Howett and Nick Andrews showed me real Antwerp hospitality. Danny Bossaer and Jan Van Snick were kind enough to share their memories of Marvin Gaye with me.

A number of experts in their respective fields gave me the benefit of their knowledge: Frank Deijnckens of the Antwerp Tourist Office, Anne de Meerleer of the Bruges Tourist Office, Luc Devoldere of Stichting Ons Erfdeel, the members of the Eine Heemkundige Kring, Marc Laridon and the Michiel de Swaene Kring, Leen Coene of Lange Nelle Gidsenkring in Ostend and Evelyn Cluyt of Vizit Gent vzw, Werner Van Hooft of the Antwerp Museum of Folklore and Yvette Kemel of Brugsche Heemkundige Kring.

I am especially grateful to Geert Vandamme of vzw De Trap in Ghent for his unstinting support with the writing of this book, and equally Filip Demeyer and Anton Stevens for their important contributions at a late stage in the writing. I learned a great deal concerning the geography and geology of Flanders from Professors Roger Nijs, Luc Daels and Marc Antrop. In French Flanders, Jean-Noël Ternynck and Jacques Messiant shared their vision of Flanders with me. John Beauval expanded my knowledge of Flemish café life. Sergei Mouraviev willingly undertook the task of sampling and describing all kinds of Flemish beer. My sister, Claire de Vries, kindly loaned me her collection of books on Flanders.

The photographs for this book come from a number of sources. I would particularly like to thank Peter De Rycke, Vicky Dens and

Marie-Jeanne Smets for their fine photos.

This book was made possibly by the timely intervention of my two muses: Dr. Betty de Meerleer shared her great knowledge of Flemish culture with me, while Bernadette Hillaert visited many of the locations in this book with me, and taught me much about grassroots Flemish culture. Mary Jackson was always there with practical help. The Centre d'Etudes Tibétaines in Brussels was as ever a home from home. I am indebted to my publisher, James Ferguson, for keeping it all going.

Finally, I should like to record my immense debt to Jacqueline de Clercq and the late René Batslé, for their many years of moral support and Burgundian hospitality.

Introduction

My Mostly Flat Country

"You Belgians of Germanic tongue, of Gallic corruption,
You non-entrepreneurial Netherlanders, you unfrivolous French persons,
You sturdy, bombastic, realistic, short-sighted folk!"
Geert van Istendael, *Vlaanderen* (Flanders), 1990

Where is Flanders?

The Brussels singer-songwriter Jacques Brel (whose family came from Ypres in West Flanders) had a popular song in the early 1960s in which he rhapsodizes about *mon plat pays* or "my flat country". Flanders is not all flat—there are hilly parts in the south-west, but flatness and the proximity of the sea have profoundly influenced its history and character. Nor has Flanders ever been a neat geographical entity. When the term first appeared in the seventh century AD, it referred only to a strip of coastline between Bruges and the North Sea, including the former Roman fortress of Aardenburg. Since then the word has taken over more and more territory, until now it is routinely used for the whole of Dutch-speaking Belgium, an administrative Region of some six million people that dominates the rest of the country both economically and linguistically. At the same time, and rather confusingly, there is the Flemish Community, an official entity established in the 1960s to deal with all matters connected with the use of the Dutch language in Flanders, in particular education and culture. The modern Flemish Region has as many as 350,000 French-speakers, who also consider themselves Flemish.

While Flanders has expanded, the term "the Low Countries" is used less and less these days. Corresponding to the Dutch "de Lage Landen", it referred originally to low-lying areas on the great river deltas of the Scheldt, Maas and Rhine between Dunkirk and Schleswig-Holstein in northern Germany. At one time the designation was taken to include the states of Belgium, the Netherlands and Luxembourg, but these are now more commonly known as the Benelux, a term coined in 1948 when the three countries entered into a customs union. The expression the Low

Countries lives on as a catch-all word for Belgium and the Netherlands and their common cultural heritage, which is somehow assumed to be influenced by the lowness of the landscape.

Flanders is both a geopolitical unit and a mythical place that lives outside its political boundaries. Part of its evocative, almost poetic presence comes from associations with the First World War, and for many the poetry of "Flanders Fields" defines the place above all else. Yet the mystique of Flanders is most fervently adopted by those who identify with the idea of being Flemish, especially those who live in the former territories of the County of Flanders in northern France or the south-west Netherlands, while many who live in Belgian Flanders are far less certain about the desirability of a future independent Flemish nation.

Blame for the vagueness of the term can be attributed to a lack of natural boundaries that might otherwise define Flanders. In his classic work on Flemish geography, *La Flandre* (1906), Raoul Blanchard refers to the "exaggerated extension of the name 'Flanders'". Borders have historically expanded and contracted. The River Aa in the French *département* of the Nord ending at the port of Gravelines was the medieval boundary. A little to the north is a long chain of hills running from Dunkirk along the Belgian border and then curving northwards to Ronse and the Flemish Ardennes. North and east there are no obstructions other than the sea and the estuary of the River Scheldt. The absence of natural boundaries has been decisive in the history of Flanders. If its early counts managed to keep Flanders independent by expanding aggressively in all directions, there was nothing in later centuries to stop foreign invaders from walking in.

Flanders Mud

The Flemish have had to work very hard to make something out of what they were given by nature. While Flanders appears to be quite fertile, the Flemish were less fortunate than those in the southern French-speaking half of Belgium. Starting 55 million years ago in the Tertiary era, almost all of Belgium was under the sea, and below the sea was a layer of clay some 330 feet deep. Further flooding over thirty million years deposited more layers of clay. The Ice Ages that began two million years ago caused the sea level to drop drastically, so much so that it would have been possible to walk from Belgium to England. The big freeze also increased

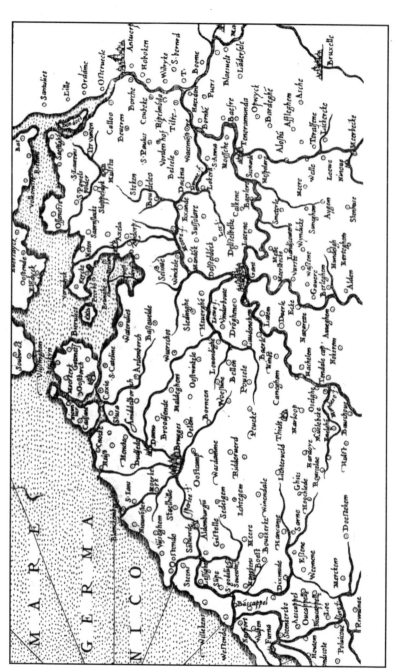

Paolo Forlani, *Flanders*, Verona, 1567.

the rate of flow of the main rivers, the Scheldt and the Leie, which in turn carved out deep valleys. These were filled by shifting sand and particles of loam blown by the north wind, but as sand is heavier than loam and travels a shorter distance, most of the sand ended up in Flanders, roughly down to a line north of Ghent, while the more valuable loam soils blew further south. Some of the better soil ended up in south-west Flanders and east of the Scheldt, with the best landing between Veurne and Diksmuide. There are also regions of heavy clay, where the original Tertiary deposits have not been covered by later wind-blown soil, in particular around Ypres and further south—as the soldiers of the First World War discovered.

The Flemish coast as it appears today looked very different in the past. A whole swathe of coast from Cap Gris Nez in France as far as the Kempen in Limburg first emerged from the sea around 2000 BC. When Julius Caesar arrived in 57 BC, the coast extended at least a mile further out to sea. In the Roman era the coastline was affected by a lengthy period of flooding caused by global warming. What is known as the First Dunkirk Transgression came to an end in the first century AD. The coastal plain was at the time mostly made up of peat, protected by a cordon of dunes. The Second Dunkirk Transgression took place in the third and fourth centuries, so that the whole coastal region had to be abandoned. At this time there were wide channels running inland as far as Diksmuide and Bruges. The channels silted up and created a new landscape of salt meadows, the *schorren*, only suitable for grazing sheep. It takes about sixty years for the salt to be washed out of *schorren*. Once the land dried out, and with the end of the Viking menace in 900 AD, there came a period of rapid economic expansion and population growth, which led to large-scale deforestation and the creation of *wastinas* or heathlands. These are visible on old maps on the border of East and West Flanders where they appear under the name of "veld", meaning not "field" but "wasteland" in Flanders.

The Third Dunkirk Transgression lasted from 1000 to 1150 and destroyed many of the sea defences that had been built. The flooding had the effect of clearing a channel almost all the way to Bruges, the Zwin, as well as widening the Scheldt estuary, making it possible for Antwerp to develop as a port. More flooding in the fourteenth and fifteenth centuries washed away islands at the mouth of the Scheldt and cleared wider channels to Antwerp.

The Name Flanders

How the region came to be called "Flanders" is the subject of some debate. The Huguenot writer Marius D'Assigny suggested in his *History of the Earls and Earldom of Flanders* (1701) that the name might have something to do with flans or *vlaaien*:

> Some are of the Opinion, that it hath borrowed this name from Flandebert, a nephew of Clodion the Hairy, second King of France. Others think it took its Name from Flandrina, the wife of Liderick, second Forester of Flanders… Others take it from the Nature of the Soil, which is wet and marshy, and because it is round and appears as a Tart, which in that Country Language is called Vlaemen or Vlayen.

Lideric the Forester (750-800?) was the semi-mythical great-grandfather of the first historical Count of Flanders, Baldwin I, and Matilda, wife of William the Conqueror, and the subject of Alexandre Dumas *père's Aventures de Lyderic, Comte de Flandre* (1842). The Counts of Flanders were very concerned with preserving their hunting forests, hence the acquisition of the name "foresters". A popular notion also suggests that the word Flanders derives from the Flemish word *vlak* or flat, but a more scholarly view has it that it really comes from *flam*, meaning a marsh. It could be that the coastal peoples of West Flanders, the Menapii, lived on islands surrounded by marshes that were often flooded by the sea and so were called *flaming*.

Who Are the Flemish?

There are two ways to define the Flemish: by ethnicity or by language. The Flemish are not purely Germanic but are in large part descended from the Franks who moved from Franconia in Germany into areas left open to them by the Romans from the third century AD. The first people of whom we have any historical record were Celts who came from southern Germany in the seventh century BC, although their original home was much further to the south-east. They were soon conquered by the Belgae, who were most likely semi-Germanic tribes speaking a Celtic language. On the evidence of place names, the population of northern Belgium in the Roman era was a mixture of Germans and Celts, who spoke Celtic languages. They cannot be described as "Flemish", nor were they Gauls. The south of Belgium was inhabited by a Celtic Alpine type, darker than the Germans. Because of large-scale population movements between different parts of Belgium, there is no longer any clear physical difference between Dutch- and French-speakers. There are almost as many blue-eyed blond individuals in Wallonia (the French-speaking area of Belgium) as there are in Flanders.

One generalization that one can safely make about the Flemish is that they do not like people making generalizations about them. Even so, there are still certain characteristic features that define Flemish culture and which are still to be found everywhere in Belgian Flanders and French Flanders, but less so in Dutch Flanders. These—for the most part icons of popular culture and folklore—include belfries (towers with bells), fancy-dress giants in processions, retables (portable shrines), certain types of café games, archery, puppet shows, beer, waffles, roadside chapels and devotion to the Catholic Church (although this is disappearing rapidly). Flemish society has become increasingly secularized, but folklore still rears its head on important occasions. The belforts or belfries remain in many larger towns as permanent symbols of independence and rebelliousness, while beer, waffles and carnival processions are timeless signifiers of Flemish identity. We shall encounter these iconic emblems of Flemishness in later chapters.

Flemings perhaps define themselves first and foremost by their language, and allegiance to their village or town. They also tend to believe that Flanders is a good place to live, where one can eat and drink well: witness the world-famous chips (or "French" fries), waffles, chocolates and beer. Significantly enough, the term "Burgundian" appears increasingly often in Flemish promotional literature for tourists, used almost as a synonym for Flemishness. While the word derives from the period when Flanders was ruled by the Dukes of Burgundy (1382-1482), it has now taken on the meaning of uninhibited pleasure and indulgence, lack of dogmatism and perhaps even lack of artificial restraints.

Flemish and French-Speakers

The dual identity of Belgium as both Celtic and Germanic was emphasized by nineteenth-century Belgian historians who wanted to promote the idea of this duality as a source of strength. The reality, alas, is rather that the two cultures have never been happy bedfellows in the unified Belgian kingdom founded in 1830. Belgium lies on the fault-line between Latin and Germanic languages and cultures; one of its unique features is the mixing of French and Dutch languages in some areas, especially Brussels, where history and politics have encouraged the imposition of French on the Dutch-speakers (namely, the Flemish). Dutch-speakers, for their part, have worked in recent times to rid their language of French influences, but these are now too deeply embedded to disappear entirely.

The Flemish have had an awkward relationship with French language and culture since the early Middle Ages, when Flanders came under French sovereignty. There is a large difference, moreover, between how the Flemish view the Walloons (the French-speaking Belgians) and the French in France. There is also some resentment against those Flemish who gave up their language and adopted French to better themselves socially, unless they were forced to do so from economic need. Hostility to the French, as opposed to French-speaking Belgians, increased during the seventeenth and eighteenth centuries, fuelled by regular invasions from France that culminated in the conquest of all of Belgium in 1794 by French revolutionaries. The French occupiers stripped Flanders of its wealth and forced its sons to serve in Napoleon's armies. A common French tactic was to take Flemish farmers' goods in exchange for worthless banknotes. The occupation of Flanders until 1814 and the French-dominated culture imposed on the Flemish from Belgian independence in 1830 delayed the revival of Flemish culture, and left the Flemish with a distinct complex in regard to their southern neighbours.

There is a nineteenth-century saying in Flanders, "Wat Walsch is, Valsch is" (Everything Walloon is false), which arose at a time when many Flemish were forced to migrate to Wallonia. Tensions between the Germanic Flemish and the Celtic Walloons continue to threaten the survival of the Belgian state. Outsiders tend to characterize this as an "ethnic" problem, but it is probably more a question of differing temperaments than ethnicity as such. The flatness of most of the Flemish landscape contrasts with the hilly areas of Belgium occupied by the Walloons. It is therefore said that there is nothing to hide behind in Flanders; you can see to the horizon and what you see is what you get. The Flemish like to contrast their straightforward manner of communicating with what they believe to be the more fanciful or rhetorical style that they attribute to the Walloons (who of course have the whole weight of French culture behind them).

It is perhaps not by chance that the Flemish Primitives, with Jan van Eyck as their greatest representative, pioneered a style of hyper-realist painting that was in complete contrast to the idealized art of the Italian Renaissance. Pieter Brueghel the Elder introduced humanism and social commentary into his painting, and in so doing created some of the most widely recognized images in the modern world. The third great Flemish pioneer, Peter-Paul Rubens, was a pivotal figure, combining Renaissance and classical models with Flemish energy and vitality. Although he has not been popular in the Anglo-Saxon world in recent times, one can find the origins of virtually every European art movement in his work. The second great wave of Flemish art came in the late nineteenth century, initially under the influence of French Impressionism, culminating with the Expressionism of James Ensor, Permeke and Gustave De Smet. While the Flemish achieved great heights as Symbolists and Expressionists in the early twentieth century, Walloons such as René Magritte and Paul Delvaux pioneered the Surrealist movement, evidence—if you believe in the Flemish/Walloon cultural divide—of the French-speakers' preference for more philosophical, conceptual art.

Flemish Revival
It is often said that Flemish culture had its heyday in the period 1400-1585. Flanders still had world-class painters in the seventeenth century, but it had certainly passed its peak after the division of the Southern and Northern Netherlands in 1585 (see p.8). The independent kingdom of Belgium was founded in 1830 on the premise that the Flemish language of the majority of the population could be eradicated. In the latter half of the nineteenth century, however, the Flemish started to fight back and gained at least linguistic equality by about 1935. With the decline of

Walloon industry since the Second World War and the rise of the Flemish economy, thanks largely to extensive US investment, excellent infrastructure and proximity to the sea, the tables have been completely turned and it is now the Walloons or French-speakers who are the poor relations. The Walloons have the French language, but not Flanders' economic muscle, founded on heavy industry as well as new technology.

Today Flanders has a standard of living that is one of the highest in the world. Although the Flemish do not like to advertise their wealth, one can see from the cars they drive and the appearance of their towns and villages that they are doing very well indeed. Even so, they are not really used to wealth, nor have they re-adopted the urban culture that they pioneered in the Middle Ages. Anyone with any money builds a villa and moves out of town, and for many the dream is to own a big backyard with chickens and rabbits. Charlotte Brontë called Belgium "Labassecour" (the farmyard) and, for good or ill, it is true that many Flemish are still close to their peasant roots. A robust peasant outlook may well be reflected in the scatological art of some of the best-known modern Flemish artists such as Wim Delvoye and Jan Fabre.

Local Identity

Town planning in Belgium hardly existed before 1980. Streets tend to be a surprising mix of incongruous architectural styles, with no one taking much notice of what has been built next door. The bad taste of some *nouveau riche* Flemish is much in evidence, as is the persistent prevalence of Art Deco design that went out in the 1920s elsewhere. G. K. Chesterton, who visited Bruges in 1909, found that:

> Flanders has the flattest and most prosaic of landscapes, but the most violent and extravagant of buildings. The fields are as flat as a paved square; but, on the other hand, the streets and roofs are as uproarious as a forest in a great wind.

Building one's own home is an important symbolic act, as a house is seen as a refuge from the vicissitudes of life as well as a good investment. The interiors of Flemish houses are generally very tidy and carefully maintained, in contrast to many exteriors.

The architectural muddle of the average Flemish street points to the individualism of the people and this extends to Flemish culture, too. There is a well-known cliché that Belgians are "particularists" or "localists" as regards culture. Belgium was cut off from the rest of the world after 1585 and even though it is in no sense cut off from the rest of Europe today, the barriers imposed by the Spanish and the Catholic Church seem to persist in the Belgian unconscious. Lack of uniformity in the designs of buildings also creates a sense of incongruity that is typically Flemish. Architecturally speaking, one certainly never knows what is around the next corner. No wonder that the Flemish have a liking for down-to-earth absurdity and deadpan humour.

Uninformed Anglo-Saxon commentators tend to have a higher opinion of the mostly Protestant Dutch than they do of the Catholic Flemish. Openness and tolerance are virtues more often attributed to the Dutch, but in truth these are just as typical of the Flemish. The Flemish—and the Belgians as a whole—do not try to appear to be something that they are not, and have not been able to present a unified image to the rest of the world, given their fragmented institutions. Many outsiders believe that French is the main or only language spoken in Belgian, whereas in reality 58 per cent of the population speak Dutch. Thus the hapless Alan Clayson, in his biography of Jacques Brel (1996):

> The main language in Belgium today is French—though Flemish continues to be a compulsory subject for its school children as Welsh is for their opposite numbers in Wales. If derived from the same Old Celtic and Low German mixture as Dutch, differences in pronunciation and dialect become more marked the further one travels across Belgium from Holland.

Confusion over identity is not restricted to foreigners. In Belgium itself there is an on-going debate about what it means to be Belgian, although it would probably be safe to conclude that there are so many identities in Belgium that one cannot pin down a single one. The leading Flemish writer Stefan Hertmans suggested in an interview that because they have had to accommodate so many foreign invaders the Flemish have had an overdose of "otherness" and have thus become less clear about their own identity.

Identity aside, the Flemish are noted as some of the best linguists in

Europe, and have no inhibitions about trying to speak a foreign language. The rest of the world has witnessed this linguistic competence in the form of Jacques Rogge, the Ghent-born President of the International Olympic Committee, who is entirely at home in five languages. Every Flemish politician can give an interview in Dutch, French or English with equal ease. This is both accommodating and helpful to foreigners, who generally do not speak Dutch, and displays a pragmatic realism about the humble position of the Dutch language as it is spoken in Belgium.

Modern Flanders

For political reasons Belgian Flanders has shrunk to the north and south since the Middle Ages, but has expanded to the east with the federalization of the Belgian state. Since the creation of the Flemish Regional government, the whole Dutch-speaking area of Belgium is now called Flanders—a historical absurdity, since Flanders now encompasses the southern halves of Brabant and Limburg, which were never before part of Flanders. The border between the Netherlands and Belgium is itself a random line drawn through the Duchies of Brabant and Limburg, so there are now North Brabant and North Limburg (in the Netherlands). Limburg was only finally divided between the Netherlands and Belgium in 1839, and was always a rather outlying part of both countries. Antwerp and the province of Antwerp historically belong to Brabant, not to Flanders. The natural border between Flanders and Brabant has always been the River Scheldt.

Stranger still, the capital of Flanders is now Brussels. The historical capital, Ghent, was not considered large enough to house the new Flemish Regional government, but more pressing was the need to acquire a large piece of Brussels to prevent it from ever being incorporated into Wallonia, or perhaps eventually into France. The present region of Flanders is, culturally speaking, very much dominated by the central axis of Brussels and Antwerp, rather as it was in the sixteenth century.

Modern-day Flanders is changing at great speed. Having thrown off the domination of the French-speakers and the Catholic Church, the Flemish have started to believe that they can take on the world and win. Flemish *haute couture*, theatre, painting, dance and music have now a high profile internationally. After centuries of negative stereotyping, it is chic to be Flemish. But modesty and discretion are still typical virtues in Flanders, and the Flemish (with the exception of some extremists) are never likely to proclaim their superiority to others. With their tumultuous history behind them, they dislike violent change but are willing to embrace new ideas if they seem useful. The Flemish are admired for their practical bent (especially by the French), but the downside is a tendency to look for short-term solutions to long-term and complex problems such as the nature of the Belgian state. Much has changed for the better, but Flanders still confronts difficult issues, not least the growth of right-wing extremism, which is considered in the following chapter.

Chapter One
War, Language and Flemish Freedom

"Of all the Gauls, the Belgae are the bravest, because they are furthest from the civilization and refinement of Provence. Merchants least frequently resort to them, and import those things which tend to effeminate the mind. They are the nearest to the Germans, who dwell beyond the Rhine, with whom they are continually waging war."

Julius Caesar, *De Bello Gallico*, Book I

Contrary to Caesar's assessment, today's Belgians are a peace-loving, if rather anarchic, people. Since independence in 1830 Belgium has been mainly successful in settling its internal disputes without resorting to violence. Indeed, one of the country's greatest paradoxes is the way that different political parties can work together in government while ignoring the intense hatred that their followers have felt for each other in the recent past. Perhaps Belgians have learnt from experience how to compromise, having often been forced to do so in the past by foreign occupiers. It is often claimed that the Flemish aversion to the centralized Belgian state is based on such experience of foreign occupation, but the attitude has hardly changed with sixty years of peace. It is the mere fact of being ruled by someone else that the Flemish dislike, regardless of the rulers' nationality.

Belgium is often called "the battlefield of Europe", and with good reason as violence and war have been a constant feature of the Flemish landscape. The Flemish, for their part, like to believe that they have inevitably been the victims of foreign aggressors and have never been the oppressors themselves, but this notion conveniently overlooks dreadful events in the Congo when it was occupied by Belgium between 1878 and 1961. Foreign occupations of Belgium, moreover, have always resulted in collaboration. The recriminations that followed the Second

Ambiorix statue in Tongeren

World War still continue over sixty years later. Perhaps not surprisingly, Belgian historians have not been keen to rake over these incidents, leaving the task mostly to British and American academics. The habit of not talking about "difficult" episodes with outsiders is engrained in the Flemish, leaving the job of remembering and rendering the truth to writers and artists.

The Romans Arrive

The prehistoric tribes of Belgium, a mix of Celts and Germans, were sophisticated and religious but also practised human sacrifice. They also had a rather un-Belgian liking for military adventures, and sent expeditions as far as the Black Sea and colonized Britain and Ireland; the Menapii of coastal Flanders gave their name to County Monaghan in Ireland. The *fir bolg* (probably meaning "blond people"), with their droopy moustaches and shaved chins, lived in a state of anarchic independence, electing kings called *rix,* who had little power until there was a crisis, and so were easy meat for Caesar when he arrived in 58 BC. One chieftain, Ambiorix, did rebel and massacred 6,000 Roman legionaries by luring them into a trap. His tribe, the Eburones, were all killed or sold into slavery and ceased to exist. Ambiorix was the first great national Belgian hero and someone whom both French and Dutch speakers could admire. Julius Caesar's praise was also a useful means of promoting the idea of a single national identity when Belgium became independent in 1830, and of justifying its existence to the rest of Europe.

After the initial bloodshed the Romans introduced more civilized habits such as under-floor heating and taking baths as well as all kinds of vegetables such as asparagus, and wine. But the Roman idyll did not last, and from the mid-third century AD the barbarians were pressing in from north and east. The Romans found it expedient to invite certain German tribes to enter Belgium as allies against the barbarians whom they viewed as an even worse evil. Their main allies were the Franks, the ancestors of the Flemish, who eventually set up their first organized kingdom in 431 after the Romans had been forced to go home. Frankish rulers carried on ferocious feuds among themselves until Charlemagne finally established his new Holy Roman Empire in 800. The centre of the Frankish empire was around Herstal near Liège and Aix-la-Chapelle (Aachen). Charlemagne's three sons took to fighting each other, and eventually agreed to split the Empire into three parts. Charles the Bald took Francia, which included those parts of Flanders west of the Scheldt, while Lothar took a central swathe covering the rest of Belgium and Holland. This division was of immense significance in Belgian history since the rulers of Flanders would owe their allegiance to the kings of France, while the rulers of Brabant and Limburg were vassals of the German Holy Roman Emperor.

Flanders went through a dark period with the Viking invasions lasting from 834 to 891. Lack of central authority during the Viking era opened the way for local warlords to stake a claim to a piece of territory, one of whom was Baldwin Iron Arm, the first Count of Flanders, who started his dynasty in 862. Baldwin's territory was small, encompassing an area between Ghent, Kortrijk, Sint-Niklaas and Bruges, but he had the advantage of being the son-in-law of Charles the Bald. His son, Baldwin II, expanded Flanders southwards all the way to Boulogne, and took control of most of the coastline between Sluis and the Somme. The policy of succeeding Counts of Flanders was simply to attack in all directions since if they did nothing then Flanders would be re-absorbed into the French kingdom. The Counts of Flanders became powerful enough to have designs on the French throne, but in 1214 the French King Philip Augustus put an end to Flemish expansionism with his victory over a combined force of Flemings, Brabanters, Germans and English at the Battle of Bouvines, and so began a tradition of foreign powers fighting battles on Flemish soil.

The Battle of the Golden Spurs

The Flemish cities of Ghent, Bruges and Ypres became wealthy from the cloth trade from 1100 onwards, but this prosperity led to conflict between the new patrician class, many of whom supported the French king, and the mass of the population who wanted independence. The Flemish patriots called themselves Klauwaerts after the claws of the Flemish lion, while the pro-French party took the name of Leliaerts from the *fleur de lys* on the French flag. Flanders was dependent on English wool to make cloth, and when in 1296 the French stopped all trade between Flanders and England, the Count of Flanders, Guy of Dampierre, was forced to enter into an alliance with the English. The French installed a governor in Flanders, but in the end the common people had their say by massacring the French in Bruges during the night of 18 May 1302.

A French army arrived outside Kortrijk on 8 July 1302, to be met by an army of Flemish weavers known as the *blauwe nagels* (blue fingernails) from the blue dye that stained their hands. The Flemish waited on a piece of dry land surrounded by marshes and rivers, having driven sharp stakes into the marshes to trap the heavy French cavalry. The French had a particularly inept leader who ordered his cavalry to charge into the marshes; the result was a one-sided massacre of the French. At the end of the day the Flemish had collected 700 golden spurs, which were hung up in the cathedral at Kortrijk. A large number of the French aristocracy had been wiped out, and Flanders was saved from being absorbed into France. The anniversary of the Battle of the Golden Spurs, 11 July, is the national day of Flanders (but not yet a public holiday for everyone). The Flemish call this the Guldensporenslag or the Battle of the Groeningenkouter (the part of Kortrijk where it took place), while to the French it is the Battle of Courtrai. In 1914, when the Germans invaded Belgium, King Albert I called on the Flemish to remember their glorious victory at the Battle of the Golden Spurs, while the French-speaking Belgians were asked to recall an incident from the history of Liège. There is no little irony in this patriotic call to arms, given that the Battle of the Golden Spurs was fought against the French and that many of the Flemish supported the French king at the time.

The van Arteveldes and the End of Flemish Independence

The Battle of the Golden Spurs was followed by less conclusive battles with the French. In 1304 the Flemish were forced to give up all of French-speaking Flanders (including Lille and Douai) by the Treaty of Athis-sur-Orge. Things took a turn for the worse when Louis of Nevers, the son-in-law of the French king, became Count of Flanders in 1322. Most of the Flemish were determined to resist the French, but they were routed at Cassel (now in French Flanders) in 1328. Edward III of England then claimed the French throne from Philippe of Valois, starting the Hundred Years' War (1337-1453). To force Flanders and Brabant to take his side Edward cut off the supply of wool to Flanders. A strongman emerged from the merchant class of Ghent by the name of Jacob van Artevelde, who argued for an alliance with England, as imports of wool from England were even more important than imports of grain from France. Van Artevelde led an independent government in Ghent from 1338 until he was murdered in 1345 (see p.72).

In 1346 Edward III won his great victory over the French at the Battle of Crécy with some assistance from the Flemish. Louis of Nevers died at Crécy on the French side and was succeeded by his son, Louis of Male (r.1346-84). Louis had every intention of remaining a loyal vassal of the King of France but for a while had to agree to an alliance with England. By playing off the English and the French against each other he successfully maintained Flanders' neutrality. Most of his reign was marked by economic prosperity and greater centralization of power, and he gained Mechelen and Antwerp from the Dukes of Brabant. In 1378, towards the end of his reign, a dispute broke out between Bruges and Ghent after Louis gave the guilds of Bruges permission to build a canal to the River Leie. A Ghent army known as the Witte Kaproenen (White Hoods) put a stop to the digging of the canal in 1379. The French king was urged to intervene by the Duke of Burgundy, Philip the Bold, who had married Louis of Male's daughter, Marguerite. The French duly obliged and defeated an army of weavers led by Jacob van Artevelde's son, Philip, at the Battle of Westrozebeke in 1382. This event ensured that Flanders would become part of the Burgundian realm.

The Burgundian Era

Philip the Bold, Duke of Burgundy, subdued the remaining Flemish rebels, who were backed by Richard II of England, and re-established peace by 1385. Philip had the interests of France at heart, while making efforts to restore Flanders to economic prosperity. By various marital alliances he ensured that Holland, Zeeland, Friesland and Hainaut also became Burgundian possessions. Philip the Bold's son, John the Fearless (r.1404-19), worked against the French king, and showed greater sympathy for the Flemish. He restored the use of the Flemish language in his state council and adopted the Flemish motto *Ik Houdt* (I Hold).

The next Duke of Burgundy, Philip the Good (r.1419-67), was ruthless with rebels but generally popular with the Flemish since he restored peace to their country. Those who harked back to the days of Flemish independence realized that they were fighting for a lost cause. The cloth trade was in decline and there was high inflation. He was able to acquire most of the areas of present-day Belgium, Luxembourg and the Netherlands he did not already control by purchasing them or with minimal military effort. His dominions also included Picardy, Artois and Franche Comté, and thus the centre of gravity of the Burgundian realm duly shifted away from the official capital of Dijon to Brussels. Philip the Good's son, Charles the Bold (r.1467-77) was a reckless character who disliked the Belgians. Charles pushed his military adventurism too far and was killed in 1477 at the siege of Nancy. The Dukes of Burgundy were now left with their possessions in the Low Countries and northern France.

Wars of Religion

Following the death of Charles the Bold, his daughter, Mary of Burgundy, decided to marry the Habsburg Archduke Maximilian of Austria to protect Flanders both from the French and from internal rebellions. Mary of Burgundy's son, Philip the Fair, married the heir to the Spanish throne, the unfortunately named Joanne the Mad, and their son, Charles V, became sole ruler of the Holy Roman and Spanish Empires. The fact that Charles V was born in Ghent was of little benefit to Flanders. With the start of the Reformation in 1519, Calvinism and Lutheranism spread rapidly among the educated classes as well as the illiterate. The natural rebelliousness of the Flemish attracted them to a new interpretation of Christianity that freed them from having to support an army of parasitic monks and nuns, but they came up against an uncompromising defender of the faith in Charles V.

The reform movement was strongest in Antwerp among the Augustinians, and they were the first to suffer when two of their number were brought to Brussels in 1523 to be executed. There were occasional executions of blasphemers and heretics in the following years, but the real explosion did not come until 1566. Charles V had abdicated in 1555, and his son, Philip II of Spain, was far less concerned about the sensibilities of the Flemish than his father had been. Protestants were by now meeting in secret in the countryside where they could listen to sermons by *hageprekers* or "hedge preachers", many of them trained abroad. A full-scale religious uprising started in French Flanders around Hondschoote in 1566, with murders of Catholic priests and the first outbreak of Iconoclasm, the deliberate destruction of religious images.

The Protestant movement spread north to Antwerp and Ghent in 1568, and most church interiors in Flanders were devastated. The rebels declared Calvinist republics in some cities but the response was not long in coming. Philip II sent in his henchman, the Duke of Alva, with an army of 17,000 to punish the heretics. Thousands were tortured and executed with the effect of bringing about a full-scale rebellion in the Netherlands.

The Northern and Southern Netherlands drew up the Pacification of Ghent in 1576, which made one state of the Seventeen Provinces with the intention of keeping out the Spanish and all other foreigners. The Calvinists became more fanatical and destructive, leading most of the southern provinces of the Netherlands to accept Spanish sovereignty and Catholicism under the Union of Arras in 1579, while the seven northern provinces created the Union of Utrecht (the basis for the modern Netherlands). With the rebels split, Philip II of Spain was able to re-establish his authority, at least in the Southern Netherlands. The final act was the fall of Antwerp in 1585 and the closure of the Scheldt Estuary, which marked the beginning of a period of isolation and cultural decline that lasted until the nineteenth century. The consequences of the Spanish victory were severe for Flanders in that all Protestants were forced to leave within two years or reconvert to Catholicism. Some cities lost half their population, as free thinkers and more progressive elements of society were forced out, along with entrepreneurs and skilled artisans. While the Netherlands and Great Britain profited from the brain drain, Belgium became a backwater of the Spanish Empire.

This era of Flemish history was fictionalized by the Brussels writer Charles de Coster in *La légende d'Ulenspiegel* (1867), written in French but against a Flemish background. Part of the book's central comic conceit is that Thijl Ulenspiegel is born at the same moment as Philip II of Spain, but grows up quite differently.

> Philip will grow up an executioner, being engendered by Charles V, the destroyer of our country. Ulenspiegel will be a great master of jolly words and youthful pranks but good-hearted withal, having had for father Claes the valiant labourer, who knows how to earn his bread bravely, honestly and simply.

In the end Claes is hanged in front of the church at Damme (see p.147). De Coster gives details of the punishments that Philip II reserved for heretics:

> His Majesty decreed, among other penalties, that the suspect might never hold honourable estate. As for those fallen again in their errors or who were obstinate in them, they would be condemned to burn by slow or fast fire, in a straw covering, or else bound to the stake, according to the judges' discretion. Other men, if they were nobles or good burghers, would perish by the sword, commoners would be hanged, and women buried alive. Their heads would be fixed on pikes as a warning to all others. The goods of all these people, if they lived in places subject to confiscation, would go to the Emperor.
>
> His Sacred Majesty accorded to all informers one-half of all the property of those executed, provided such property did not exceed one hundred pounds of Flanders money.

Flemish society is still profoundly marked by this so-called "Spanish lobotomy", firstly because many of its most creative and dynamic people emigrated, and secondly because Flanders was physically and intellectually cut off from the rest of the world for the next 250 years.

French Invasions
The seventeenth and eighteenth centuries were the least glorious of Flanders' history. The city of Antwerp, the world's cultural capital for a few decades until 1585, was cut off from the sea by the Dutch, and gradually went into decline (see Chapter Nine). From the time that the French King Louis XIV (r.1643-1714) tried to expand his kingdom in all directions, Flanders was subjected to regular invasions. One of Louis XIV's more extreme acts was to bombard Brussels in 1695, with the result that there are almost no buildings there from before that date. In 1701 the Spanish King Charles II made the grandson of Louis XIV heir to the Spanish throne in his will, setting off the War of the Spanish Succession which pitted the British, Dutch and Holy Roman Empire against the French. While the French first took over Belgium by trickery, the British general, the Duke of Marlborough, drove them out again. The consequence was that Belgium was transferred to the Austrian

Crown in 1714 by the Treaty of Utrecht. The French occupied Belgium again between 1745 and 1748, but had to withdraw. Although the French could not take Belgium militarily, their cultural influence was enormous, and this was a period when the use of the French language increased steadily.

The Austrians were concerned with the economic development of Belgium, but hampered by the opposition of the British and Dutch as regards expanding foreign trade from Flemish ports. The reign of Empress Maria Theresa (r.1740-80) has been turned into a mythical golden era by Flemish schoolbooks. Her successor, Joseph II, wished to impose enlightened despotism on the Belgians, but antagonized his subjects by removing many of the Catholic Church's privileges and reforming the judicial system without consultation. Although he had good intentions, Joseph II's heavy-handed style finally pushed the Belgians to revolt in 1787 and, to the surprise of the rest of the world, they succeeded in defeating the Austrians at the Battle of Turnhout in 1789. Inspired by the example of the American Revolution and the fall of the Bastille, the Belgians declared independence as the United States of Belgium the following year, but the Belgian dream of independence was thwarted by the French revolutionaries, who captured Belgium in 1794.

The Belgians soon found that the French were far worse masters than the Austrians. Churches were closed down, and priests who would not swear allegiance to the Revolution were thrown out of their houses. The forced conscription of young men was one reason for the revolt against the French known as the Boerenkrijg (Peasants' War), which started in October 1798 at Overmere in East Flanders. Many of the rebels were farmers, armed only, so legend has it, with scythes and pitchforks. The greatest centre of resistance was in the Kempen and Limburg. The Flemish briefly took Mechelen but soon lost it because of lack of military experience. This episode provided the material for the Antwerp-born writer Georges Eekhoud's *Les fusillés de Malines* (Shot at Mechelen, 1891). The revolt came to an inglorious end in Hasselt in 1799. The pioneer writer in Dutch Hendrik Conscience published his account in *De Boerenkrijg* (1853). There is a museum dedicated to the Boerenkrijg in Overmere, while many Flemish villages and towns also have monuments to the Boerenkrijg, erected on the centenary of the revolt in 1898 or on other anniversaries.

The Boerenkrijg was accompanied by an outbreak of banditry that was aimed more at Flemish farmers than at the French. The life of the brigand Louis Bakelandt (1774-1803) has provided endless material for the Catholic press and hundreds of strip cartoons, as the rebellion against the anti-clerical French has been picked up by the Church as a perfect theme for impressionable Flemish youngsters. Under the French several gangs of "brigands", as the French always called them, operated in Flanders. The Binders in Brabant were so-called because they bound victims to their chairs. (They were also reputed to be able to fly through the air.) The Bokkerijders in Limburg and over the German border were reputedly Satanists.

Matters improved with the Concordat between Napoleon and the Pope in 1801. Some churches reopened and priests were treated less harshly. There was also some improvement in the Belgian economy. Napoleon was never popular, as he was always viewed as anti-Catholic, but his rule ended in 1814. After his defeat at Waterloo it was time to consider what to do with Belgium. Some Belgians would have been happy to return to Austrian rule, but the British decided that Belgium should be joined with the Netherlands.

Independent Belgium

The Belgians found they had exchanged one set of foreign masters for another with the arrival of the Dutch. While the Dutch King William I did much to help the Belgian economy, he lacked diplomatic subtlety. The Catholic hierarchy could not accept domination by a Calvinist country, and the French-speakers would not accept the imposition of the Dutch language. In August 1830 Belgian discontent erupted during an opera in Brussels. The revolt gathered enough support from around the country to make it hard for William I to re-impose his authority, and so he wisely consented to grant Belgium its independence. The Belgians chose as their new king an ambitious German prince, Leopold of Saxe-Coburg, who turned out to be an excellent ruler. The Belgians still had to fight the Dutch, however, and only survived with help from the French and British. In the end they had to give up their claim to Dutch Flanders (Zeeuws Vlaanderen), north Brabant, north and east Limburg and the German-speaking area of Luxembourg. Belgium declared itself eternally neutral in 1839, with the Great Powers as guarantors of its neutrality.

Belgium did not have to contend with foreign invasions for the rest of the nineteenth century, and soon became one of the world's most prosperous countries. Leopold II had imperial ambitions, which were fulfilled from 1878 onwards when, with the help of Henry Stanley, he was able to take over a vast and wealthy tract of central Africa, the Congo. This became his private colony, a source of immense wealth. The reign of terror imposed by the Belgians on the indigenous population brought condemnation from the rest of the world, with Mark Twain leading the campaign against the Belgian king. It has been estimated that as many as twenty million Africans may have died in the process. Belgium itself was not at peace either. The industrial revolution created a huge underclass of oppressed workers, and from time to time their protests were violently suppressed by the army and the *gendarmerie* or militias.

Language Struggle

> *De taal is gansch het volk.*
> "The language is the people entire."
>   Prudens van Duysse, 1836

The Flemish have their own term for the struggle to assert their rights in the single Belgian state, namely *ontvoogding* or "emancipation". This word suggests that the Flemish were under a "guardian" or *voogd* and thus had to grow up to become adults, their oppressors or guardians, it seems, being the French-speakers.

There were doubts in 1830 about whether Belgium should exist at all. Perhaps the British were primarily behind the creation of this hybrid country as a way of weakening the Dutch. Under the threat of invasion from the Netherlands and France, Belgium's political parties, the Liberals and Catholics, joined into a coalition government and the country took the motto of *L'Union fait la force*, Unity is Strength. (This was also the motto of the Dutch Republic in the sixteenth century.) Slogans aside, it seems that few in 1830 anticipated the problems involved in trying to force two different cultures and languages into one state. The revolt by the Belgians against Dutch rule in 1830 arose partly from the fear of the French-speakers that they would be forced to use Dutch rather than from an objection by the Dutch-speakers to using French. The small elite who voted on the Constitution were, in any case, all French-speakers regardless of which part of the country they came from.

The first Belgian Constitution stated that the "use of language is free (*facultatif*)", which became a pretext for the French-speaking elite to marginalize the Dutch language. Dutch was the language of servants and peasants and could not serve as a medium for serious writing, or so they believed. Dutch was, moreover, not standardized in Belgium, with the population mostly speaking dialects of Dutch that are often referred to as Flemish. The first prime minister of Belgium, Charles Rogier, informed Leopold I: "Our government must make efforts to destroy the Flemish language to prepare Belgium to be absorbed into our great fatherland, France." It was an appropriate irony that Rogier was shot in the tongue by his political rival Charles Gendebien during a duel.

Flemish and Dutch

The terms Flemish and Dutch are the source of much confusion. The Salian Franks, who settled in the northern part of Belgium from 300 AD and retained their Germanic speech, started to use the term *diets* to distinguish their language from that of their kinsmen who had become romanized and adopted what was later to become French. The term *diets* means nothing more than "of the people"; it was replaced by Nederduits from the sixteenth century. While the Dutch in the Netherlands started to use the term Nederlands from the eighteenth century, there were many Flemish who were not keen to be identified with the Calvinists and who preferred to use the term Vlaams or Flemish for their language. By 1900 it was generally accepted that there would have to be a common Dutch language in Belgium and the Netherlands, in spite of resistance from some die-hard Catholics like the poet Guido Gezelle (see p.130). It was not until 1973, however, that the Belgian Constitution started to refer to Dutch (Nederlands) rather than Flemish (Vlaams). Nowadays almost all Belgian Dutch-speakers say that they speak Nederlands. The Dutch written in Belgium is officially the same language as that of the Netherlands, Algemeen Nederlands, even if in practice it displays considerable differences.

Flemish became a prestige language in the thirteenth century, thanks to the works of great writers such as the mystical poets Hadewijch and

John of Ruusbroec and the author of the *Reinaert the Fox* saga (see pp.99-102). It became the official language of Brussels from 1350, but in Flanders official documents were already drawn up in French from 1250, and the elite tended to use French. The official use of Flemish declined after the Burgundians took over Flanders and Brabant in 1382, from when there was greater pressure to use French. With the isolation of Belgium from the rest of the world from 1585, the position of Flemish came increasingly under threat. The domination of French culture and French invasions in the eighteenth century all worked against the use of Flemish.

It was only at a late stage that some Flemish realized the danger that French could pose to their language. The dawn of the Flemish Movement is usually seen as the publication in 1788 of the *Verhandeling op d'onacht der moederlyke tael in de Nederlanden* (Memoir on the Neglect of the Mother Tongue in the Low Countries) by the Brussels lawyer J. B. C. Verlooy (1746-97). He pleaded for the creation of a Dutch culture on French Enlightenment lines, and praised the beauties of the Dutch language. Commentators like Verlooy were not taken very seriously, if indeed anyone was aware of them at all. The Flemish Movement started on a small scale, under the influence of Enlightenment and Romantic thinkers, premised on the belief that languages should be purified of foreign elements, and that every people should speak its own language.

In the early days of the Belgian state the pauperization and apathy of the Flemish population played a major role in leaving the field open for French. In another sense, however, the Flemish speakers' lack of education was a factor in saving their language from extinction, if only because one could hardly teach French to illiterates. A more serious threat was the mass migration from Flemish-speaking areas to Brussels and to the industrial heartlands in French-speaking Wallonia. Speaking French became necessary to advance in the world, and even helped the Flemish from different parts of Flanders to understand each other more easily.

It required dedicated work by scholars and writers to create a standardized Dutch literature in Belgium that could appeal to a wide audience. The main mover in this process was Jan Frans Willems (1793-1846), who edited and published classic medieval Flemish texts and worked to bring some order to Belgian Dutch. The pioneer writer,

Hendrik Conscience (1812-83) from Antwerp, wrote the patriotic classic, *De leeuw van Vlaanderen* (The Lion of Flanders, 1838) and encouraged many Flemish to read in their own language. Still, the Flemish Movement in its early stages was very much the preserve of a small group of *petit-bourgeois* scholars and civil servants who felt excluded from power by the political system, and hoped to advance their careers by spreading the use of Dutch. In 1875 there was a student protest in Roeselare led by the poet Albrecht Rodenbach (1856-80), marking the start of the Blauwvoet movement and its well-known rallying cry "Vliegt de blauwvoet, storm op zee" (When the blue-footed fulmar flies, there is storm at sea). Blauwvoeterij ("blue feetism") is no longer a current term. Supporters of Flemish autonomy and the Dutch language were also for a long time known by the French term of Flamingants. This has negative overtones, being a French word, and the Flemish generally prefer to use the term *vlaamsgezind* (pro-Flemish).

Attempts to redress the flagrant repression of the Dutch language in the new Belgian state were slow to take shape. A number of Flemish intellectuals organized a "pétitionnement" in 1840 asking for Dutch to be used in some areas of the administration and law-courts, but the authorities quickly realized that these requests had no real popular backing and took no action. The main movement against the use of French came, not surprisingly, from Antwerp, where hardly anyone spoke the language. A case in which two Dutch-speakers were guillotined after a trial of which they had not understood a single word caused widespread anger. In 1873 the first reform of the Constitution took place, allowing the use of Dutch in the administration of Flanders. In 1878 Dutch became one of the official languages of Belgium, but the French-speakers retained the right to use their language in the law-courts and the administration in Flanders. Progress was slow because the connection between the struggle for universal suffrage, higher wages and better working conditions, and the Dutch language had not been made. The decisive shift only came with the cataclysmic changes of the First World War.

The First World War
The Belgian government received an ultimatum on 2 August 1914, demanding that it allow the German armies to pass through Belgium

Flemish casualties, First World War

into France. King Albert I resolved to resist the German invaders, who resorted to acts of unprovoked violence against civilians in their rage at being held up on the way to France. Whole towns were destroyed and, as an ultimate act of vandalism, the great library of Louvain University was burnt down. All of Belgium fell to the Germans, except for a small triangle of land behind the River IJzer in the west. The Belgians and their allies were only able to hang on by opening the dikes, making it impossible for the invaders to pass through the flooded countryside. The war had immense consequences for the future of Flanders, not least because the majority of the lower ranks were Flemish rather than French-speakers, fighting for a country that discriminated against their language.

Life in occupied Belgium was far from pleasant. To stop Belgians escaping to the neutral Netherlands in the north, the Germans erected an electric fence along the border, where many Belgians died while risking the passage. The United States and other countries came to the aid of the starving Belgians by organizing food supplies. There was also a determined propaganda campaign waged by exiled Belgians to win sympathy for their country. The Nobel prize-winner Maurice Maeterlinck contributed an anti-German play, *Le bourgmestre de Stilmonde* (The Burgomaster of Stilmonde, 1916), while the poet Emile Verhaeren published *Villes meurtries de Belgique* (Shattered Towns of Belgium, 1916) and travelled around France giving patriotic talks. England, at least at the start of the war, was gripped by pro-Belgian fever. In the music halls there were songs in the vein of:

> Bravo! Little Belgium, it's proud we are of you
> Bravo! Little Belgium, you'd the pluck to see it through
> Hats off to little Belgium,
> You're a fighting race sublime!
> Your flag is still unfurled
> In front of all the world
> And we're with you—all the time!

There was also a vogue for lurid cartoons of Belgium depicted as a scantily clad maiden threatened with rape by German monsters. Yet the propaganda campaign eventually backfired, as the British public grew tired of tales of atrocities, and the French press picked up the theme of Belgian collaboration with the Germans. Belgium received little from the Treaty of Versailles beyond a small amount of German territory and a large amount of sympathy.

Flemish Activism

The idea of federalism or independence for Flanders was hardly considered before the First World War. The official ideology peddled by schoolbooks was that Belgium had a hybrid Latin-German identity, and that this was a source of strength. The decisive shift in the debate occurred during the war. The German occupiers tried to play off the Flemish against the Walloons by making Dutch the sole language of administration in the Flemish territories in the vain hope that Flanders would be unified with Germany. This only resulted in administrative chaos because local officials were not prepared to cooperate or were not capable of working in any language other than French. The real action in the Flemish nationalist struggle took place both within the Belgian army, which continued to fight behind the River IJzer in the west of the country, and groups of Flemish activists in the occupied remainder.

The second half of the war saw a growing pro-Flemish Frontbeweging (Front Movement), a response to discrimination against the Flemish in the Belgian army. In particular, all orders were given in French, even though probably some seventy per cent of the rank and file were Flemish. The percentage of Flemish in the army is, it should be said, a matter of hot debate; at the start of the war there were naturally more French speakers in the upper echelons and the administration of the country who were exempt from military duty, while Flemish peasants supplied the bulk of the cannon fodder. More nationalistic Flemish writers put the figure as high as ninety per cent. Later studies show that about two-thirds of casualties were in Flemish units. There had been protests against the anti-Flemish discrimination in the army for many years, but there was also the fear that splitting the army into Dutch and French-speaking units would encourage separatism.

The illegal discrimination against the Dutch language led a group of soldiers to write an open letter to Albert I on 11 July 1917 (the anniversary of the Battle of the Golden Spurs), asking him to intervene. The outcome was the introduction of some bilingualism, which was in any case required by law, but also hostility towards Flemish agitators. In occupied Flanders there were very few who would go along with the German plot to split Belgium, the so-called Flamenpolitik (Flemish policy). The French press outside Belgium carried on a campaign of anti-Flemish propaganda with the support of the exiled government, and this was enough to make the Flemish militants carry on working for the Flemish cause, regardless of the war. From August 1915 the slogan "the Belgium of the future will be Latin or it will be nothing" was popular with French speakers. A group of Flemish activists elected a Council of Flanders and asked the Germans to split the Belgian administration into Dutch and French-speaking sectors. This group went as far as to declare Flanders independent at the end of 1917 (the Germans took no notice of them). Brussels received a Dutch-speaking governor, and the University of Ghent was Dutchified. Most Flemish activists in occupied Flanders preferred to await the outcome of the war before doing anything.

The defeat of the Germans posed a problem for the Flemish

militants. While they welcomed the end of the war, their leaders were now put on trial, and all the work that had been done to further the Flemish cause seemed to be lost. Everything Germanic was now rejected, and everything French was in vogue again. Albert I, who feared for the unity of his kingdom, forced the Catholic Party to accept the principle of one-man one-vote (the so-called Castle of Loppem Incident) on 11 November 1918 (for women the vote only came in 1948). The repression of Flemish activists during and after the First World War created the basis for a new type of Flemish Movement, ready to press for complete independence for Flanders.

This Damned War
One might have though that the First World War would have provided ideal material for Flemish writers. But if many future Flemish militants and literary figures fought at the IJzerfront, including Cyriel Verschaeve, Ernest Claes and Joris van Severen, the conflict did not generate the quality of literature that was found elsewhere, either because these figures were too young at the time or because Flemish literature had not developed sufficiently beyond the didactic stage. The future leader of the 1930s fascist Verdinaso party, Joris van Severen, wrote a diary of his time at the front, during which he was sent to a French labour camp for distributing pro-Flemish leaflets, *Deze vervloekte oorlog—dagboek 1914-1918* (This Damned War, 2005). Van Severen was murdered by French police in May 1940. The major work of Flemish literature from the war is *Eer Vlaanderen vergaat* (Before Flanders Fails, 1927) by Jozef Simons (1888-1948), a semi-fictional history of the Frontbeweging, the campaign by Flemish soldiers for equal rights (see above). The ambivalence of the Flemish towards the Belgian state during the war and the campaign of denigration against them afterwards stifled literature in Dutch about the Great War until recently.

While the war continued at the front, a new and innovative voice was emerging in occupied Antwerp, that of Paul van Ostaijen (1896-1928). During the war he was involved in the Activist movement, aiming to promote Flemish equality if necessary by cooperating with the Germans. A period of exile in Berlin after the war brought him into contact with new currents in the arts and reinforced his position as an avant-garde poet and critic. He is best known for his *Bezette stad*

(Occupied City, 1921), a collection of poetry that uses revolutionary typography as part of the text and challenges many prevailing taboos (see p.214).

Progress between the Wars

The Flemish Movement took on a strongly pacifist colouring after the First World War as banners inscribed with the slogan "Nooit meer oorlog" (No more war) appeared at annual commemorations of the war dead. In 1920 the first IJzerbedevaart (Pilgrimage to the River IJzer) took place, a meeting to commemorate the dead and to affirm Flemish identity. The slogan AVV-VVK (All for Flanders—Flanders for Christ) carved onto a huge cross by the IJzer was a naïve way of expressing Flemish sentiments, while ignoring the political blandishments of the Socialists and Liberals.

The Flemish turned to using education, newspapers and culture to promote their cause. Little by little new laws were enacted giving them some of what they demanded, in particular a half-Dutch university in Ghent and more Dutch-medium schools in Flanders from 1925. A decisive event came in 1928, when the people of Antwerp voted overwhelmingly in favour of the imprisoned collaborator August Borms and against the Liberals. The pro-Flemish parties now had huge support, and since the majority of the Belgian population now spoke Dutch, a more radical programme of monolingual regions was forced through in 1932. By 1935 French and Dutch had equal status as administrative languages, if not as regards culture. Brussels was officially made a bilingual city, although in practice the laws have never been properly enforced.

The economic crisis of the 1930s and disillusionment with central government resulted in major gains by new ultra-right parties, mainly the VNV or Vlaams Nationaal Verbond and Verdinaso, in the 1936 elections. The Rexist party (named after Christus Rex and not because it was monarchist) had its roots in Wallonia but also had a following in Flanders. The Catholic Party was accordingly forced to show more enthusiasm for the Flemish cause to try to win back votes from the far right (as it is at the moment). The Catholic Party, however, has always found it difficult to give up its allegiance to the Belgian state and the established social order.

The Second World War

Arguments about greater autonomy for Flanders were rendered irrelevant by the German invasion on 10 May 1940. This time the Belgians were unable to hold on to any of their territory, and the campaign was over in a mere 18 days. King Leopold III decided to remain in Belgium, while Queen Wilhelmina of the Netherlands wisely decamped to London. Leopold III has been judged very harshly by both the British and the Belgians, for although he did nothing more than lead a comfortable life under the German occupation, he effectively destroyed the prestige of the Belgian monarchy. The Germans, meanwhile, adopted different tactics in their second occupation by attempting to win over the civilian population and by interfering less in the country's administration, but the intention was still to absorb Flanders into the Third Reich. The ultra-right wing parties that had sprung up in the 1930s, the VNV, Rex, Verdinaso and numerous other small groupings, saw advantages in collaboration. In 1940 many assumed that Germany had won the war and sincerely believed that a new era had dawned. Some 16,000 young Flemish volunteered to join the SS and fight the Bolsheviks on the Eastern Front. The result was a campaign of assassinations in Belgium between collaborators and the resistance.

One of the main weapons used by the collaborators was the anonymous letter passed to the Germans, accusing neighbours of harbouring Allied airmen or of other crimes. These incidents are still remembered. Everyone was mixed up with the black market in some way or other; some became wealthy from trading in goods stolen from Jewish individuals or businesses or from smuggling food. Since the Second World War the Flemish and Walloons have continued to accuse each other of being the worse collaborators. The Belgian government in exile in London declared open season on collaborators when it returned in September 1944, under the slogan *Ieder zijn zwarte* (Everyone their collaborator). More than 561,000 people were investigated, 2,940 sentenced to death and some 242 executed (as well as those who were killed by the resistance at the end of the war). Some Nazi sympathizers spent the rest of their lives in exile. Major economic collaborators with friends in high places escaped unharmed, while those who had been duped by the Germans into supporting their New Order were locked up in the concentration camp at Breendonk, driven out of their jobs and homes and deprived of pensions and civil rights, and so inevitably had to rely on each other for support. There was a vogue for smashing up the houses of suspected collaborators, or those who were unpopular with their neighbours.

Belgium as a whole became even more polarized between a monarchist Catholic Flanders and an anti-clerical Socialist Wallonia after 1945. After a brief period of keeping their heads down, those who had been persecuted and their sympathizers formed a new political party in 1954, the Volksunie, with an explicit programme of independence for Flanders and an amnesty for collaborators. The VU was backed by a large section of the Flemish intelligentsia and became a serious threat to the Christian Democrats in the 1960s. It was disbanded in 2001 after it became known that one of its leaders had attended a meeting of SS veterans.

Collaborators and Victims

As in the First World War, the Belgian government in exile started a propaganda campaign to win support from the Allies, the most successful manifestation being the Belgian Information Center, which ran for 25 years in New York under the writer Jan-Albert Goris (pseudonym of Marnix Gijsen). This organization published works on Belgian culture and Belgian poetry in translation from a nationalistic standpoint. It was also responsible for publishing Robert Goffin's *The White Brigade* in 1944, intended to inform Americans about the resistance to the Nazis. Goffin makes skilful use of semi-fictional tales of resistance exploits and evokes Belgium's resistance to the Spanish occupation.

> In that place and on that day Belgium's history rolled back for hundreds of years to another scene of horror and solemnity. While the truck had stood, the blood of its cargo had dripped to the street; the truck rolled away, and all that remained of the heroism of these men was a red puddle on the cold stones. Then the praying people rose and came forward; knelt again and, almost with awe, dipped their handkerchiefs in the sacred blood—blood no longer of any one man, blood of a nation united, in anguish and in death, before the enemy.

Breendonk concentration camp

Goffin is referring to the execution of the Counts Egmont and Horn on the Grand' Place in Brussels in 1568.

The Second World War was something best forgotten for most of the Flemish. Those who had compromised themselves with the Germans felt guilt or resentment at their treatment by the resistance militias, the White Brigades, after the war. At the same time, the myth of the Flemish as underdogs and victims gained more strength the more the French speakers (including Jacques Brel) vilified them as crypto-Nazis. The persecution of Flemish collaborators created a powerful new group of nationalists, of whom the most articulate spokesman was Gerard Walschap (1898-1989), the leading novelist of the inter-war years. He gives a clear account of the kind of moral choices that confronted the Flemish during the war in *Zwart en wit* (Black and White, 1948). Presented as the musings of a young Flemish Nazi sentenced to die in the morning, the story tells how the prisoner was a socialist at the age of seventeen, but chose to go to Berlin to study and was indoctrinated into volunteering for the Russian front. A short piece by the anarchist writer

Louis-Paul Boon, *Hij was een zwarte* (He Was a Collaborator, 1986), blames Catholic teachers for brainwashing their pupils to support ultra-right wing parties.

The classic novel about collaboration and repression is the mainly autobiographical *Het verdriet van België* (The Sorrow of Belgium, 1983) by the West Flemish writer Hugo Claus. The central figure, Louis Seynaeve, was born in 1929 like Claus and is brought up by nuns from the age of eighteen months to eleven, when he is taken back home. Louis' family are Nazi sympathizers. Claus' father was a printer and a member of the VNV, and was locked up in 1944 for six months on suspicion of being a collaborator. *The Sorrow of Belgium* is full of reflections on small-town life in the suburbs of Kortrijk, where Claus spent his youth. He identifies a connection between Catholic brainwashing and an inability to see the evil nature of fascism. Louis Seynaeve ends up joining the Hitler Youth, but after the war begins to understand the dangers of all forms of ideology. A much shorter and more readable reflection on the after-effects of collaboration in Flanders is *Marcel* (1999) by Erwin Mortier, which is also available in English. Here a young boy comes across a letter from his uncle who died at the Russian front and discovers that his family and schoolteacher all have skeletons in their cupboards from the Second World War.

Hugo Claus had already dealt with the effects of war on the Flemish subconscious in his phantasmagorical *De verwondering* (Amazement, 1963); this is available in French as *L'étonnement* but not in English. The novel concerns a language teacher in Ostend by the name of Rijckel who goes mad, sometimes identifying himself as an SS man and sometimes as his victim. According to Claus, the Flemish have a "ruler mentality", related to their patriarchal culture, in which they want to emancipate themselves from the domination of the French speakers, but still oppress the weak in their own society. Claus' rejection of the Catholic Church and small-town West Flanders should be seen as a reaction to his own experience of being placed in an institution at the age of 18 months. Much of his work concerns incest and the Oedipus complex and implies a general rejection of what he sees as the complacent, narrow-minded provincial Flemish bourgeoisie. A reading of *The Sorrow of Belgium* gives a certain insight into Flemish society, even if the style is, to say the least, challenging.

Legacy of Occupation

Numerous occupations have made the Flemish wary of dealing with authority, or exercising it. There is accordingly a strong tradition of *laissez-faire*; things run more smoothly when everyone does as they please. Weak central government has meant a lack of resources for the judiciary and police, with undesirable effects. Although there are some who say that Flanders is a "police state", this view is based on the plethora of official forms that must be filled at every turn. In reality, the Flemish prefer to take short cuts and circumvent authority completely if they can, with tax evasion seen as an almost civic duty. On the other hand, trust and reciprocal solidarity are important Flemish values, fostered by the need simply to survive through numerous harsh occupations. Hoarding food is another habit that is thought to have been acquired after the First World War.

More generally, the Flemish do not tend to show off their wealth and those who can have an entrenched habit of concealing their assets in foreign countries. The more conservative among them dislike "otherness" or deviance from conventional behaviour and are susceptible to the appeal of authoritarian groupings that seem to offer protection against the outside world. In the past it was the extended family and the Catholic Church that gave them their sense of security; now that families are shrinking the Flemish feel the need to find new forms of social organization.

Flemish society was until recently *verzuild* or "pillarized" in the sense of being split into three main compartments: Catholic, Socialist and Liberal. Up until the 1960s it was entirely the norm to spend one's whole life in close association with one of these groupings. There are Catholic boy scouts, sickness funds, trade unions, theatre groups, football clubs and, of course, the same for Socialists and Liberals, although the Catholics are by far the best organized. Until the 1960s Catholicism was virtually the only religion in Belgium. The rapid secularization and internationalization of Flemish society since then have rendered such affiliations less meaningful, although they still count for something outside the main cities. Until 1961 Catholic priests told their parishioners to vote for the Catholic Party and which writers not to read—something they can no longer afford to do if they want anyone to come to church.

Flemish Victory

The battles of the post-war period were first fought over the issue of linguistic censuses and the long running "schools struggle" over Catholic education. The census of 1947 contained the question: "What is your first language?" This seemingly innocuous query raised intense hostility among the Flemish, as it was an invitation to pro-French Flemish to claim that they had become French speakers, with potentially serious consequences for any future division of the country and allocation of resources. The results were published in 1954, and some municipalities were indeed transferred to Wallonia. The main social change after 1945, meanwhile, was the economic and demographic decline of Wallonia, which had always relied on heavy industry and coal, and the increase in the population of Flanders, which by the 1960s accounted for nearly sixty per cent of the population of Belgium. Huge post-war foreign investment was increasingly channelled towards Flanders, and especially to Antwerp and other cities close to the main ports. The Catholic Flemish dominated the scene by their weight of numbers and new economic muscle, even if industries were often still owned by outsiders. The struggle now became more clearly defined: the Flemish demanded cultural autonomy (the elimination of French domination), while the Walloons wanted to maintain the unitary state and the freedom to run their own economy (meaning more subsidies).

The census due in 1960 had to be postponed to 1961 after massive protests by the Flemish, and the question about language was scrapped (it has never been asked again). As the communes to the south of Brussels had seen a steady influx of middle-class French speakers it was widely felt that the question about language would be used to bring these communes under French-speaking administration, with the result that Brussels would be joined to French-speaking Wallonia. After more demonstrations on the streets of Brussels in 1961 and 1962, it was finally decided in 1963 that Brussels would be limited to the existing nineteen communes, but that there would be a further six Flemish-run communes with "protected" French-speaking minorities around the periphery.

Picking up from the hesitant beginnings just prior to the Second World War, the first reform of the Belgian Constitution in 1970-71 created three cultural councils (for Dutch, French and German speakers). These councils could pass decrees in areas relating to culture and language use and received funds from the state. This reform created a new political entity, the language Community, or Gemeenschap in Dutch. More important was the reform of 1980 creating the Regions of Flanders, Wallonia and Brussels. At this point the competencies of the Communities and the Regions were laid down, and the geographical border between the Regions became inalterable. The Flemish Region and Community merged, as they were to all intents and purposes identical, except for the 140,000 Dutch speakers living in Brussels who are represented in the Brussels Parliament. The status of Brussels was fiercely contested and could not be settled until 1988. Regional assemblies with legislative powers were then created, and Regional governments with executive powers. The state thus handed over powers to the Regions in three main areas: daily life (town planning, education, environment, housing, etc.), the economy, and control over local administration. The federal state retained control over pensions, social security, defence and foreign affairs.

The fourth reform, the St. Michael Accords of 1993, instituted direct elections to the Regional parliaments, the first of which were held in 1995. At that point it seemed wise to allow the new system to settle down and to see whether it was enough to satisfy the demands of the Flemish majority. After all, for the first time since the fourteenth century the Flemish were free of foreign rulers and able to determine their own destiny. Even so, having their own political institutions is not, as yet at least, enough to change Flemish attitudes towards politicians, whom they traditionally call *zakkenvullers* or people who line their own pockets. It is a moot point whether the Flemish are less interested in politics than other nations, and now that they have their own government, a healthier attitude is likely to develop towards the political process. There was a further change in political culture with the large-scale demonstrations in 1996 against official corruption and incompetence in the case of the Walloon paedophile Marc Dutroux.

The Christian Democrats have been out of government since 1999, and appear to be in irreversible decline. The long-accepted system of political appointments and backroom deals has been curtailed, while subsidies for cultural activities are also being channelled less through political groupings. The main issue in Flemish politics now is whether to maintain the welfare state or to accept globalization and economic liberalism, rather than the age-old dispute between clericalists and anti-clericalists.

The Revival of the Extreme Right

Having reached a point where Flanders is now one of world's wealthiest countries (in terms of per capita income and quality of life), one might expect the Flemish to be satisfied—yet this is far from the case. A significant sector of the population either appears unconvinced of the value of democracy or is simply politically naïve, voting in increasing numbers for the neo-fascist Vlaams Blok, or Vlaams Belang as it became in 2004. The VB is not part of any regional or local government but has influence through committees as well as members of the European Parliament. In 2004 it gained about one-third of the vote in Antwerp and it is close to being the largest party in Flanders. Most of its support is concentrated in the central swathe of Flanders between Antwerp and Brussels. Vlaams Belang was built on the grievances of those who were persecuted at the end of the Second World War as well as on a simplistically nationalist platform. Now that the issue of amnesty for collaborators has been resolved, the VB has shifted its emphasis onto immigrants and irrational fears that foreigners will take away the new-found wealth of the Flemish. One of the stranger features of the VB is the way that many Flemish Socialists have taken to voting for them, as well as some Brussels French-speakers who dislike immigrants more than they do the Flemish. Some of the electorate, it is said, even support the VB to show their irritation at being forced to vote on a Sunday, and without compulsory voting its support would probably fall by half. More generally, the Flemish have a habit of springing to the defence of anyone who resists authority. By attacking the VB, the state has created a new type of underdog and so unintentionally encourages its growth.

Now that the Flemish dominate Belgium, they would naturally like to stop French-speakers from taking a large part of their taxes. It is estimated that US$12 billion is transferred every year from Flanders to Wallonia, a staggering amount given that the population of Flanders is less than six million. Even so, there is no question that most Flemish do not want Flanders to become an independent country, and that there is a significant difference between being pro-Flemish and supporting Flemish independence. Nor is telling the two positions apart too difficult; the out-and-out nationalists use only two colours in the Flemish flag: black and gold. Those who wish to remain within the Belgian state keep the red tongue and claws of the Flemish lion. One can also gauge ideological leanings from the way that people spell Dutch words: the more nationalistic Flemish use a so-called "advanced" spelling that substitutes a Germanic "k" for the Latin "c": thus *komitee* for *comité* (although this does not necessarily mean that they are right-wing).

The Flemish can no longer complain about the domination of French culture, as the issue long ago ceased to have any meaning (if it ever did) and they are now free to choose their own cultural preferences. The move towards full independence has also come to a halt, with over seventy per cent of Flemish preferring to remain within the Belgian federal system. The extreme right, meanwhile, has fallen back into the mindset of the 1930s, trying to isolate Flanders from the rest of the world, which it finds threatening, by appealing to the so-called *bange blanke man* (scared white man). There is also a much wider section among the Flemish who simply dislike anyone or anything that disrupts their ordered and predictable lives. Given that this stability was achieved after so much upheaval, it is perhaps something for which they cannot be entirely blamed.

Chapter Two
Religion and Folklore

"Stop talking about a particular value for one generation and that value will no longer exist. Religion is a matter of nerve. It's made in the first place for cowards."

Jef Geeraerts, *De goede moordenaar* (The Good Murderer), 1972

Flemish Tradition

Guide books often inform visitors to Flanders that there is a great deal of "traditional folklore" in the region, but this should perhaps be taken with a grain of salt. What is certainly true is that there is no shortage of "folklorism" rather than folklore, in that much of what is presented as traditional only appeared after 1830 and was deliberately introduced by the wealthier classes of society for commercial gain, to legitimize a certain historical incident or simply to distract workers briefly from their harsh day-to-day lives. Many of these new traditions were based on some earlier precedent; sometimes, as with the Eine Fietel (see p.39), they emerged from the people as a revived saturnalia, a chance to express ambivalent or negative feelings about the Church and the ruling class. There has always been a tension between the need to regulate and police carnivals and the desire to release pent-up frustrations, as can be seen very clearly in the present-day Aalst Carnival (see below).

Flemish society is as secularized as any other; no more people go to church than in Britain. There are those who have completely rejected the Catholic Church but are still troubled by their experiences at its hands, whom one might call "ex-Catholics", and those who no longer believe but still recognize the importance of Christian ethics and culture in Western society, who are "post-Catholics". The Catholic Church controlled the hearts and minds of the Flemish for hundreds of years. Its ideological hegemony waned in the twentieth century, as urbanization cut off the previously docile peasants from their roots. The Church's failure to prevent the Catholic University of Leuven from going over to the use of Dutch in 1967 was the final blow to its authority. The reaction to its decline was rather like that of a country emerging from decades of totalitarian rule, and continues to manifest itself in grossly tasteless cartoons and public displays of obscenity that would not be tolerated in other European countries. Some writers feel that they have to put their anti-Catholic credentials on display through crude satire; one such is Herman Brusselmans, the most popular writer in Flanders (in reality an innocuous bourgeois from Hamme in East Flanders). In a passage in the semi-autobiographical *Ex-minnaar* (Ex-Lover, 1998), Brusselmans is riding on a motorcycle through Merelbeke, near Ghent, in the middle of the night:

> At a certain moment I noticed a little chapel built in a ridiculously small copse. I stopped, parked and ran to the chapel. It was nothing more than a stone pillar with above it a box and a glass frontage, through which you could see a statue, representing, as the notice said, "Our Lady of Seven Sorrows". "Actually it's Eight Sorrows," I said to myself, "the eighth one being that Our Lady could get Her Holy Gob stamped on."
>
> I turned words into deeds, smashed the glass to bits with my helmet, ripped out the wooden statue, looked into the eyes (where I saw nothing) and smashed it against one of the dying trees. The head fell off its body. With my left foot I gave it a tremendous kick. It flew between two trees, and disintegrated against yet another tree... "Goal," I mumbled with pain in my heart.

Small wayside shrines or *kapellekes* are still lovingly looked after in the countryside and towns. Many are on the sites of pre-Christian sacred trees or crossroads and have miracles associated with them. The notion that someone would vandalize a wayside chapel is far-fetched, even in modern irreligious Flanders.

The Catholic Church Today

The Spanish occupation has given the Catholic Church in Belgium its strongly Mediterranean flavour. The cult of the Virgin Mary and the multitude of shrines on street corners and in the countryside have led some to dub Belgians the "Spaniards of the North". Visitors are generally struck by the Baroque Spanish style of decoration in churches where images of the extravagantly tormented Christ have a feel redolent of the Inquisition and the Spanish Terror of the sixteenth century, and for many there is a distinctive smell of death in Flemish churches. Older Catholics still display images in their houses of an eye in a triangle (representing the all-seeing Holy Trinity) and the words: *God ziet u. Hier vloekt men niet* (God is watching you. No swearing here.). In the past these warning signs were put in cafés; a few remain in place.

Once dominant in Flanders, the Church is now rapidly declining. Most priests are over fifty and hardly any new clergy are being trained. If it is generally said that Flanders is Catholic and that Wallonia is not, this simplification obscures significant variations across Flanders as regards religious faith. West Flanders is socially conservative and the most Catholic of all the provinces, while Limburg and the area north of Antwerp are also traditionally strongly Catholic. Least Catholic are the big cities of Ghent, Antwerp and Brussels. The rest of East Flanders is a mixture of Catholic and Liberal. Leuven in Flemish Brabant has Europe's largest Catholic university, but the rest of the province is less religious than East Flanders, even if it has Belgium's largest pilgrimage site at Scherpenheuvel-Zichem.

Many Flemish continue to consider themselves Christians but cannot stand the institution of the Church itself and the diktat of Rome. Important institutions in Flemish life, as we have seen, have their roots in the Catholic Church or are still run by Catholics. At the same time, the Belgian Church has recently become less authoritarian and is often at odds with Rome. The ageing clergy and shortage of new priests mean that responsibilities are increasingly devolving onto lay preachers and deacons, but Rome still prohibits women from becoming deacons and, as a result, women are particularly dissatisfied with the current situation. Many Catholics have simply stopped going to church except for births, marriages and funerals. Church attendance has fallen dramatically, going down to as little as eight per cent of the population in 2005.

For those who do not want to deal directly with the Church, the bizarrely named Rentapriest organization will send a suitably qualified person, who may or may not be an ordained priest, to carry out a ceremony in the home. One advantage of such services is that a child can be christened at home and have a certificate to that effect, so that he or she can still take first communion later in life. Divorcees who remarry can also receive religious blessings, much to the distaste of the more conservative clergy. Rentapriest was started by a gay priest and a married priest from East Flanders with the guiding principle that everyone should think for themselves.

Catholicism has left a lasting impression on the Flemish, for good or ill. Part of the Flemish self-image is bound up with charity and compassion, but as in Latin countries the Flemish prefer to restrict their charitable giving to local causes rather than the welfare of those who live far away. While there is certainly a connection between the low crime rate in Flanders and the past imposition of Catholic morality, Christian belief has sometimes been replaced by unadulterated materialism. Others who still feel a need for spiritual devotion turn to alternative Asian religions. The well-known cliché that the Flemish live between materialism and mysticism is perhaps vindicated by the fact that Flanders still produces quite a number of self-sacrificing Catholic missionaries. There is a genuine tradition of contemplative mysticism that remains alive today and which was not imposed from outside. This is clear from the writings of the great Flemish mystics of the thirteenth century such as Hadewijch and John of Ruusbroec. The Flemish are still susceptible to religious impulses, even if now they are not always of the Christian variety. Flemish literature has also traditionally included a didactic or moral message, something that has not helped its writers to gain success abroad.

While modern Flanders is increasingly secularized, there are also remnants of an earlier paganism, and in more backward areas there is still belief in witchcraft, the so-called "evil hand" rather than evil eye. A farmer whose cow falls ill or milk turns sour may believe he has been bewitched. If an exorcist is required, Jesuit, Franciscan or Dominican priests are preferred, as they are reckoned to have more power than an ordinary parish priest because of their greater discipline. The Volkskunde (Ethnological) Museum in Antwerp—which will move to the Museum Aan de Stroom in 2008—has a remarkable collection of tools used by witches collected in the Kempen around 1900, donated by the writer Max Elskamp.

The Schools Struggle

The Flemish are very proud of their education system. In terms of results and discipline it ranks with the best in the world, on a par with Korea and Hong Kong. This success, however, has been achieved at the cost of equality. Pupils are rigorously selected and moved into vocational courses if they are not academically bright, and there is a strict correlation between educational attainment and social status. Until the Second World War anyone who could afford to would send their children to a French-medium school. Nowadays about six per cent of the population of Flanders speak French at home, but their children will generally go to Dutch-medium schools to ensure that they are not disadvantaged later on in life. In Brussels, Dutch-medium schools are full of French-speaking children, to the extent that they are now limited to 65 per cent of the intake. This is partly because North African immigrants send their children to French-medium schools.

Most schools in Flanders are in the so-called "free" sector (*vrij onderwijs*). The name is misleading since they charge for various items that are free in the state sector. If a village has one school, then it is almost always Catholic, and some eighty per cent of schools are in the Catholic sector. Their high charges discourage the children of poorer immigrants from going there, but those who can afford to prefer to send their children to Catholic schools where they will learn better Dutch at the price of having to undergo compulsory religious instruction in Christianity. These communities make up for this disadvantage by sending their children to out-of-hours Muslim tuition. There are very few private fee-paying schools.

The so-called *schoolstrijd* or "schools struggle" dominated Belgian politics during certain periods when the Catholics were out of government, especially in 1878-84 and 1954-58. Attempts by the Liberals to impose state education all over the country in 1878 led the Catholics to set up an alternative system. There were violent clashes and the Belgian government severed its relations with the Vatican. The Liberals had gone too far out on a limb and were rejected by the electorate in 1884. A similar incident took place in 1954 when the Socialists attempted to reduce subsidies to the Catholic sector and took discriminatory measures against graduates from Catholic schools who wished to become teachers in the state system; they were again rebuffed at the following elections. It is still the case that teachers in the state system do not work in Catholic schools, or vice versa.

Partisan Publishers

Dutch literature in Flanders since independence in 1830 has suffered from both a lack of readers and a lack of publishers. Major Belgian writers writing in Dutch are now published by Amsterdam-based firms such as De Bezige Bei, Prometheus and De Arbeiderspers. In the nineteenth century the Belgian book trade was dominated by two politically inspired publishers, the Willemsfonds and the Davidsfonds. The Willemsfonds was founded in Ghent in 1851 and named after Jan Frans Willems, the great promoter of the Dutch language in Belgium and the "Father of the Flemish Movement". The 38 founders were mostly liberals or moderate Catholics. When the anti-clerical Julius Vuylsteke became general-secretary in 1862, the organization expanded greatly as well as becoming more explicitly liberal. The Willemsfonds published books intended to enlighten the backward Flemish masses, ran free libraries and organized lectures—all of which were a thorn in the side of conservative Catholic priests who did their best to frustrate their liberal rivals.

The Catholics accused the Willemsfonds of corrupting youth with atheistic and immoral literature. In 1875 the rival Davidsfonds (named after a Catholic priest) was established with its base in Leuven, while the Willemsfonds continued to operate from its headquarters in Ghent. Both the Davidsfonds and Willemsfonds ran people's libraries (Socialists had their own libraries). The Catholic Church did not want its followers to read novels at all, as these usually presented an alternative view of the world to its own. Books about history, especially the defeat of the Protestants, or crude propaganda against freemasons and free-thinkers were the staple diet of the Catholic book clubs. The Davidsfonds quickly gained complete control in the countryside, while the Willemsfonds found itself limited to the larger cities. The collections eventually ended up in municipal libraries. The Willemsfonds, Davidsfonds and three smaller funds are still active as socio-cultural organizations.

Perhaps the most surprising story in Flemish publishing is that of Angèle Manteau. Originally a French-speaker from Dinant, she took lodgings with the Dutch poet Jan Greshoff in Brussels when she was a student and developed a passionate interest in Dutch literature. In the 1930s up-and-coming Flemish writers had great difficulty in finding publishers, and there was no one who would even consider publishing experimental fiction. Manteau took over a book import business from a Dutchman in 1932 and started the Angèle Manteau imprint in 1938. By bringing out Dutch translations of commercially successful writers from outside Belgium as well as non-fiction, Manteau had the resources to launch the careers of many Flemish writers. Manteau remains a prestigious publisher.

Carnivals and Processions

The processions and marches around towns and villages that mark the year's calendar are among the most typically Flemish of cultural events. At the most basic level, these may consist of little more than a brass band marching down the street, seemingly just for the fun of it, but there are many different types of procession. An *ommegang* (literally, "going around") is a profane procession around village or town, often featuring costumed giants who are there to make the proceedings more impressive. Different groups and associations within the community can take part in the *ommegang*. The Brussels Ommegang has become a tourist event with magnificent costumes and historical re-enactments.

A *processie* is purely religious and involves a parade with a saint's relics and other religious symbols. The classic example is the town of Veurne's Boeteprocessie or Procession of the Penitents, started in 1644 (about which Rilke wrote a poem). The tradition of *boeteprocessies* was a Hispanic import, introduced when Spanish troops wished to recreate their own processions on Maundy Thursday and Good Friday. This meant a procession of hooded penitents carrying a wooden cross or iron bar and whipping themselves with iron hooks. The Flemish not unreasonably found this spectacle repellent, but after the Protestants had been finally driven out, the authorities wanted more Catholic manifestations and the cities duly instituted their own processions, albeit in slightly less extreme forms. Bruges had the first procession in 1626. These events were then suppressed by the Austrians and the French and turned into processions of the Holy Sacrament without great drama. Only the Boeteprocessie in Veurne has continued to the present day. A *processie*, moreover, can turn into an *ommegang*, but not the other way round. Taking part in the preparations for a procession or parade is an important way of confirming one's sense of identity and belonging in the community.

A third type of procession is the *carnaval*. Carnivals go back to Roman times or earlier, and the occasion is the start of Lent (the word *carnevale* means "goodbye to meat".) Mardi Gras is known as Vet Dinsdag (fat Tuesday) or Vastenavond (eve of fasting) in Flanders and is an excuse for a rowdy street party. Even so, the tradition of carnival is in decline. Many such carnival parties reappeared in the mid-nineteenth century after a long period of being suppressed by the Austrians and French occupiers, but they cannot be compared to the raucous celebrations of the Middle Ages. Instead, they were revived by the notables of a town or village to foster a sense of civic pride and because they were popular with café and restaurant owners who made a large part of their annual profits from the carnival.

In the traditional scheme of things, people in a town belong to a *carnavalvereniging* (carnival society) and pay dues to finance the building of a decorated float. The winner of the competition for best float or costume receives the title of Carnival Prince or Emperor, much as in Germany. It is very much the older generation that belongs to carnival societies such as the Orde van Neptunus in Ostend and many other "Ordes". Most processions are subsidized by municipalities and are particularly successful in coastal resorts like Heist and Blankenberge as an important part of the tourist season. The Ostend Carnival, for instance, lasts three days. On the Friday the Cimateire Stoet takes place when candles are placed in pumpkins to recall the time when there were no lighthouses and people stood on the shore holding torches to guide boats home. Sunday witnesses the Kloeffeworp or clog throwing, when clog-shaped sweets are thrown into the crowd from the town hall (among them is one made of gold). The first Sunday in July is the date of the Zeewijding or Sea Blessing for the protection of fishermen.

Fietelen
Two festivals take place each year in the East Flemish village of Eine, near Oudenaarde. On the last Sunday in June the Ruiterommegang (horse-riders' procession), also called the St. Pieterskermis because it was traditionally held on the name day of St. Peter, fills the streets. It is now the festival of Eine's patron saint, St. Eligius, or St. Elooi in Dutch. St.

Eligius was a silversmith and an early Christian missionary to the area who also shod horses and thus became patron saint of horses, farmers and railways. During the festival horses and riders are blessed with the silver hammer the saint holds in his hand. The hammer allegedly contains a relic and may also be a religious throwback to the Norse god Thor.

The Eine Fietel started in 1852 as a joke, but not with any obvious anti-religious connotations. In that year a village woman apparently told her husband to stay at home and "watch the door", so he took it off its hinges and went around the village cafés with the door in a wheelbarrow. There is a statue of this scene near the church. A *fiertel* is a reliquary carried around a village or town, except that here it is pronounced *fietel* (the word derives from the Latin for a portable shrine, *feretrum*). The original patron saint of Eine was St. Eleutherius, the patron saint of Doornik; he was then replaced by St. Eligius. This process of substitution was quite common in the past, for if one saint became more popular or was shown to be more effective in answering prayers, then he could take the place of the original.

The Fietel is held on the fourth Sunday of September, when the reliquary of the Holy Cross obtained by crusaders in 1204 is also brought out for worship. During the Fietel local groups are expected to produce a short performance piece making fun of various events or figures from the previous year. (The verb *fietelen* means to satirize or to make a performance out of events or rumours that have done the rounds, in particular subjects that cannot be openly discussed. It is said that locals are brought up *al fietelend,* or joking as they go along. There are also special songs: *fietelliederen.*) Participants inform the festival committee of the chosen title, but the actual content of their performance has to remain a secret. Other items are fixed, such as the giants, people dressed up as horses or performing bears, and so on. The biggest of the giants, which can reach thirty feet, are pushed around on wheels.

't Ros Beiaard in Dendermonde

Dendermonde is a conservative Catholic town in East Flanders on the River Dender, named after the Celtic god of thunder. Dendermondenaars are known as the *kopvleesfretters* (literally devourers

"Beiaard the giant horse was black as pitch,
but his broad chest as white as hail."
Felix Timmermans, *De vier heemskinderen,* 1922

of compressed pig's head or brawn), and their liking for this typical Flemish dish is apparently legendary. At the centre of local folklore is the mythical horse, Ros Beiaard, colloquially called *'t peird* (the horse) and the Vier Heemskinderen (Four Home Children). The story goes back to the time of Emperor Charlemagne, when a certain Reinout, nephew of Charlemagne and one of four brothers, was playing chess with Charlemagne's son Louis. Reinout suspected Louis of cheating and so cut off his head in a rage. The magical horse, Beiaard, allowed the four brothers to flee but in the end his owner had to give him up to restore peace with Charlemagne. Ros Beiaard drowned himself in the Dender after he thought that his master had abandoned him.

Where four brothers are born in one family with no girls in between, they qualify to ride Ros Beiaard on one of his ten-yearly outings. They have to be aged between seven and twenty-one when they ride the horse, and both they and their parents must be born in Dendermonde. The last outing was in 2000 and the next will be in 2010. The same tradition exists in Lier, near Antwerp. The story itself originated in Wallonia, but the bards who told it always situated the action in the town they were visiting. The name of the horse comes from the French *baie* (for a bay horse) and is not related to the Flemish word for a carillon, which is also *beiaard*. The bay-coloured horse is carried, with coats of arms on the skirts that hide the frame; it can be up to thirty feet tall, while the four children on top have to hang on for dear life.

The last Thursday of August marks the Katuit or Reuzenommegang (giant *ommegang*) in Dendermonde. This is a major festival and is heavily promoted by the Flemish tourist office. Three giants by the names of Indiaan, Mars and Goliath dance around the town accompanied by numerous floats and 800 costumed performers. Dendermonde has also acquired an international reputation for its jazz festivals and is now home to the Jazz Centrum Vlaanderen. A number of Belgian festivals have been declared part of the world's cultural heritage by UNESCO. In Flanders these include 't Ros Beiaard and the Giants of Mechelen.

Carnival in Aalst
Aalst considers itself the carnival capital of Flanders, with three days of riotous festivities around *vastenavond* (eve of fasting) or Shrove Tuesday and Ash Wednesday. The traditions around *vastenavond* go back to Germanic and Roman celebrations such as Saturnalia, when the world was turned on its head, the master became the servant and women ruled over men. In the pre-Christian tradition there was also the invocation of new growth during the winter months, while the tradition of the *steekspel* (jousting), where winter and summer battle it out, is age-old. In the Christian version this became a joust between Carnival and Lent, a common theme in prints and paintings. The Brussels Museum of Fine Art has a Brueghel painting of the joust.

Such events could take place any time between 11 November (Martinmas) and Easter. In Flanders fasting or *vasten* is naturally

connected with Ash Wednesday, the start of Lent. The Sunday before the start of Lent is Vette Zondag or Quinquagesima. The big party then takes place on Shrove Tuesday or Vetten Dinsdag (Mardi Gras). The Sunday after is Sotternyensondag (Fools' Sunday) or Quadragesima. In pre-Christian times there was feasting rather than fasting. The older dialect word *vastelauved* is still used in Aalst, *vastelen* meaning "to wander about talking incoherently," a more accurate term for the celebration than "the eve of fasting". There is also the Halfvasten Foor (Mi-Carême in French), literally "mid-Lent fair", which goes on for several weeks in Ghent and elsewhere. Another type of festival is the *kermis* which was originally held annually to commemorate the dedication of a church or chapel.

The medieval Aalst Carnival was a tumultuous affair, with societies of young men organized by district running amok in the city. Too much exuberant revelry was a threat to public order, and so the authorities tried to organize festivities rather than let them carry on for weeks on end. By 1733 it was said that the people started to wear fancy dress only eight days before Ash Wednesday rather than weeks before. There was always also a tradition of putting on profane plays during the carnival. From a

Christian point of view, the whole event was little more than an exercise in showing people how not to behave.

The present tradition of the Aalst Carnival dates more precisely from 1851, when a group of traders set up the carnival society with the intention of providing entertainment for the locals and promoting the city and its businesses. This was the first year when there was an organized parade or *carnavalstoet*, and the tradition of fancy dress was also revived. Poorer people who could not afford to make costumes would borrow their spouse's cast-off clothes, so the men acquired the name of *Voil Jeanet* (Dirty Janet) as they generally had only their wives' dirty old clothes to wear. The tradition has become ever more popular with the young and the costumes increasingly sophisticated. Interestingly, *jeanet* is these days a term used all over Flanders for a homosexual or effeminate man.

The Aalst Carnival is now a huge event with thousands of participants and expensive and elaborate floats, satirizing politicians, the Church and almost everything, it seems, but the Belgian royal family. There are strict rules about the construction of the floats and images. Work starts on 11 November every year, and no float may be used more than once. The techniques used are on display at the Aalst town museum (Stedelijk Museum). The event especially appeals to heavy metal fans who appreciate an excuse to put on make-up, and the most enthusiastic participants in the parade are generally teenagers or in their twenties. Things can get rowdy in the evening; some shops board up their windows, trees are protected with boards and the police maintain a sometimes heavy-handed presence.

A West Flemish Saint

The Flemish saint *par excellence* is St. Godelieve, whose pilgrimage place is at Gistel near Ostend. She was from Boulogne in northern France and was married off to one Bertolf, the son of a local lord. Her mother-in-law took a dislike to her, in particular to her black hair, and not only called her "black crow" but arranged for her to be strangled with her own scarf by two henchmen. When she took a long time to die, she was held down head first in a pool. The water where Godelieve was drowned subsequently assumed miraculous powers, especially when applied to the throat or eyes. Her unappreciative husband's daughter by his second wife was born blind, but was cured by the water from her well. Around the spot where she was drowned there then appeared white stones that were believed to have formed from the mixing of her blood with the water, so-called *bloedstenen* (blood stones). Fourteen years after her death her husband had a vision of her sewing shirts for him, and she was immediately canonized in 1084.

These days there is a thriving pilgrimage place and an abbey with eight Benedictine nuns, a museum, the well itself and the miraculous water. In a pleasing touch of modernity, the site boasts automatic dispensers for candles, rosaries, prayers and images of St. Godelieve. The Kraaikapel (crow chapel) on a small hill recalls an event in her life: on one occasion St. Godelieve was sent to the fields to act as a scarecrow by her mother-in-law. When she heard the bell for mass, she ordered the crows to go and sit in a barn and they obeyed. There is a Naaikapel (sewing chapel) with the miraculous seamless shirt dating from the eleventh century supposed to have been made by St Godelieve herself. Her skeleton is still preserved in a reliquary, and the museum has a fine collection of material relating to her cult. The chapel has the usual tiles decorated with expressions of thanks to the saint, with just a few of the old-fashioned ex-votos (metal plaques) representing the eyes of the cured left in gratitude. There are also reliquaries studded with small pieces of saints' bones in the so-called "prison" of St. Godelieve. The power of saints is believed to reside in their bones, while St. Godelieve is also invoked by women praying for a peaceful marriage.

The present Abdij ten Putte (Abbey of the Well) dates from 1891. The original abbey was destroyed by Protestants in 1578 and the sisters had to flee to Bruges. The row of trees silhouetted against the whitewashed abbey buildings is reminiscent of the Begijnhof in Bruges. In the summer there are plenty of pilgrims, and on the second Sunday in July the St. Godelieve Procession takes place in Gistel, which has expanded into a major festival with 1,000 costumed participants. The nuns themselves lead a life of work and prayer (*ora et labore*), as laid down by the Rule of St. Benedict, getting up at five in the morning and praying several times a day in between work.

Chapter Three
Food, Drink and Popular Culture

"Those good Flemish: they have got to eat."
Victor Hugo

A long line of foreign authors like Hugo have remarked that the Flemish enjoy eating, indeed that the alleged habit of overeating renders them unfit for the higher life of the mind. Thus in "Une excursion en Belgique", in the French *Magasin pittoresque* (1836):

> The fog which weighs on this country and oppresses the inhabitants forces them to eat five meals a day, and obstructs the vigorous exercise of the imagination. Finally, the narrowness of its boundaries and scarcity of resources destroy the desire to emulate others and puts obstacles in the way of large designs.

Belgians live to eat, or so goes the cliché, and they want both quality and quantity. Brueghel's village feast goes on and on and on, and the Belgian medical profession laughs all the way to the bank.

Chip Van Culture
Visitors to Antwerp will be glad to know that there is a museum on the Groenplaats dedicated to chips (or French fries) in the emporium known as Fritkot Max. Named after two pioneering Walloon chip merchants called Fritz and Max, Fritkot Max houses part of the unique collection of chip-related artefacts built up by the Antwerp art lecturer Paul Ilegems, who is the author of three books on *frietkots* or chip vans. He has also brought out a CD with songs relating to chips, *De Zingende Friet* (The Singing Chip). Ilegems regards *frietkots* as a metaphor for *belgitude*, an expression of nonchalance and proof of an ability to improvise when faced with challenges such as converting old buses or sheds into chip vans.

Finch singing competition in Moeskroen

The temporary nature and, let it be said, occasional ugliness of the *frietkot* have elicited hostility from some, and they are in danger of dying out, victims of ruthlessly bureaucratic hygiene inspectors. The colourful and individualistic *frietkot* is a symbol of independence and uninhibited pleasure, but the authorities are more concerned with the smell and litter they create and so want them removed from the vicinity of public buildings such as churches where they might disturb tourists. In most places the *frietkot* now has to be housed in a permanent building; the old-style van can no longer stand on its own on the square. Only Antwerp seems willing still to tolerate *frietkots* in open areas.

Belgians are so closely identified with potatoes that the Dutch call them *pattatekes* or "little potatoes". As a joke the British advertising agency Saatchi and Saatchi staged a notorious stunt in 1994, which is now repeated annually. A Paris café, La Jatte in Neuilly-sur-Seine, announced: "In Belgium the 14th of July is on the 21st. To celebrate the event the Café de la Jatte is offering two portions of French fries for the price of three. This offer is open to all Belgians. No proof of identity required." The Belgian government protested at this racially insulting gag and unwarranted slur on Belgian intellect, but to no avail.

There is no evidence that the French invented chips, nor can one be certain that it was the Belgians either, but it is known that they were being sold in the streets of Belgium from the 1830s. The introduction of potatoes into Belgium around 1700 had a dramatic effect on the population, as potatoes were easier to grow than wheat (to say nothing of their alleged aphrodisiac properties). The Flemish peasants suffered severely as a result of the potato famine of 1845, and many migrated to Brussels and Wallonia, but the effects were far less severe than in Ireland.

No Joke

The Flemish are the first to admit that there is something comical about some of their food. Witness the Mechelse Koekoek (Mechelen cuckoo), a kind of chicken or *vogel zonder kop* (headless bird) of ground pork with strips of beef around it held together with toothpicks. Sold ready-made by butchers and known also as a *blinde vink* (blind finch) or *loze vink* (fake finch), the gourmet does not need to assemble these strange parcels himself. Many traditional dishes are under threat, in particular the *frikadel* (or *fricadelle* to French-speakers). This ground beef and pork

(sometimes only beef) meatball could be likened to a Flemish hamburger, but is eaten with tomato sauce and not in a roll or bun. The *frikadel* conjures up images of a mother's home cooking; you would not expect to find it in a takeaway. The real *frikadel* is often confused with a more dubious kind of sausage, the *frikandel* or *curryworst,* an indescribable mix of pureed offal disguised with curry powder, sometimes termed a Flemish hot dog (in Limburg it is known as a *lange frikadel* or long *frikadel*). The *curryworst* (pronounced *kerryworst*) is specific to Antwerp and is also termed "Hollandse *frika(n)del*".

Linguistically the *frikandel* is certainly inferior to the *frikadel* ; a *frikandel* is long and a *frikadel* is round. The Flemish say *frikandel* because it trips off the tongue more easily than *frikadel*. Uncertainty about the contents of the *frikadel* has led to its decline, and fewer and fewer are being eaten. In the cosmopolitan and post-modern playground of the Flemish *frietkot*, meanwhile, one may now enjoy supposedly more honest Turkish pittas (with döner kebab inside), *shoarmas,* hamburgers, pizzas, Indonesian *loempias* (spring rolls) and *satés* (pieces of chicken on a stick with peanut sauce) and *merguez* (Moroccan spicy sausage).

The traditional Flemish blood sausage—the *bloedpens*—is also going out of fashion. This is a kind of haggis, but sausage-shaped. In Ghent a staple food was once horse and garlic sausage, *peerdeluukworst,* not much eaten these days although the nearby town of Lokeren still specializes in *peerdeluukworst* with French fries. The thinly sliced *charcuterie* (salted and thinly sliced meat) known as *filet d'Anvers* (Antwerp fillet) is usually horsemeat but sometimes beef. (Horsemeat is clearly labeled *paardevlees.*) A stock item is Flemish pork sausage (*Vlaamse worst*), a kind of endless sausage that is fried and served with boiled potatoes and red cabbage (cooked with brown sugar and vinegar). This very basic dish was a favourite of King Baudouin I (r.1950-93). In *Tijl Uilenspiegel* an emissary from Flanders offers the newly-born King Philip II a Ghent sausage five cubits long and half a cubit round and expresses the wish that the future king will develop a thirst for Ghent Klauwaard beer after eating the sausage because, he concludes, anyone who loves the beer of a city could not hate its brewers. Note, however, that there are now no breweries in Ghent because the Germans removed all the copper from the city during the First World War. Just as odd is the story that in the seventeenth century all the butchers of Ghent were descended from the illegitimate offspring of Emperor Charles V, so they were called "Sons of Princes". The truth is that only a few people could obtain a licence to operate as a butcher and those who did became wealthy. There were no butchers' shops as such; all meat had to be sold from the central market where it could be closely monitored.

At the bottom of the food chain (in Ghent at least) is the very traditional *hoofdvlak.* Take a pig's head, clean thoroughly, boil in stock, remove all the meat, mince it and press into a shaped tin. To most Dutch speakers, *hoofdvlak* is a term in geometry, meaning "principal plane"; only in Ghent does it mean "reformed pig's head" or brawn. Elsewhere it is called *kop, varkenskop, kopvlees* or *Gentse kop;* in Antwerp there is even *Breughelkop.* The people of Aalst, we have seen, call the inhabitants of Dendermonde *kopvleesfretters* (*kopvlees* eaters); they swear that the Dendermondenaars fish dead dogs out of the Dender floating downriver from Aalst to make into *kopvlees.* Ghent *kopvlees* is best eaten with local mustard from the Tierenteyn shop on the vegetable market. The mustard is made on the premises by machines in the basement that work all day long while the customers are served above. The Antwerp novelist and publicist Willem Elsschot composed a ditty to advertise Tierenteyn mustard after he had become friendly with the owner:

In the desert you find coconuts
And savages on their naked feet.
For whiskey you need to be in England

The best mustard is here in Ghent
Go to the Bisschop Seghersplein
And ask for Ferdinand Tierenteyn.

In past times the poor had little meat, at best some salted bacon and the occasional rabbit or chicken in the countryside. In French Flanders one can still find *potjevleesch*, officially consisting of pieces of four "white" meats—veal and rabbit, along with a choice of poultry and beef—preserved in jelly. This was originally a Dunkirk recipe that spread to the rest of the Nord-Pas-de-Calais after the Second World War when *potjevleesch* had been forgotten in most places, now even turning up in Veurne as *potjesvlees*. The people of Dunkirk are credited with inventing *potjevleesch* when in the sixteenth century there was a plague of rabbits in the dunes nearby. When locals were given permission to exterminate them, there was so much rabbit meat that it had to be preserved in jelly complete with the bones.

Frietkot Blues

The blues singer Big Bill Krakkebaas—the pseudonym of Armand Hombroeckx—scored his only major hit with *Eene me hesp* (Ham Sandwich). The song had its origins in a real-life existential crisis: Big Bill was wandering the streets of Leuven after a heavy night's drinking and had to choose between a cheese or ham sandwich. *Eene me hesp*, which owes much to Chuck Berry, is actually the B-side of a single of which the A-side was *Stoose blues* (Station Blues)—*stoose* being the Leuven dialect word for *station*. Perhaps typecast by *Eene me hesp*, Big Bill has not reached the same heights again, even with his *Frietkot blues*—an all but incomprehensible Leuven dialect rant about French fry stalls.

> There's a frietkot by the station
> Where they have good mayonnaise
> The pickles they are mouldy
> And the mussels they are grey.
> And if you want to order a Stella
> People, it's just apple mush.

Stella Artois, of course, is the well-known Leuven beer, much drunk in Britain. Big Bill once ran the Café Allee in Leuven; now he plays his blues there. Another band who seized on the comic potential of food is Wawadadakwa from Antwerp, a group of jazzers who went to perfect their art in Cuba before releasing their popular *Broodje préparé* ("Raw ground beef bound with raw egg and capers in a white bread roll") in which they repeat the words *broodje préparé* over and over to a heavy driving beat. Fans of the raw may also like the notorious *filet américain*, uncooked ground beef without the bread. Items worryingly labelled *toast cannibale* and *steak tartare* also contain raw minced beef.

Classic Meals

At the top end of the gastronomic market stands *waterzooi*: chicken cooked in cream sauce, rather sophisticated and not much eaten, found also in French Flanders. Next down is *paling in 't groen*—river eel in a slimy green sauce of eighteen herbs including spinach, chervil, tarragon, sorrel and parsley. Donkmeer Lake near Dendermonde is famous for its eel restaurants. The most popular local haute cuisine dish is *stoverij* or beef stewed in dark beer for hours, known outside Flanders as *carbonades flamandes*. It is certainly simple enough to make: stew chunks of beef in onions and (optionally) a dark beer or even red wine.

Waterzooi is less well known abroad. The word *zooi* means "a mess" or mixture of ingredients. Originally *waterzooi* was made with freshwater fish such as eel, bream or pike perch and was poor people's food. Freshwater fish often had a bad taste, so they were first marinated in milk, thus giving the *waterzooi* its typical white colour. At the coast fishermen made *waterzooi* from the fish they could not sell at the market, and the ingredients consisted of whatever came to hand. These days *waterzooi* is more often made with chicken and is usually cooked with cream, but until quite recently chicken was a luxury food. A popular television programme, *Gentse waterzooi*, features the actor Gène Bervoets travelling around the world trying to make *waterzooi* with whatever local ingredients he can find. The French operatic composer Jules Massenet (1842-1912) liked Ghent chicken *waterzooi* so much that he wrote a *Cantate au waterzooi* in homage. For the full story of Flemish cuisine there is no better book than *Everybody Eats Well in Belgium* by Ruth van Waerebeeck, a Ghentite chef who teaches cookery in New York.

Beer Paradise

The Belgians have worked hard in the last few decades to promote their beers around the world with the result that they dominate international beer rankings. Most are bottled beers, which travel well but cannot be brewed anywhere other than in Belgium. Delirium Tremens, brewed by Huyghe in Melle near Ghent, has the reputation as the world's best beer since it was rated top by the American author, Stuart A. Kallen, in his *50 Greatest Beers in the World* (1997):

> Words simply cannot describe the intricate flavor of this beer, but that won't stop me from trying. The color is golden and the head creamy and light. The first sip warms my throat and belly like an old woodstove does a log cabin. It's lightly hopped and surprisingly malty for such an airy, sunshine beer. With a nose somewhat reminiscent of Orval, the aftertaste is fruity, almost cherry. A warming alcoholic glow works its way down the throat to the stomach.

With its fermentation using three different yeast cultures, Delirium Tremens is sold under the more reassuring name of Mateen in the US (Mateen was an early Flemish brewer in America). The *tripel* beers can reach a lethal 15 per cent in alcohol content. Westmalle Tripel is rated by many as the world's best beer although it rather obviously tries to make you drunk. A third contender for best Flemish beer is Duvel, brewed in the Antwerp suburb of Mortsel.

Flemish Brabant has many of the best breweries in Belgium such as Grimbergen and Affligem. The valley of the River Senne on the western side of Brussels is the only place where one can brew naturally fermented *lambic*, the basis of *gueuze*, *kriek* and *faro*. The process relies on bacteria that float in the air known as *brettanomycis bruxellensis*. A widely exported beer is the *witbier* or "white beer" of Hoegaarden, near Leuven. A summer drink, not too alcoholic and best served with a slice of lemon, Hoegaarden is a cloudy beer based on wheat with a lemony taste from its coriander flavouring. Other kinds of *witbier* are Brugs Tarwebier or Dentergems Wit. One can ask for a *witteke*—the diminutive of *wit*.

The dregs should never be drunk of any kind of *dubbel* (brown beer) because they are an effective laxative. In the case of *tripel* (also called *blond*) the problem is rather that the dregs are likely to cloud your drink. A Flemish bartender will always take care not to serve the dregs of any kind of bottled beer.

The beers known as Trappist are brewed by Trappist monks in only a few places in Belgium. The most popular Trappist beers in Flanders are Westmalle Dubbel and Tripel and St. Sixtus. Westmalle is north-east of Antwerp, while St. Sixtus is in West Flanders. There are three other Trappist monasteries but they are not beer producers. The recipes are strictly secret and no one is allowed inside the breweries. The more common *abdijbieren* or "abbey beers" are not usually brewed by monks and are often simply commercial trademarks, with many of the workers lay people. The name *abdij* carries a certain cachet, but the beers are less stable and consistent than the famed *trappistes*.

Flemish beers often have humorous names with religious themes such as Moeder Overste (Mother Superior); the beer's advertisements convey "greetings from Mother Superior". Others are Verboden Vrucht (Forbidden Fruit), Duvel (devil in Flemish dialect), Judas, Satan, Paranoia and so on.

Waffle Iron Politics
The aroma of hot waffles is a defining feature of life in Belgium and northern France, an intense and almost mystical pleasure in something uncomplicated. Belgians favour the lighter, bigger variety, with deep indentations. There is no such as thing as "to waffle" in Dutch, in the sense of talking meaninglessly, but the expression *wafelijzerpolitiek* or "waffle iron politics" does exist, meaning that the government has to spread its subsidies evenly all over the country just as the batter flows evenly into a waffle iron. These tools of the trade conceal deep meanings that are eloquently explained in folklore expert Jacques Messiant's *Le temps des gaufres* (Waffle Time, 2002). The lozenge shapes or stars, for

instance, are male and female symbols and therefore represent the ideal of a happy marriage. "Luikse wafels" or Liège waffles—the basic rectangular type made of flour, eggs, and sugar, and eaten hot or cold—are normally to be found in shops and around railway stations. Other varieties are less commonplace, perhaps because the elaborate waffle irons used to make them are no longer manufactured. Old waffle irons are cheap to buy in the Sunday market in Bruges, and Het Huis van Alijn, the folklore museum in Ghent on the Kraanlei, has an excellent collection.

In the Flemish-speaking area of France—Cœur de Flandre—visitors may well be offered *stryntjes* or small hard waffles with coffee. The word is related to the French *étrennes*, a New Year's gift, and it was the custom around Steenvoorde for women to make *stryntjes* at New Year to offer to poor people who came to the door to sing a song wishing the owners good health and happiness. If *stryntjes* were first made as a charitable act, it then became the custom for children to visit friends' houses to have *stryntjes* (or in Boeschepe, *lukjes*) every Saturday in January and February, which became *stryndag* (*stryntjes* day). Nowadays *stryntjes* are eaten every day of the week and are available in Belgian Flanders as well. French Flanders also has the full range of other waffles.

Café Games

One of Flanders' many peculiarities is the survival of traditional café games that have disappeared elsewhere, except perhaps in northern France where there is a similar culture. Games vary from region to region, along with their rules. A generally popular game is *krulbollen* or curved bowls. The bowls are like Dutch Edam cheeses, flattened on both sides so that they run in an elliptical course. Rather like French *pétanque* the purpose is to get one's bowl as close as possible to a *stek* or "stake" while at the same time knocking opponents' bowls out of the way. The game was taken by settlers to the US and Canada and is still played there under the name of *rollebolle*; there is even a world championship.

Skittles, or *kegelen* in Flemish, is another popular game, played both indoors and outside. In general there are nine skittles. There is also table skittles or *tafelkegelspel*, where the ball that knocks over the skittles is attached to a string on a stick. Another variant is the *mannetjesspel*—where you knock over "little men" on a metal rod using a ball on a rope

in a cross between table football and skittles. Or you can use a top to knock over skittles on a hexagonal board as they do at 't Blauwershof in Godewaersvelde, near Steenvoorde in north-west France, where W. Somerset Maugham was stationed as an ambulance driver in the First World War. Another popular game at 't Blauwershof is the "frog game"—*pudebak*—where contestants shoot a ball into the mouth of a metal frog.

Tonspel, throwing a coin through various sizes of holes in a barrel, is still very popular at the Quinten Matsijs café in Antwerp's Moriaanstraat, for instance, where the writer Willem Elsschot liked to play. The wooden *tonspel* is reputed to be 250 years old, and looks it. The well-known British game of shove ha'penny or pushing a coin at a target—known here as *bakschieten*—is also still played in the western half of Flanders. A more generally popular café game is *pitjesbak,* played using dice that are thrown into an octagonal box. There are three dice, with a 1 being worth 100 or *de piet* (slang for penis), and a 6 being worth 60. With salacious logic, the highest score is 69, a throw of 4 + 5 + 6. Small cafés in the countryside are the most likely to have a *pitjesbak* set. These days various kinds of billiards such as *tap-biljart* and *carambol* are the most widespread café games, and there are snooker halls in every town.

Card games were once very popular in Flanders, but they have declined in the face of television and the internet. The Flemish tend to prefer hybrid forms of bridge, especially in Ghent, while the game called *bieden* is a type of whist with bidding and *rammi bridge* features only cards from the 7 to the ace to make sequences of three consecutive cards. In the recent past there were cafés entirely devoted to card games, but these have mostly disappeared. The town of Turnhout, close to the border with the Netherlands, has long been the home of the card manufacturing industry in Belgium and also has a museum of playing cards, the Nationaal Museum van de Speelkaart.

Football and Red Devils
The official national sport of Belgium is archery, although the most popular sports are cycling or football. The classic archery contest involves placing a wooden target—the *gaai* or *papegaai*—on top of a wooden pole or attached to the side of a building. The *papegaai* is a defining icon of Flemish culture, along with a number of other games.

But football, as elsewhere, is a national obsession. Rather like Manchester United, the Belgian national football team is known as *De Rode Duivels* or Red Devils. There is little doubt that football (or soccer) was introduced to Belgium by the British and Irish. The earliest known football team was set up by an Irishman named Cyril Bernard Morrogh at the Jozefienencollege in Melle outside Ghent in 1860. English students in Antwerp started the Antwerp Football and Cricket Club in 1880 and played matches against sailors from visiting British ships. The oldest Flemish football clubs such as Club Brugge and Daring Club Brussel have their roots in Catholic colleges frequented by English-speaking students.

The Flemish were initially taken aback by the perceived brutality of the sport, but soon took it to their hearts. The Belgian Football Federation (Belgisch Voetbal Verbond) was set up in 1895 and was one of the founders of FIFA in 1904. Belgium won the Olympic Games football competition against Czechoslovakia in 1920. The best performance by the national side thereafter was in 1986, when Belgium came fourth in the World Cup.

Belgian footballers did not officially become full-time professionals until 1974, which meant that the sport was for a long time less developed than elsewhere. The only club that is well-known outside Belgium is RSC Anderlecht in Brussels, which is regularly eliminated in the first round of the Champions' League. Their main rivals are Standard Liège in Wallonia and Club Brugge, the leading Flemish club. While Club Brugge has won the Belgian First Division fifteen times, its greatest moment in European football was in 1978, when it lost the European Cup final to Liverpool FC. Club Brugge fans consider RSC Anderlecht their main rivals, partly on linguistic grounds, since Anderlecht is largely French-speaking. It is also entirely natural that the tough, anti-Brussels West Flemish would dislike a big-money club like Anderlecht. The other main club in Flanders, KAA Gent—for a long time known even in Ghent by its original French name, La Gantoise—has been less successful over the years, even though Ghent has twice the population of Bruges. The club's fans are known as "Buffalos" and the team's shirt bears the head of a Red Indian; this strange iconography can be traced back to the stay of Buffalo Bill's Circus in 1906 near the club's stadium in the working-class suburb of Gentbrugge.

The only Flemish club to achieve great things in Europe was KV Mechelen, who won the Cup Winners Cup in 1988 and went on to win the European Super Cup against PSV Eindhoven of Holland. Anderlecht won the same trophy in 1978 against Liverpool. Flemish players have from time to time tried their luck in the UK, but without making a great impact. Franky Van der Elst played for West Ham United in the 1980s and for New York Cosmos later in his career, as well as appearing in four World Cup tournaments.

It is generally believed that Belgian football fans have been corrupted by contacts with their British counterparts. The first organized group of football hooligans in Belgium, the O-side, appeared after Anderlecht's successful season in Europe in 1974-5. Other groups followed suit. Thus Club Brugge has the East-side (founded 1980), Antwerp the X-side and KAA Gent the Rebels. The members of "sides" are "siders", small groups of skinheads and right-wing extremists who imitate English models, with English songs and English calling cards. Trouble at football matches is nothing new, however, as in 1908 *Le Soir* reported on fighting between Club Brugge fans and Antwerp players.

Folk Music

Karel Waeri (1842-98) is the best-known Flemish folk singer of the past. There is a statue of him next to the Sint-Jacobskerk in Ghent, carved by another well-known but contemporary folk singer, Walter de Buck. The figures around the column are characters from Waeri's songs, while the central figure at the top is Waeri himself, with a socialist realist expression. Waeri was a weaver who started his political career with the Progressive Liberals and then switched to the Socialist Party. His anti-clerical views, as well as his bawdy songs, made him very unpopular with some and he was banned from Catholic circles. Waeri performed in well-off bourgeois homes, playing the fiddle while his wife sang. (By all accounts he had an unpleasantly nasal voice and never sang while fiddling.) His songs commented on political events, often starting with the trademark *'t Gaat al om geld en macht* (It's all about power and money) and then moving on to deal in unflattering terms with individuals. After eleven in the evening, and with the permission of the ladies in the audience, Waeri would sing *vetjes*, more ribald songs. One of his songs makes fun of the vogue for giving Flemish cafés French names:

Café Français, café des Arts,
Café Royal, café Renard,
Café de Paris, café de Rome,
Café de Lille, café Vendôme,
Café Parci, café Parlà,
Café Kaka, etcetera.

Interestingly, a century later a grouping of Flemish organizations, De Draak, has introduced an annual prize to any café or other shop that chooses an original Dutch name and promotes a genuine Flemish ambiance.

The Ghent folk-singer Walter de Buck is the main living interpreter of Waeri's songs and made much use of his name to promote the revival of the Gentse Feesten, the ten-day festival in July. This event was first instituted by nineteenth-century Ghent factory-owners, who thought that if the workers had ten days of solid drinking in July they would be more likely to turn up for work on time on Mondays during the rest of the year.

Popular Song

New forms of music produce new artists. The 1960s witnessed the so-called *kleinkunst* movement, directly inspired by the American folk boom. The term is somewhat pejorative, as it literally means "lesser art" though it could be loosely translated as Flemish *chanson* or "singer-songwriter" music. There have also always been singers who use Dutch or their local dialect to make a particular political or cultural statement. The three main exponents are Wannes van de Velde in Antwerp, Walter de Buck in Ghent and Willem Vermandere in Bruges. Only the latter is still actively producing new albums. The more sophisticated songs from this repertoire are called *het betere lied* ("better songs"), *luisterlied* ("songs to listen to") or *het Nederlandse lied* ("Dutch song"). This trend has faded somewhat since the 1980s, however, faced with competition from the many American- and British-influenced groups that have come to prominence. Some Flemish, meanwhile, choose to sing in English and have had limited success abroad. The group Soulwax from Ghent has become internationally high-profile since 2005, while in Flanders itself Clouseau has been the most popular group since 1985, with Deus and

Novastar also big names. As regards the folk revival, Kadril is the main force, reviving Flemish bagpipes reconstituted on the basis of Brueghel's paintings and contemporary Galician bagpipes.

There are all sorts of imitations of English music, but Germany also exerts a powerful influence with the *schlager* (hits) genre dominated by unsophisticated crooners like Will Tura and Willy Sommers. Bizarrely, Flanders even boasts its own country-and-western genre whose main exponent, Bobbejaan, has his own version of Tennessee's Twitty City, an amusement park named Bobbejaanland in Lichtaart in the Kempen. Bobbejaan Schoepen became a star in the 1950s by wearing a cowboy outfit and singing songs such as *Lights of the Scheldt* and *Café without Beer*. He has gained no fewer than 25 gold and platinum disks (an artist has to sell only 50,000 records in Flanders to be awarded a gold disk); to the younger generation he is only known for his amusement park.

Altogether different but still with mass appeal is Helmut Lotti (real name Lottigiers), who is actually from the working-class Ghent suburb of Gentbrugge, where his mother at one time sold soup from a van. A respected classical tenor who has sung alongside Pavarotti, Domingo and Carreras, he has sold 15 million records worldwide but still goes to his *stamcafé* (regular bar), the Middenstandhuis in Merelbeke, when he is in town.

Opera with Soup

Flemish opera receives little support from the regional government, which in thirty years has sponsored only four new operas. What money there is goes into the safely traditional repertoire put on by the Flemish Opera House in Ghent and Antwerp. On the margins is the highly energetic De Rode Pomp in Ghent, based in a small hall for chamber music and chamber opera, which has premiered more than 200 Flemish works. New operas are often written in English in the hope of reaching a larger audience, as there are those who feel that the Dutch language is not suitable on account of its excessive number of guttural sounds.

The fervently post-modernist Flemish composer Boudewijn Buckinx had the original idea of combining opera with food. The Buddhist scripture, the *Dhammapada,* is sung in Pali (an ancient Indian language) while the singers cut up vegetables and make soup. The smell of celery is supposed to have an intoxicating effect on the audience;

everyone eats the soup at the end of the performance.

Flemish composers have banded together into the Comav organization (Componisten Archipel Vlaanderen), united in outrage at lack of support from the Flemish government. They are conscious that any composer whose music is judged to be "difficult" struggles to be heard. More successful is Wim Mertens, who wrote the music for Peter Greenaway's film *The Belly of an Architect* (1987). His music is repetitive but melodic.

Phallic Symbols

Asparagus was brought to Belgium by the Romans and has always been valued for its (theoretically) aphrodisiac properties. It is grown in Mechelen, Boom, Rupelmonde and the Kempen among other places. The original name comes from the phallic-shaped holy water sprinkler (aspergillium) used in the Catholic Church. The Flemish writer Hugo Claus showed his appreciation with "Asperges":

Asparaguses are mostly old gentlemen
who like to stick together.
There are certainly ladies as well
who bear berries in the late summer
and others grow wild and free in Venice
in the first days of May.
Sometimes I imagine I am such a lord,
rebellious and with uncertain conscience.
You cannot eat all of me;
you must first gently peel my skin.

•

But while I am alive
I am tied up by a princess
steamed straight up, upright
and glide into her mouth.
A whole winter's evening her still water
smells of my deep earth.

The Flemish artist Thierry de Cordier submitted a painting of a penis ejaculating over a crucifix for an exhibition in Athens in 2004 with the title *Another Asperges Me* (referring to the title of Psalm 50). The work was withdrawn and the organizer prosecuted for obscenity.

Pigeon-milkers and Singing Birds
"Milking pigeons" or *duivenmelkerij* is the traditional term for pigeon fancying in Belgium, the leading country in this arcane competitive pastime. Belgium, or rather Flanders, owes its elevated position in the pigeon world to the crossing of birds bred for speed in Antwerp and those bred for endurance in Liège, which created the Belgian *reisduif,* the most sought after in the world. The craze grew in the industrial cities until there was a pigeon fanciers' office on every street corner. The pigeons were originally kept in lofts in the centre of towns, but this is no longer possible and they now live in back gardens in the countryside. They are taken by truck to a far-off point, generally in northern France, and released to fly back home but first have to be trained over short distances and then further away. Some are released from Barcelona in the morning and may be home by evening in Flanders. The prize money consists of a percentage of a pot made up of the bets placed by the pigeon fanciers, but the big money is to be made from breeding winning pigeons. Sadly, those pigeons that do not make the grade are likely to have their heads ripped off if they arrive home too late from a flight. The large amounts of money involved have also led to suspicions of doping, but very few pigeons ever test positive. In any case, the best birds are those that can fly in a straight line rather than the fastest. One way to encourage the male pigeons is to keep them separated from their pregnant female partners for a few days before the race, a practice that is called *spelen op weduwschap* (to play on widowerhood).

Finch singing contents have been going on for over a century in Belgium and the Netherlands. The male finches are kept in cages and separated in February each year when the young bird is kept with a teacher or a cassette recording is used. The objective is to make the finch "sing" as many times as possible—up to 1,000 times in a session. A row of *vinkeniers* or finch enthusiasts sit by the roadside with cages that have one side of frosted glass while another person records the number of songs by cutting notches into a branch (see picture, p.46). The winner is the finch that has sung the most during a fixed period, and the prizes are either a paper flower or a small sum of money. The sport is under threat from environmentalists and the law against catching finches in the wild.

Flanders also lays claim to *krieleniers*—people who keep crowing cocks. Sometimes bets are placed in advance on the number of times the cock will crow in a certain period. Both sports have national associations and their own magazine. To see the *vinkeniers* in the flesh the visitor should go to the Astoria café in Lauwe near Moeskroen on the French border.

Chapter Four
Ghent and the Gate to Hell

"Orpheus, this city is built on twenty-six islands.
Do you know how much water there is in this city?
For that reason this is the city of dread,
because water is the realm of the unconscious, of death."
Lieven Tavernier, Over Water, 1986

Many Flemish consider Ghent, with its unrivalled cultural facilities and superb architecture, the best place to live in Belgium. Its people, the Gentenaars, are very much aware of their history and take great pride in the city, where the absence of skyscrapers and modern buildings in the centre does much to keep its historic atmosphere intact. This is also the most French of Flemish cities; at one time it was said that the best French in Belgium was spoken here, although the city has also been the butt of many jokes about its tendency to mix French and Dutch. It was the home of Maurice Maeterlinck, Belgium's only winner of the Nobel Prize for Literature (1911), who wrote in French. There is still a substantial French-speaking bourgeoisie, but they keep a low profile and have to use Dutch in their dealings with the rest of the population. There are few shops or restaurants where French is spoken; the second language is now English.

Ghent is the historical capital of Flanders, a city that demanded respect from great rulers until it declined in the fifteenth century. In the previous century the French historian Jehan Froissart claimed that Ghent could put an army of 80,000 into the field. Gentenaars perhaps still feel they inhabit a capital city and tend to think big, if not quite as big as the Antwerpenaars. They also like to see themselves as eternal rebels and are well known for their motto: "Voor den duivel geen stap achteruit" (For the devil not one step back). Ghent's dark history also weighs heavy on its people, for the city has a less attractive legacy of violence. Between soaring Gothic monuments are sombre back streets, once witness to

A 1950s view of Ghent's three towers

enormous deprivation. This is also a city of docks, the scene of bitter industrial strife in earlier times.

Early Years

Whether Ghent existed in Roman times is a much-debated question. There must have been a settlement here from early on, since Celtic artefacts are still being found and the city's prehistory written. Ghent owes its existence to its position at the confluence of the Lys and Scheldt, Flanders' two main rivers. The original name, Ganda, is usually interpreted as "meeting of two rivers" in Celtic, or it could mean the same as Scheldt, i.e. "thrusting". The Blandijnberg, a hill that rises all of ninety feet above sea level, forms a natural strong point near the two rivers and once had a Roman villa. On its windy top is the Boekentoren or Book Tower, a classic piece of modern (1935) architecture by the Antwerp-born architect Henry van de Velde, and one of Europe's earliest skyscrapers. It now houses some two million books belonging to the University of Ghent. To the north there was a lower, marshy area, and then another small hill, the Zandberg (now one of Ghent's most authentic little squares) near the Stadhuis or Town Hall.

The constant risk of flooding required large-scale work on straightening out and dredging the rivers. The Lys, or Leie in Dutch, divides into two at Drieleien, following a tangle of channels before flowing into the Scheldt on the eastern side of the city centre. The medieval port of Ghent was situated in the heart of the city on the various branches of the Leie, hence the names of the quays ending in "lei" such as Graslei and Korenlei. New channels such as the Ketelvest (by the Opera) were carved out to create new quays and make it easier to keep out unwanted visitors, and so Ghent became known as "the city on twenty-six islands".

Ghent's location meant that it could levy taxes on ships loading and unloading. The right to levy taxes on warehousing or *stapelrechten* guaranteed a steady income. Along the canal quays were the *stapelhuizen* or warehouses, and the names of the quays record what was unloaded by what were originally large wooden cranes operated by six or eight men on a treadmill. One of these cranes has been recreated and can be seen on the edge of Bruges on the Sasplein. The Kraankindersstraat next to the Stapelplaats recalls the crane operators, known as *kraankinderen* (crane children). The *pijnders* or sack carriers also have a street named after them. The former power station at 2 Kraankindersstraat has been turned into a cultural centre—De Centrale—with a wide offering of world arts and music at subsidized prices.

Romantic Beginnings

St. Amand first convinced the hostile locals to adopt Christianity by raising a hanged criminal from the dead while he was staying here between 629 and 639. With St. Bavo, St. Amand founded the Abbey of St. Peter (Sint-Pietersabdij) near the university, and the Abbey of St. Bavo (Sint-Baafsabdij), which has one of the three towers that Ghent has adopted as its symbol. For some time the settlement could develop in peace, but during 851 and 879-83 Vikings sailed up the Scheldt and destroyed the monasteries. The inability of the Frankish kings to protect monasteries and towns gave local rulers an opportunity to assert themselves. At this time Baldwin Iron Arm, the first Count of Flanders, appeared on the scene and proved his worth. Judith, daughter of King Charles the Bald of France, had been married off to King Ethelwulf of England and then to his son, both of whom died soon after. In 860 she was only seventeen and a widow for a second time. Baldwin had heard of her beauty and gained access to her, but knew that her father would never agree to her being married to his vassal, a mere Flemish count. The couple ran off together across the border to Lotharingia, the kingdom of Charles' nephew, with the king's curses doubtless raining down on them. Baldwin then let it be known that he was going to seek an alliance with the Vikings. The Pope intervened on his behalf, and the couple were duly married.

Baldwin's territory was small, encompassing an area between Ghent, Kortrijk, Sint-Niklaas and Bruges. Under Charlemagne's rule, the County of Ghent (*Pagus Gandensis*) was separate from the more westerly County of Flanders (*Pagus Flandrensis*). Baldwin established his castle at Bruges and also brought the relics of St. Donatian there, so that the Church of St. Donatian became the most important religious institution in his realm. No one knows exactly why he was called Iron Arm, since he did not fight any wars and was able to survive a Viking invasion simply by staying behind his castle walls. His son, Baldwin II "the Bald", expanded Flanders to the south as far as Boulogne and took control of most of the coastline between Sluis and the Somme. His victory over the Vikings in 890 made him a force to be reckoned with in the French kingdom. By this time Flanders had some major religious institutions, including the abbeys of Saint-Vaast and Saint-Omer in French Flanders.

The Counts' Castle

The Gravensteen or Counts' Castle is a remarkable building that has dominated the city of Ghent for over a thousand years. Located on the left bank of the Leie, the first castle built by Baldwin II corresponds to the surviving donjon (*slottoren*), while the larger part of the castle was completed by Count Philip of Alsace by 1180; there is a Latin inscription above the entrance with the date. The entrance looks quite new because it is made of quartzite, a much harder stone than the rest of the castle.

The Counts' Castle played a part in the handing down of the legend of the Holy Grail. When Abbot Dunstan of Glastonbury sought the protection of Count Arnulf I in 950 and stayed for some time at the Abbey of St. Peter, he left behind some mysterious manuscripts including one of the Holy Grail story. Some two centuries later, Count Philip of Alsace passed on the text to his court poet Chrétien de Troyes, who made use of it to create the French version, *Perceval*, a model for Malory's *La morte d'Arthur*.

The Counts' Castle was a place of terror for most of its history. The exhibition of instruments of torture is not for the faint of heart as it seems that Count Baldwin VII could be creative when punishing wrongdoers. In 1113 he asked anyone who had a grievance to come forward, while at the same time the executioner was heating up a cauldron of boiling oil. An old lady complained that a knight by the name of Pieter van Orscamp had stolen her cow and destroyed her cottage. He gave the order to have the miscreant thrown into the oil; the executioner hesitated, so the Count threatened him with his axe. By throwing the errant knight—complete with armour—into a cauldron of boiling oil, Baldwin showed that not even the mighty could escape his justice, and with that he was given the name of Hapkin (Little Axe) by the crowd. (There is now a brand of beer called Hapkin.) On another occasion he decided to hang ten knights who disturbed the peace at a fair in Torhout and insisted that they line up and hang each other. When he came to the last unfortunate he made him stand on a stool with the noose around his neck, and then kicked the stool away himself.

The Gravensteen lost its military importance after the sixteenth century and more and more houses and shops were built up against the walls, but around 1880 the decision was made to demolish all these accretions and to rebuild the parts that had been damaged. The result has been to recreate perhaps the most sinister building in Belgium. Outside the wall is a large metal spider's web made by the German artist Stefan Kern in 2000 for the street art exhibition, *Over the Edges*. Opposite the castle is the Sint-Veerleplein, where public executions were carried out under the Inquisition, and in the corner the seventeenth-century Vismijn or Fish Market. Above the entrance is a statue of Neptune, flanked by two figures representing the Scheldt and Lys rivers. The other side of the Vismijn is the Groentenmarkt or vegetable market, which was the original fish market. The lion holding a pennant was made in 1913 for the Ghent Universal Exhibition and recreates one of four markers that once stood at the corners of the fish market. For reasons of public health, it was illegal to sell any fish outside these four markers. The long building is the Vleeshuis or meat market, now a covered market, and the small wooden lean-tos are the *penshuisjes* or "sausage huts". To prevent contamination, sausages had to be sold separately from meat.

Across the street is the Kraanlei with the superb folklore museum, Het Huis van Alijn, housed in a former hospice. Here local Ghent marionette Pierke Pierlala, dressed up in red and white like a figure from the Commedia dell'Arte, acts out his adventures on Wednesday and Saturday afternoons. The stories are for children and feature witches and simple tales of good triumphing over evil. Pierke, supposedly a baker by trade, is perhaps rather subversive but entirely honest and good-natured. Purists bemoan the fact that he is the only character to speak in a Ghent accent (one could hardly call it a dialect any more), while the rest of the characters speak a pure standard Dutch for the benefit of the youngsters.

Jacob Van Artevelde and the Friday Market

From 1100 there was relative peace, and the city of Ghent began to assert itself against the control of its remote French overlord. By digging canals between the Lys and the Scheldt and building city walls, an area known as the *kuip van Gent* (Ghent basin) was established, with its own set of laws. The city became hugely wealthy through its role in the cloth trade, based on weaving high-quality English wool. The growth of the textile trade meant a rapid increase in population, so that by the fourteenth century Ghent was the second largest city north of the Alps with 65,000 inhabitants—only marginally fewer than Paris. (At the time London was considerably smaller and Antwerp no more than a village.) The three cities of Ghent, Bruges and Ypres had a monopoly on weaving fine cloth, which they defended with tooth and nail against the rest of Flanders. The rise of the cities also saw increased social tensions between various classes, mainly between the *poorters* or patricians and the guilds of weavers and fullers, who were responsible for removing the grease from woollen cloth with fuller's earth. The Count of Flanders owed his allegiance to the French king and was bound to fight on his behalf, even if his sympathies were with his own people. The *poorters*, who invested their capital in risky trading ventures, often sided with the French, while the guilds, which had few political rights, tended to support the Flemish cause. Ghent was also often at war with Bruges, Brussels and Antwerp.

A model of Ghent's rebellious spirit was Jacob Van Artevelde, a patrician who tried to take on the French and make the king of England the overlord of Flanders. His statue stands on De Vrijdagmarkt or Friday Market, which has always been the arena for protests and demonstrations. The other centre of gravity was around the Veldstraat and the Cathedral of St. Bavo, with its patrician mansions going back to medieval times. Ghent and Flanders were sucked into the Hundred Years' War, starting from 1337, when Edward III of England claimed the French throne from Philip of Valois (see Chapter One). To push Flanders and Brabant to take his side, Edward claimed a monopoly on the trade in wool in 1336. The Flemish Count Louis of Nevers took the side of the French king, and so the English stopped all exports of food to Flanders, swiftly reducing the Flemish to starvation.

At a time when there seemed to be no solution to the English embargo, a junta of patricians took over the city in early 1338 under Van Artevelde's leadership. His policy was to seek alliances with England and her allies on the Continent, which included Brabant, Hainaut, Zeeland and Holland. Edward III soon lifted the embargo on wool exports and destroyed the French fleet off Sluis in 1340. Edward stayed in Ghent and was acclaimed as king of France, but Van Artevelde relied too heavily on

Pointing towards England? Van Artevelde

promises of assistance from England and recklessly wasted his energies trying to regain former Flemish territory in northern France. While Van Artevelde was negotiating with the French, the weavers massacred hundreds of fullers in the Friday market in 1345. As the leader of the fullers, Van Artevelde lost his popularity and it was no great surprise when he was murdered on his return to Ghent. The story is told in *James Van Artevelde: Man of Ghent* (1980), by Patricia Carson.

Van Artevelde's statue on the Vrijdagmarkt points in the direction of England, it is said. There was a statue of the hated Emperor Charles V here until 1792, when the French hauled it down and replaced it with their own Marianne. This, in turn, was succeeded by a statue of the Roman goddess of war Bellona until the Van Artevelde statue was put up in 1863. Near the Vrijdagmarkt is the Groot Kanonplein (Big Cannon Square), home of the ancient cannon named Dulle Griet (Mad Meg), whose title seems to derive from the cannon's roar rather than from a particular person. Pieter Brueghel the Elder painted Dulle Griet in a style reminiscent of Hieronymus Bosch as a woman wearing armour who rushes out of the gates of Hell bearing her loot. The painting, meant to depict greed personified, is in the Mayer van den Bergh Museum in Antwerp. When Victor Hugo visited Ghent he complained that the local people were in the habit of putting their rubbish inside the cannon (it is now securely protected against litterbugs). He also made a fine drawing of the cannon and the Friday market.

The Final Rebellion
The Holy Roman Emperor Charles V was supposedly born in Ghent at the Prinsenhof in 1500 and was named after his reckless great-grandfather Charles the Bold, the last Burgundian ruler of Flanders. It is more likely that he was born in the small town of Eeklo, but the birth was kept secret because Eeklo was on French territory, while the Prinsenhof was neutral. This was once a palace with 300 rooms; the only visible remnant is the Donkere Poort or Dark Gate that led from the Prinsenhof into the Bachtenwalle between the Gravensteen and the nearby Rabot, three round towers standing on a lock built to control the waters of the medieval Lieve Canal that runs to Sluis. Charles V was well acquainted with the Flemish, without having much sympathy for their concerns, and kept them under control by exploiting their fondness for official titles and honours. In 1539 an uprising erupted, as the Gentenaars objected to their loss of privileges and demands for taxes to finance foreign wars. In 1540 Charles V took harsh measures to put down the revolt, firstly by executing the ringleaders and then by making the city's dignitaries walk barefoot through the streets in their nightshirts with nooses around their necks.

The black and white noose or *strop* has now become a symbol of Ghent, and anyone born in Ghent is known as a *stropke* or *stroppendrager*. For a long time the people of Ghent were ashamed of this title and there was even a law passed in the same year (1540) making it a crime to call anyone by that name, but by the mid-nineteenth century the name was accepted as a badge of honour. Black and white nooses are nowadays sold in souvenir shops near the castle. As a further punishment, the original Abbey of St. Bavo (Sint-Baafsabdij) and its surrounding houses were torn down and the Spanjaardkasteel or Spanish Castle erected in its place. This has also been demolished. Parts of the Abbey of St. Bavo (in an area of social housing around the

Spaanskasteelplein) are sometimes open to visitors. Edward III's son, John of Gaunt, was born here in 1341 to Philippa of Hainault.

In 2000 a large exhibition was organized at the Abbey of St. Peter to mark the 500th anniversary of Charles V's birth. Gentenaars have mixed feelings about "Keizer Karel" or "Charlequin" (the name Charlequin rhymes with Arlequin—harlequin in French—which makes him sound less threatening). The exhibition tellingly featured a model of him circling the world while roasting on a spit. His statue on the Prinsenhofplein, a gift from the Spanish city of Toledo, had a sign around its neck: "We will put up with you but without enthusiasm."

St. Bavo and the Adoration of the Lamb
The Cathedral of St. Bavo started out as the Sint-Janskerk or Church of St. John the Baptist and is first mentioned in 942. The powerful patricians of Ghent had their mansions or *stenen* around the church. Most of the twelfth-century Romanesque church on the site was demolished in the late thirteenth century and gradually a much larger church was built here. The central part of the Romanesque crypt remains and is open to visitors; it holds reliquaries and some medieval wall paintings that survived the Iconoclasts' attack in 1578. The Scheldt Gothic aisles were completed in 1353 in blue Doornik limestone. The outer chapels and ambulatory are at least fifty years later and in a whiter limestone. The 270-foot tower is in the more sophisticated Brabant Gothic style with a brick-lined interior, and was only finally completed in 1534.

After the closure of the Abbey of St. Bavo in 1540, the Church of St. John the Baptist became the Church of St. Bavo, and then the Cathedral of St. Bavo in 1559. The church has suffered from fires and other disasters over the centuries. The wooden spire was destroyed by lightning in 1586, 1587 and 1602. Some believed that the fire was caused by witches giving off sparks by riding their broomsticks too fast around the tower; one woman was tortured and put to death as a witch. In the end reason prevailed and a lightning conductor was installed, but the spire was never rebuilt. The Cathedral of St. Bavo with its spire intact can be seen in the van Eyck brothers' masterpiece, the *Adoration of the Lamb* (or *Mystic Lamb*), which stands in a separate corner of St. Bavo's.

The Cathedral of St. Bavo also contains two other great

masterpieces: the *Conversion of Saint Bavo* by Rubens and the Calvary triptych by Ghent painter Joost van Massenhove (also known as Justus van Gent, 1435-80). The Rococo pulpit by Laurent Delvaux from 1741-5 and the Baroque high altar in white and red marble (1702-82) contrast with the Gothic architecture in a way that is typical of Flemish churches, as their interior decorations were mostly destroyed by Protestant Iconoclasts in the sixteenth century.

The *Mystic Lamb* was commissioned by a wealthy Ghent couple, Joos Vijd and Elisabeth Borluut (shown kneeling in the outer panels) and begun by Hubert van Eyck in 1420. He died in 1426 and the painting remained uncompleted until his brother Jan van Eyck took it on in 1430. It was unveiled on 6 May 1432, on the occasion of the baptism of Count Philip the Good's son. The inscription at the base of the outer section gives the credit to Hubert van Eyck: "there has never been a greater painter." The van Eyck brothers had a modest motto: *Als ic can* (The best I can). The symbolism is extremely complex and could only have been painted under the guidance of a priest.

The painting has been substantially restored, and some parts were lost along the way. The three main panels show the Virgin Mary, Christ and St. John the Baptist, although there is much disagreement over whether the central figure really is Christ. One view is that the Lamb is Christ and the dove is the Holy Spirit, thus making the central figure God the Father. The three central panels were painted over in 1550 apparently to correct a previous unsuccessful restoration. The smaller figures along the top of the upper right and left panels are minor prophets and sybils who foretell the coming of Jesus Christ. The musicians either side of the three central figures are not angels (they have no wings); they may not even have been an original part of the whole. Next to the musicians are Adam and Eve; the latter has the wording: "she did harm by bringing death." Eve holds an exotic Asiatic citrus fruit in her hand. At the extreme left and right are the figures of the Angel Gabriel and the Annunciation of the Virgin Mary.

At the centre of the composition is the Lamb (the Christ) below the dove or Holy Spirit, with fourteen kneeling angels around him. To the right and left of the angels are groups of female martyrs and male "confessors" or men who suffered for the faith without being martyred. Below the female saints is a group of apostles, popes and male saints. The lower left group consists of Old Testament figures accompanied by a number of exotic potentates and pagans who converted to Christianity. Many of these cannot be identified. To their left are the Just Rulers (although they are usually incorrectly referred to as Judges) with the Soldiers of Christ in front of them bearing flags. The Just Rulers also cannot be readily identified; they may represent various Counts of Burgundy and local magistrates. On the right side are two panels with those who have renounced the world: pilgrims, saints and hermits.

During the religious conflicts of the 1560s the painting was hidden in the tower. Two parts—the Just Rulers and St. John the Baptist—were stolen during the night of 10-11 April 1934. The thief sent messages demanding a ransom, along with cryptic drawings indicating where the paintings might be found. St. John the Baptist was found in a luggage locker, but the original of the Just Rulers has never been found. The robber intended to hand it over to an Antwerp priest, but the Belgian authorities did not agree to his terms. It is generally assumed that the thief was a certain Arsène Goedertier, a foreign exchange dealer from Wetteren and a sacristan of St. Bavo who knew all the comings and goings of the staff in the cathedral. To carry out the robbery he locked himself in the cathedral in the evening and took the paintings out in a coal-merchant's cart. The exact facts, however, could never be established, as Goedertier died in November 1934, nor could his motivation for stealing the paintings. There was already a replica in existence of the Just Rulers, but this was considered too much like the original, so another was made, and this time the artist painted the face of Leopold III, King of Belgium, on one of the Just Rulers so that no one could have any doubts that this was a modern copy.

The theft of the panels has provided much material for novelists and conspiracy theorists. Albert Camus made use of the *Mystic Lamb* in his novel *La chute* (The Fall, 1956). A Paris lawyer, Clamence, has left for Amsterdam and is hiding the missing panel in a cupboard of his room. He calls himself a "penitent judge" and hopes that the police will arrest him so that he can confess to having the missing painting.

Theatres and Opera
Between St. Bavo and the Belfort is the Nederlands Toneel Gent (Ghent Dutch Theatre), formerly the Koninklijke Nederlandse Schouwburg,

opened in 1899. The building itself goes under the name of Het Groot
Huis (The Big House) and is also sometimes home to a company called
the Publiekstheater. Four figures representing chambers of rhetoric or
rederijkerskamers appear on the frontage, namely De Fonteyne, Sint
Agnete, Sint Barbara op Sint Pieters and Maria ter Eere. There is an
allegorical mosaic in the centre depicting Apollo and the Muses. Not far
away, in the direction of Sint-Jacobs at 18 Koningstraat are the offices of
the Koninklijke Academie van Nederlandse Taal en Letteren (Royal
Academy of Dutch Language and Letters). This foundation promotes
literary research, dialectology, Dutch linguistics and literature as a whole.
The Royal Flemish Academy of Sciences at 1 Rue Ducale in Brussels
does not deal with literature.

Ghent had a Dutch-speaking theatre from 1847, with the Minard
Schouwburg on the Walpoortstraat, near the university. This fine
neoclassical building has now been restored and belongs to the city of
Ghent. The Ghent Opera House or Vlaamse Opera is not far away on
the corner of the Schouwburgstraat. The architect Louis Roelandt
(1786-1864) also designed the nearby Justitiepaleis and the original
University of Ghent buildings on the Voldersstraat. Roelandt trained in
Paris and used French decorators for the lavish interiors that were meant
to show off the wealth of Ghent. The opera house was finally completed
in 1842.

The most significant figure by far in the history of Ghent opera was
the soprano Vina Bovy (1900-83), who was born near Sint-Pieters
station. She was orphaned early in life and was discovered singing in a
factory by a music-hall owner. Arturo Toscanini saw her at the Paris
Opera House in 1925 and arranged for her to learn Italian and made her
into a star. She was fêted at the Metropolitan in New York, La Scala in
Milan and in South America but always had a hankering to return to her
roots to speak Ghent dialect and eat Ghent food. On her retirement
from the stage she was appointed artistic director of the Ghent Opera in
1948, a post she occupied until 1955. The rest of her days she spent in
an apartment in the Kortrijksesteenweg. Her funeral resulted in a
scandal, as she had asked to be buried in a pauper's grave, with no
ceremony, which was misinterpreted by outsiders as an insult by the city
authorities. During her earlier life she had been married to an Italian
nobleman and lived in the palace of the Empress Eugénie in Monte

Carlo, and it was widely rumoured that she had lost her fortune gambling and really was a pauper. Finally, in 1984 her remains were re-interred in the working-class Brugse Poort cemetery with a magnificent gravestone paid for by the Gentse Sosseteit, a local cultural organization, satisfying all concerned that Ghent's favourite daughter had been given the send-off she deserved. There is a bust of Vina Bovy in the entrance to the Opera House.

The main annual musical festival, the Festival van Vlaanderen, uses the Stadhuis or Town Hall as one of its venues, right across from the Belfort. The music season in Flanders begins at the end of August, with September the peak month. The Festival van Vlaanderen officially carries on from June to October every year.

Bells and Dragons

The view of the three towers of Ghent that now form the city's symbol was obscured until 1913 when a new square was created by the burgomaster Emile Braun, and the entire street from the Sint-Michiels Bridge to the Zuidstation was cleared of obstructing buildings, all with the intention of making the city more attractive for visitors to the Universal Exhibition of 1913. The Belfort or belfry is a typical symbol of Flemish independence, a soaring, self-confident tower that is taller than the nearby Cathedral of St. Bavo. The Belfort received a new spire in 1913, also for the Universal Exhibition.

The *draak* or dragon on top of the Belfort is meant to guard Ghent's civic freedoms, as well as being a pagan symbol. It was long believed that the dragon was brought from St. Sophia in Constantinople by Count Baldwin IX, but it was made in 1377 in Ghent (the original invoice is still preserved). The dragon has to be remade in gilded bronze from time to time because of corrosion, the latest version dating from 1980. Having the dragon replaced is a traumatic event for superstitious locals; on the last occasion it had the traditional black and white *strop* or noose temporarily hung around its neck before it was lifted into place by helicopter.

Flemish belfries always have a set of bells or carillon (*beiaard*). Bells were used to warn of danger or joyful events, and to regulate the working day and call the curfew. The main bell in the Ghent belfry is Klokke Roeland (Roland Bell), named after Charlemagne's nephew Roland.

Albrecht Rodenbach (1856-80), who was from Roeselare and a cousin of the Symbolist Georges Rodenbach, wrote some verses about the bell, which are now a Flemish anthem:

Suddenly his bronze voice
Rings out for the city
Ghent's heroes shudder in their graves
You Jan Hyoens, you Artevelden
My name is Roland, I call out fire
And sound storm in Flandersland.

For centuries no ruler dared to touch the great bell, until 1540 when Emperor Charles V hanged the man who sounded the alarm from Klokke Roeland's clapper (at least according to Charles de Coster's *Thijl Uilenspiegel*). He also ordered the bell to be confiscated, but his orders were never carried out. The original Klokke Roeland lasted from 1314 until 1659, when it was broken up to be recast. The second Klokke Roeland (which weighed six tons) cracked in 1914 when an electric hammer was used to ring it. This bell remained silent until 1948 when it was taken down and placed next to the Belfort on the Emile Braunplein. The present Klokke Roeland is the third of the name and was put in place in 1949. The carillon in the tower can be seen from close up by climbing the Belfort. It is operated manually with a keyboard or otherwise by a rotating copper drum with wires attached to the bells, forming a sort of giant music box. A number of people have hanged themselves from the rope attached to Klokke Roeland's clapper, but the story in *Thijl Uilenspiegel* is probably fictitious.

On one side of the Belfort (to the right of the tourist information office in the crypt) is a grey building with one of Ghent's best-known statues on the tympanum, the Mammelokker. This was originally the entrance to the city's prison, and shows the Roman legend of an old man Simon (or Cimon) who was condemned to die by starvation, but who never weakened because his daughter suckled him through his prison bars. In the popular imagination it is believed that the incident happened during the Middle Ages in Ghent. His daughter prayed to God and the Virgin to give her milk, as a miracle was needed since she was unmarried and had no children. It used to be said that one only became a real Gentenaar after spending at least one night in the city's jail beneath the Belfort.

The third of Ghent's famous trio of towers, along with the Cathedral of St. Bavo and the Belfort, is the Church of St. Nicholas (Sint-Niklaaskerk), an austere and apparently unfinished building as old as St. Bavo. The church was built on uncertain foundations between 1220 and 1250 and started to crumble almost immediately. This is a typical Scheldt Gothic church, with the tower above the crossing rather than over the western entrance, a feature of later Brabant Gothic architecture. Also typical of Scheldt Gothic is the use of blue Doornik limestone. During the French occupation the church was humiliatingly used as horse stables, and until the 1960s there was a serious risk that it would collapse altogether. St. Nicholas was finally declared safe in 2000 after 700 years of almost continuous repairs. The interior is much lighter than that of St. Bavo, and there is little decoration. Much of the exterior is new restoration.

Veldstraat

Ghent experienced a long period of stagnation with the final victory of the Spanish in 1585, only recovering in the late eighteenth century with the advent of renewed economic growth under the Austrian rulers Maria Theresa and Joseph II. The most significant cultural development of the seventeenth century was the appearance of the flamboyant Flemish version of Baroque architecture, but otherwise Ghent remained very much a backwater of the Spanish Empire. Many of the city's finest buildings are in a classical style from the latter half of the eighteenth century, when Belgium was prospering under the rule of the Austrians. Ghent's economic fortunes changed with the mechanization of the spinning industry, largely as a result of the efforts of Lieven Bauwens (1769-1822), who smuggled British spinning machinery into Belgium during the Napoleonic blockade. He could equally be said to be responsible for much of the poverty and exploitation experienced by Ghent's working class, and he was so unpopular in his lifetime that he had to spend most of his time in France.

The most impressive of the eighteenth-century buildings, the Herenhuis d'Hane Steenhuyse (1768-73) in the Veldstraat, once accommodated Louis XVIII during his exile in Ghent. The outside gives little if any clue to the wealth of decoration inside. Chateaubriand wrote at length about his stay in Ghent during "The Hundred Days", the period in which Louis XVIII had to remain outside France until Napoleon was defeated. The ordinary Gentenaars dubbed the obese Louis *Lowie die zwiet,* a pun meaning "sweaty Louie" in Ghent dialect. On the other side of the road is the Arnold Vander Haeghen Museum at 82 Veldstraat (also known as Hotel Clemmen) where an exhibition is devoted to Maurice Maeterlinck, Belgium's only winner of the Nobel Prize for Literature. Near the Herenhuis d'Hane Steenhuyse a plaque commemorates the negotiations held here between an American delegation under John Quincy Adams and the British to end the British-American war of 1812. The Treaty of Ghent was signed on Christmas Eve, 1814.

The leading contemporary Flemish writer, Hugo Claus, lived at 13 Predikherenlei behind the Veldstraat from 1955 to 1964 (the house is now an art gallery). At the time he was a member of the international COBRA art movement; the Dutch artist Karel Appel painted murals on the walls. In the 1980s Claus lived on the Sint-Jansvest (also overlooking a canal) and frequented the Hotsy Totsy Club, a freemasons' café much favoured by the Ghent literati at 1 Hoogstraat. The eccentric Claus believes that Gentenaars have the miasma of the canals in their clothes, that it has infected their brains and their way of speaking. In *Het teken van de hamster* (1979)—translated as *The Sign of the Hamster*—he gives his idiosyncratic view of the good people of Ghent:

"Goodbye to Ghent"
In Ghent the houses are grey and serrated.
Their skin is like a woman with smallpox.
The half-wit residents squat good-naturedly,
Static river water fouls my street.
My house is like all the houses here;
Visitors are amazed at the stench.

It should be said that Claus has little good to say about anywhere in Flanders (or humanity in general). His *bons mots* include: "Ghent is a good place to stay in a hotel, as long as you have enough money in your pockets to leave when the demons strike," and "stupidity is congenital in Flanders."

For many years canals and water were considered unhealthy and best hidden away. In the Middle Ages plague sufferers were housed next to canals, where they would have access to water supplies. Recently, however, there has been a vogue for reclaiming old canals and waterways and turning them into desirable urban features. The city has recently been uncovering the spot where the Leie and the Scheldt meet between the Bisdomplein and the Nieuwbrugkaai. Between the Cathedral of St. Bavo and the Bisdomkaai is the Geeraard de Duivelsteen, or House of Gerald the Devil, which now houses the city archives, dating from 1245. The building was named after Gérard Vilain, a descendant of the *châtelains* of the Counts' Castle; whether he was a satanic character or not is debatable, but the building itself looks sinister enough.

Maurice Maeterlinck and his Hothouse Flowers

Ghent can claim three Nobel Prize winners, one of whom is Maurice Maeterlinck, who was honoured in 1911 (the other two were chemists). Maeterlinck (1862-1949) was never very popular with the Flemish, as he wrote exclusively in French. He was born at 6 Peperstraat in Ghent to a wealthy family of landowners. In the memoirs of his youth, *Bulles bleues* (Blue Bubbles), he calls it by its French name of Rue au Poivre (Pepper Street). Maeterlinck studied under the Jesuits at the Collège Sainte Barbe (now Sint-Barbara College) in the company of several well-known writers, in particular Grégoire Le Roy and Charles van Lerberghe. In 1895 the three of them went to meet Georges Rodenbach (author of *Bruges-la-morte*), who had also studied at Sainte Barbe and was already a well-established writer. It has been suggested that the gloomy atmosphere of the Collège Sainte Barbe had a detrimental effect on Rodenbach and turned him into a morbid character. The present-day Sint-Barbara College, situated in the Savaanstraat parallel to a canal, is no longer run by Jesuits but is still the most prestigious school in Ghent. It can also count the leading Symbolist poet Emile Verhaeren, and the novelist Franz Hellens, among its alumni.

Maeterlinck is known mainly for his children's play, *The Bluebird* (1909), which had its origins in a story he wrote while still at school. When he was thirteen one of his teachers, a young French Jesuit priest, introduced him to some of the better French writers. As an exercise in

creative writing, Maeterlinck wrote a piece about the animals in his grandmother's farmyard. The teacher suspected that Maeterlinck had copied it, but as he had written it in the class under the teacher's eye he had to admit that this was a precociously brilliant piece of writing.

The Bluebird is a Symbolist extravaganza with no fewer than 116 characters, many of them in the shape of forces of nature or inanimate objects such as Light, Water, Air, Bread and so on. The play goes something as follows: two poor children, Tyltyl and Mytyl, have fallen asleep after a disappointing Christmas and dream that a fairy sends them to find the Bluebird of happiness. In the cave of Fate there are millions of bluebirds but only one that can survive in daylight. The fairy needs the Bluebird for her dying children and only Light will help the children to find it. Finally, her children recover but the bird escapes and the children ask the audience to return it. *The Bluebird* is an expression of Maeterlinck's agnostic and eclectic views on religion, with references to Plato's caves and pantheism as well as to the dangers of science and progress. While Flemish playwrights such as Cyriel Buysse were imitating contemporary realist models from France, Maeterlinck went to the other extreme with his dreamlike symbolic fantasies. *The Bluebird* was first produced by Stanislavsky in Moscow in 1908.

Maeterlinck's father was greatly interested in horticulture and trees, a common preoccupation among the Flemish middle classes in the late nineteenth century. He had extensive greenhouses in his garden at Oostakker and tried to grow peaches for export to England. During his first stay in Paris Maeterlinck wrote the collection of poems that was to become *Serres chaudes* (Hothouses, 1889). In his memoirs he says:

> The title Serres Chaudes was quite natural, because Ghent is a city for horticulture and above all flower-growing and cold, temperate and hot greenhouses abound. The foliage and exotic flowers, the heavy and lukewarm temperatures of my father's greenhouses always attracted me. On a hot summer's day, when I was knee-high to a grasshopper, nothing seemed more agreeable or mysterious than those crystal palaces where the sun's power reigned. I imagined that I was travelling the tropics and that I was Paul Bernardin de Saint-Pierre awaiting Virginie.

The hothouse symbolizes the soul trapped in a glass case where it experiences unnatural intensities of feeling:

O hothouse in the forest deeps!
And your doors for ever closed!
And all there is beneath your dome!
And under my soul in your analogies!

The thoughts of a princess who is hungry,
The weariness of a sailor in the desert,
A brass band at the windows of incurables...

Maeterlinck's early literary success with the revolutionary Symbolist play *La Princesse Maleine* (also 1889) and *Serres chaudes* was not entirely to his advantage as it disqualified him from becoming a judge, the career that he was expected to follow. An effusive article by the French writer Octave Mirbeau in 1890 in which he compared the 27-year-old Maeterlinck to Shakespeare made the city authorities fear a scandal if such a person were appointed a judge, so Maeterlinck was obliged to write for a living.

Edward Anseele and the Socialist Movement

Ghent is the birthplace of the three mainstream Flemish political parties, currently the Socialists, Liberals and Christian Democrats. (The ultra-right Vlaams Belang is more identified with Antwerp; the people of Ghent dislike being associated with extremism and intolerance). It has always been a politically active city, with its role as the traditional capital of Flanders, its social conflicts going back to the Middle Ages and its concentration of heavy industry making it a breeding ground for political movements. Gentenaars have traditionally been protesters, ready to defend their "rights" and "privileges". The workers of the industrial age, meanwhile, lived in such dire conditions that they had to protest to survive.

The Flemish socialist movement originated in the former factories between the Zuivelbrug and the Krommewalbrug along the Achterleie, the river behind the Vrijdagmarkt, and especially on the Edward Anseeleplein nearby. The socialist leader Edward Anseele Sr. (1856-

1938) was a printer of humble origins who started the Flemish Socialist Party in 1877 with a few associates as a branch of the Belgian Workers' Party. Anseele was a moderate socialist with a particular interest in cooperative forms of ownership. He translated Emile Zola's *Germinal* (see p.272) into Dutch for the benefit of the workers.

With the economic muscle of their mass membership, the socialists were able to set up workers' pharmacies, bakeries, breweries, clothes shops and cigarette factories as well as strike and unemployment funds and even a hospital. The socialist sickness fund, Bond Moyson, whose offices are all over Ghent, is named after Emiel Moyson, an activist who died young. In 1910 the movement bought a brewery, the Vooruit, and land on the Sint-Pietersnieuwstraat (close to the university and Sint-Pietersabdij) with the aim of building a palace of culture for the workers. Evening classes and cultural activities were of central importance to the workers' movement, even if not directly related to the Flemish language struggle. The Vooruit (1911-14) was designed by Ferdinand Dierkens, who was given the job after his successful work on the magnificent socialist AVC building on the Vrijdagmarkt. Edward Anseele became a powerful government minister but his authoritarian style made him many enemies. There is an ugly statue of Anseele Sr. urging on the toiling masses in a constructivist style by Jozef Cantré (1890-1957) to the right of the city council offices on the Woodrow Wilsonplein.

Patershol and Jules de Bruycker

Between the Counts' Castle and the Rabot is the former slum district around the Patershol, an abandoned Carmelite abbey. The district was peopled by lawyers and functionaries in medieval times, but the growth of industry in the early nineteenth century and the need to build more housing transformed Patershol (which means "monks' den") into a warren of fetid alleyways around the crumbling medieval monastery. Bohemians and artists started to move in around 1900, attracted by the cheap lodgings and colourful local characters. The Ghent etcher Jules de Bruycker (1870-1945) took up residence in Patershol in 1902. He grew up in the Jan Breydelstraat near the Counts' Castle and worked for his family's upholstery and wallpapering business for most of his career. In 1905 the Ghent writer Franz Hellens chose de Bruycker to illustrate his first novel, *En ville morte* (1906), his attempt to give Ghent the same treatment as Georges Rodenbach had done with *Bruges-la-Morte* (see p.143). De Bruycker had a major influence on Hellens, showing him the seamy and grotesque side of life in the Ghent slums, but *En ville morte* sank without trace and has never been reprinted.

Leading Flemish writers were fascinated and inspired by the seediness of Patershol. Karel van de Woestijne, the ideological leader of the Sint-Martens-Latem school of artists (a group that moved out of Ghent to escape what they saw as its squalor) wrote in *Jules De Bruycker* (1922):

> The principal building in the Patershol, which lay right across from a suspicious inn that was full of deathly quiet until ten o'clock at night—and then the nightly screaming commenced as if someone had been murdered under the final command of hellish powers. To the left, under the old slate roof that declined on a handsomely carved rafter, a steep stone stairway turned, with the help of a rope shining with grease, where the painters' ateliers opened up. They were large blue-plastered spaces, furnished with a singularly eloquent slovenliness. There was no single hole through which you could see the slightest decoration. On the other hand, unmade beds with dubious sheets offered a hospitable sleeping accommodation. The lack of paintings was noteworthy: impoverished painters rarely think of work. But one noted unwashed plates here that suggested that something was eaten now and then. (translated by Stephen H. Goddard)

De Bruycker accurately depicted the hellish conditions in Ghent's slums, his account of their deformed denizens reminiscent of the works of Brueghel the Elder and Bosch, as well as his own contemporary, James Ensor. His *Rond het 's Gravensteen te Gent* (Around the Counts' Castle, 1913) constitutes one of the most memorable images of Ghent. After spending the war in London, he returned to Ghent and rented a studio in the alleyway called Het Pand by the Carmelite monastery, now turned into social housing and an exhibition space. De Bruycker steadfastly refused to leave Ghent or its proletariat, and so failed to receive the international recognition that he deserved.

The area of Patershol was used as a backdrop for the film version of Jean Ray's horror classic, *Malpertuis* (1971). The area was cleaned up in the 1990s and is now full of expensive restaurants and arty shops interspersed with social housing. In the corner of the Trommelstraat can be seen what some interpret as the original "Patershol", a low rounded gateway through which the monks had to pass before curfew. Next door is the small park called Kaatsspelplein with the derelict sixteenth-century Drongenhofkapel, a chapel used by monks fleeing the religious troubles of the time. The stained-glass window at the back is made up of X-rays taken in hospitals by the West Flemish artist Wim Delvoye, one of a collection called *Trans Parity* bought by the city of Ghent. The only way to see the X-rays is to peer through a crack in the green entrance doors when the light is shining through them. Delvoye has on occasion made X-rays of people or animals engaged in sexual activity but, happily perhaps, it seems that the window in the chapel is more innocuous. Delvoye has also courted controversy by tattooing pigs in China, but is most famous for his digesting machine, the Cloaca (see p.224).

The Citadel Park, MSK and SMAK

The Citadelpark is home to the Ghent modern art museum, the SMAK (Stedelijk Museum voor Actuele Kunst) next to the Congrescentrum, and also on the edge of the park the Museum voor Schone Kunsten (MSK) housing older works. The MSK was designed by Charles van Rysselberghe, brother of the painter Theo van Rysselberghe. The museum reopens in 2007 after extensive renovation. Among its treasures is the *Carrying of the Cross* by Hieronymus Bosch (1450-1516), depicting Christ tormented by deformed figures, with St. Veronica in the lower left.

Bosch lived in 's Hertogenbosch in Brabant at a time when there was no border between the Netherlands and Belgium, and was a major influence on Pieter Brueghel the Elder, not to mention Salvador Dalí. The sensibility in his work is very Flemish; like Brueghel, it deals mainly with sin and human failings, containing symbolic commentary on contemporary events, but pushed to a greater extreme. There is speculation that Bosch was a member of a heretical sect, under the influence of drugs or even mentally deranged.

Another Bosch picture in Ghent is *St. Jerome at Prayer*. Here the hermit St. Jerome lies on the ground in the desert, symbolizing the world, while around him are the symbols of Satan whose temptations he is too weak to resist. Another exceptional piece is Théodore Géricault's *Portrait of a Kleptomaniac* (1820). There is a good selection of Flemish painters here, but Old Masters are thin on the ground, with Antwerp, Bruges and Brussels holding far larger collections.

Across the road from the MSK, the SMAK is a rather undistinguished maze of white rooms but the exterior belies the significance of the exhibitions. A movement for a modern art museum in Flanders started in 1957, but it was only in 1999 that the SMAK finally opened in the Citadel Park as a separate institution. The museum exists largely thanks of the efforts of one man, Jan Hoet—the "art pope" of Flanders—who worked for 25 years to create a modern art museum in Ghent. In 2003 the SMAK took the radical step of appointing a Ukrainian-American, Peter Doroshenko, as its director but the experiment was short-lived and he left in 2004, due more to differences of opinion on policy than to his lack of Dutch. His replacement, Philippe van Cauteren, was chosen from the in-house staff.

Jean Ray

The Ghent horror writer Jean Ray (1887-1964) was born Raymond de Kremer, the son of a port official. The family was sufficiently well off to buy a newly-built house at 48 Ham (meaning "hamlet"). This house took on enormous significance for Ray, who was day blind and could not stand bright lights. He referred to it as "dark" (even though it had large windows) as the shutters had to be kept closed all the time. As with many who suffer from this affliction, Ray had green eyes, which terrified his sister. The kitchen, meanwhile, was in the basement and was flooded from time to time when it rained heavily. During what was, to say the least, a bizarre childhood his parents engaged a nursemaid called Elodie, who was a *vertelster* or traditional storyteller. At the end of the nineteenth century it was a custom to use the services of a storyteller to teach children about history or to entertain people outdoors on warm summer evenings.

All of Ray's tales start in the area of Ghent that he knew best (usually disguised) between the Sint-Jacobskerk and the port before spinning off into ever more incredible fantasies. At the end of the nineteenth century the area was much more sinister than one might imagine it now, with dark narrow alleyways and a fog of industrial pollution hovering over the canals.

Ray worked in lowly positions in the city administration while writing for magazines. Even so, he led a life of luxury, since as the nephew of the powerful socialist minister Edward Anseele he wanted for nothing and was wealthy enough to send his daughter to school in a chauffeur-driven car. This privileged existence changed abruptly in 1926 when he was charged with fraud along with a stockbroker for whom he was working. He had obtained some 1,500,000 Belgian *francs* (equivalent to US$5 million today) from potential investors in bogus companies. He was sentenced to six years in prison but served only three.

Ray claimed to have a Dakota Indian grandmother, that as a young man he had served on tramp steamers in the South Seas, smuggled mother-of-pearl and been a pirate, that he could tame tarantulas and lions, that he was involved in the Prohibition-era liquor trade known as Rum Row, that he had been shot, and so on. Many writers (especially French) have accepted these fanciful inventions, which were purely intended to cover up the fact that he had been in jail and was now excluded from conventional society. Indeed, Ray most likely never went to the places that he writes about so effectively, but rather used street maps to give authentic-sounding names to places, often translated literally from Dutch or French into English. Thus he set some of his stories in the London suburb of Sevenoaks because there is a Zeveneken (meaning exactly the same) near Ghent. The audience Jean Ray was aiming at, whether young or old, wanted stories set in exotic locations such as South and North America or, maybe less so, England—places in any case synonymous with adventure.

On leaving jail, Ray had little chance of finding a respectable job and had to write for a living. He wrote in Dutch under the name of John Flanders (the name was a tribute to Moll Flanders) and adopted many other pseudonyms such as King Ray and Alix R. Bantam for comic strips, but his main job was rewriting some 100 stories about an American detective—*Adventures of Harry Dickson, the American Sherlock Holmes*. These were pre-1914 German booklets that an Amsterdam publisher had asked him to translate, which he reworked in a style that is a mixture of Nick Carter, Sexton Blake and H. P. Lovecraft. These were first published anonymously but later collected and issued under the name of Jean Ray. His stories for the newspaper *Het Volk* about another American detective, Edmund Bell, were illustrated by the Ghent artist

Frits van den Berghe (1883-1939), who inspired many modern cartoonists. Van den Berghe, who was born in the same street as Ray, had a doom-laden style of proto-surrealism that showed the influence of Max Ernst and Flemish Expressionism. Ray also became involved with Dutch children's magazines, mainly *Vlaamse Filmkens* (Flemish Films), published by the ultra-Catholic Averbode publishing house. This connection with Averbode has resulted in Ray's Dutch work disappearing from view, as few expected anything of worth to have originated with the publisher in question. Yet Ray started to gain recognition in France after the Second World War, with his classic *Malpertuis* republished in 1956 as a sci-fi novel. By 1961 he was internationally acclaimed as a master of the fantastic novel and his work became popular in the US; the collection *Ghouls in My Grave* appeared there in 1964, the same year that he died. He had already written his own epitaph (in English):

Here lies Jean Ray
A gent sinister
Who was nothing
Not even a minister.

Ray is buried at the Campo Santo, the cemetery for artists and writers in Sint-Amandsberg. Today there is growing interest in Ray's life and work, and a non-profit organization, De Vrienden van Jean Ray, works to perpetuate his legacy.

Malpertuis

Malpertuis is Jean Ray's only full-length novel, one that he wrote and rewrote over some twelve years. It has only recently appeared in English. It is constructed, or rather reconstructed, with great attention to detail and multiple narrators and stories within stories. Ray spent much time rearranging sections of the novel and the result is not easy to follow. It was completely rewritten with the help of a better French speaker, by the name of Jules Stéphane, to whom the novel is dedicated. Ray bases the house named Malpertuis on several places in Ghent as well as houses in Germany (whether he actually went there is open to doubt). The real Malpertuis (meaning Gate to Hell) is traditionally the lair of Reinaert the Fox and can be accurately located as the twelfth-century estate in Destelbergen, near Ghent, of a certain Siger III, *châtelain* of the Counts' Castle. But Ray probably did not have a particular place in mind: "Keep searching for Malpertuis. But don't forget that, if you don't find it, that accursed infernal house might find you… and then…"

It is possible that the house that he describes is what is now the socialist cultural centre, the Vooruit on the Sint-Pietersnieuwstraat, conspicuous as you go up the hill from the Minard Theatre on the Walpoortstraat, next door to the University of Ghent's administrative offices:

> Again I see rising before me the excessive bay windows and balconies, its landings with stone balustrades, the towers crowned with pointed weathervanes the windows built in pairs in the shape of crosses, its crumbling reliefs, representing winged serpents or Aztec heads, and the doors needlessly reinforced with square-headed nails.

The film *Malpertuis* (1972), directed by Antwerper Harry Kümel and featuring in minor roles pop stars Sylvie Vartan and Johnny Hallyday, could have been one of the high points in the Belgian cinema and remains the most expensive film made in Belgium. A young blond sailor, Yann or Jean-Jacques, is spirited away from a bar in the 1920s and wakes up in the house of his uncle, Cassavius, acted by a bloated, cigar-smoking Orson Welles. Cassavius is on his deathbed and it is time to read his will. Jean-Jacques finds that he is trapped in a castle with endless underground chambers and secret passages. Then he is bewitched by three women, all of them acted by Susan Hampshire. Jean-Jacques decides to unravel the secret of Malpertuis and discovers that he is on an island where the ancient Greek gods of Olympus are kept alive by the faith of a few believers. Even more bizarrely, there are gruesome murders and the appearance of a mad taxidermist. The film's startling mix of classical myth, horror and the surreal has endeared it to fans of the fantastic, even if it did not find favour with the critics. It has appeared in several versions, and a director's cut may be issued soon. It would be reasonable to see *Malpertuis* as a satire on the decline of socialism, which is only kept alive by the belief of its supporters, not least because the characters are based on the Anseele family, who were once Ray's sponsors.

The film set for *Malpertuis* was based at the former Carmelite nunnery in the Vrouwebroerstraat in the slum district of Patershol (see above). Various locations were used including the white house on the corner of the Graslei (now being turned into a hotel), the Klein Begijnhof, Patershol, Sint-Jacobs and the Academisch Ziekenhuis hospital. Bruges was used for the medieval street scenes. The first version of the film was edited by Richard Marden and shown in English and French at the Cannes Film Festival in 1972. Harry Kümel put out a Dutch version in 1973; in his view, Marden had mixed up the scenes in the film and thus made it even more confusing than it was originally. In 2004 Nicholas Royle took up the theme of *Malpertuis* in his novel, *Antwerp*, which revolves around an attempt to make a film in that city.

Kümel's previous film was a lesbian vampire movie, *Daughters of Darkness* (1971), on the strength of which he was given the chance to direct *Malpertuis*. Kümel believes that his *Daughters of Darkness* was a forerunner of the successful *Emmanuelle* soft porn series. While *Malpertuis* won two prizes at film festivals, it did nothing for Kümel's career. After the debacle of *Malpertuis*, he directed *De komst van Joachim Stiller* in 1976, based on the magical realist novel by Antwerp writer, Hubert Lampo (translated as *The Coming of Joachim Stiller*), but most of his career has been in television.

Original Flemish *Noir*

Horror fiction is strikingly popular in Flanders and Belgium, and many Belgian writers like to play with the theme of death by evoking memories of the Spanish Terror and other occupations. The Brussels writer Michel de Ghelderode (1898-1962), who was Flemish in all but language, set virtually all his plays in the sixteenth century, and death features prominently in virtually every one of them.

The original Flemish horror story is the tale of Heer Halewijn, which goes back to the early Middle Ages and is well known in other parts of Europe. The classic version from the fourteenth century begins with:

Heer Halewyn sang a little song
And all who heard it went along.

Halewyn is a serial killer who attracts his women victims by singing. One day a princess decides—in the words of the song—to go along to his house, naturally against the advice of her family. When she arrives she sees a row of women strung up on a gallows. Halewyn asks her how she wants to die, and she chooses the sword. But fortunately she has a trick up her sleeve, suggesting that he take off his coat so that it will not be stained with blood. While Halewyn takes it off she grabs the sword and cuts off his head. A moral conclusion, we are led to believe, but Halewyn is not finished yet, as his head starts to talk and asks the princess to call his friends. She sensibly refuses, and the head then asks her to apply ointment to its severed neck but she refuses this as well, saying, like a good Catholic girl: "I won't follow the advice of a murderer." Finally she takes the head home and serves it up on a platter at a banquet, in the style of John the Baptist.

Roger d'Exsteyl: Supper with Bats
A leading member of the Ghent school of *roman noir*, Roger d'Exsteyl (real name Roger Martens, 1926-79), was born in the working-class area

of Ledeberg. After taking a degree in German and English, he spent time in Paris before returning to work as a journalist on various Flemish newspapers. Like Jean Ray, he was immensely productive during his twenty-year career, writing hundreds of short stories but no full-length novels and also translating Edgar Allan Poe and Oscar Wilde among others. He was certainly influenced by his friend Ray, who appears alongside Sherlock Holmes in one of d'Exsteyl's short stories, *The Old Curiosity Shop*. He uses the same approach of starting out with a well-known location and then luring the reader further and further into his own demonic world. D'Exsteyl was a firm believer in the occult and the supernatural, but his over-sensitivity got the better of him and after several physical and mental breakdowns he burned to death in his own house in 1979.

For d'Exsteyl there could be a horrific event waiting to happen at any moment on any street in Ghent. His first major work, the novella *De dames Verbrugge* (The Ladies Verbrugge, 1953) opens next to the Cathedral of St. Bavo:

> Pausing briefly, Hugo looked down at the street below him: frozen image of grey patrician houses with spiny wooden balconies and highly significant screens over the windows. It seemed to him that one or other demonic spirit had swept the street away to a bygone time of war and occupation and that the anxious citizens were sheltering behind the suspiciously closed blinds against the threatening bullets of a patrolling detachment. Above this gloomy scene rose the ethereal white torch of the lit-up cathedral in the fairy-like glow of searchlights.

De dames Verbrugge remains d'Exsteyl's most important work, prefiguring his main themes of anxiety, fear of the irrational in a rationalist age and the banality of death. It is also a social critique of a family of wealthy French-speaking Ghent bourgeois who care more for their good name than about life and death. D'Exsteyl uses the street name Kruiswegstraat (Calvary Street) in many of his stories; the original is the Hoofdkerkstraat, a dark little alley between St. Bavo and the Bisdomplein, a perfect setting for a murder in a cold mist. The Kruiswegstraat appears several times in d'Exsteyl's collection *Souper met vleermuizen* (Supper with Bats), where London smog is transmuted into Ghent fog:

> When the mist hung—thick, greyish yellow mist like a huge, stretched out jellyfish clamped onto houses and people—I sometimes went for a walk in the Kruiswegstraat, one of those small, dead quiet side streets that are woven like so many threads of a spider's web around the town centre. It seems as though all the male inhabitants have long since died out, except for a couple of mummified old gentlemen, who only leave the protective lap of their houses when it's mild spring weather.

De dames Verbrugge was filmed as *6 rue du Calvaire/Kruiswegstraat 6* (1973) by Jean Daskalidès, a member of the well-known chocolate-making Daskalidès family (who are of Greek origin, as are their Ghent rivals, the Leonidas family). Daskalidès backed his production company Daskafilms with his personal chocolate fortune. He had already won several prizes with his short films and decided in 1970 that he would make a full-length film, no matter what. A man of multiple talents, he was a practising gynecologist and led a jazz orchestra during the Second World War.

Romeo and Juliet with Cats

One of word cinema's most unlikely episodes took place in Ghent: the filming of a version of *Romeo and Juliet*—acted entirely by cats. This 1970 oddity was the brainchild of Armando Acosta, a Spanish-American director and son of Hollywood scriptwriter Mercedes Acosta. Acosta Jr., who also runs a religious sect and has taken the name of Ganapati (after the Indian elephant god) after spending time in the 1960s following a Hindu guru, used his disciples to produce the film. The only human actor, meanwhile, was John Hurt, cast in the unlikely role of "La Dame aux Chats", an eccentric boatwoman. (In an understatement Hurt later described it as "a fairly extraordinary film".) The feline cast was voiced by actors, including Ben Kingsley, Quentin Crisp, Maggie Smith and Vanessa Redgrave.

Even without special effects the cats put in a remarkably good performance, especially when at one point two hundred of them were released across the Sint-Michiels Bridge in the direction of the Belfry.

They had been kept indoors for the winter to be trained as extras and half of them did not bother to return. According to the director's wishes, the film can only be shown to the accompaniment of Prokofiev's ballet *Romeo and Juliet* with a live symphony orchestra. After the release there was a tour of world capitals, but the film has rarely been shown since. The Ganapati sect's restaurant, The Medici Steps, is on the Michielsstraat, near Sint-Michiels Bridge.

"As the mist, wind and winter cold parted
The place gained the soft tints of a watercolour
The Scheldt slowed its course through the green irises
And the willows bent their branches into umbrellas."

Emile Verhaeren, *Les flamandes*, 1883

Chapter Five

East Flanders and the Scheldt

"A small village square and a few streets,
A statue of Christ at the crossroads,
The grey Scheldt and then the tower
Which mirrors itself in the ill-tempered water."

Emile Verhaeren, "Mon village", 1904

With Ghent at its heart, East Flanders stretches from near Antwerp to the French border, while the suburbs to the north of Ghent are but a few miles from the Dutch port of Terneuzen. East Flanders can be divided into three parts: the sandy, infertile Meetjesland around Eeklo along the Dutch border; the marshy Waasland in the north-east; and the south with its richer farmland. The river valleys were the first areas to be settled by the invading Franks in the fifth century following the departure of the Romans. The areas in between were largely left uninhabited (except in the south). In prehistoric times all of East Flanders was covered with forests, most of which had been cleared away by the eleventh century, creating *wastinas* or *heide*, often infertile heathland populated by those who could not find any place in conventional society. To survive, the small farmers of the heaths had to take on seasonal jobs in northern France's sugar beet harvest and in the polders of West Flanders, while their wives stayed at home and made lace. The rich diversity of Flemish dialects in the countryside can be largely explained by the isolation of rural communities until the coming of the railways in the 1830s. If the heaths were reforested with pine trees in the eighteenth century, these days they are increasingly infested with luxury villas rather than robbers.

Waasland and Reinaert the Fox
If you head north-east out of Ghent along the old Antwerpse Steenweg, you enter the Waasland. The first town you come to is Lochristi (Grove of Christ), the begonia-growing capital of Belgium—and probably the

world. The begonia is the national flower of Belgium, and in spring the fields of the Waasland are full of the delicate blossoms of begonias and azaleas. (The rest of the year one is likely to see little else but hundreds of glasshouses.)

This is the land of Reinaert the Fox, the cunning anti-hero of the saga *Van den Vos Reinaerde*. There are statues dedicated to this sadistic animal in various locations, including outside the Heidekapel in Waasmunster and two in Stekene, while the area is covered with cycle routes named after the animals in the saga—although in truth there is not a great deal to see here. The village of Hijfte, near Lochristi, is one of the places mentioned in the medieval work in which the animals plot against the life of Noble, the Lion King: "Between Hijfte and Ghent they met on a dark night to make their plans. Under the sway of the devil and his powers, all five swore to kill the king on that inhospitable heath."

The author of *Van den Vos Reinaerde*, the greatest work of medieval Dutch or Flemish literature, was known simply as Willem. He spent his life, around 1200-1250, in East Flanders, including Ghent, which he mentions twice in his works. No one knows who Willem was, although he has been identified with a certain Willem of Bruges, Canon of Kortrijk Cathedral. At the start of *Van den Vos Reinaerde* he tells us that he wrote *Madoc*, about a Welsh prince who was supposed to have discovered America in 1170, but the work is lost.

Willem, die Madoc maecte,
Daer hi dicken omme waecte,
Hem vernoyde so haerde
Dat die avonture van Reynaerde
In dietsche onghemaket bleven.

Willem, who wrote Madoc,
As he often took such care
It troubled him so much
That the adventure of Reinaert
Had not been written in Dutch.

The story of *Van den Vos Reinaerde* has Germanic roots. The French books consulted by the author are themselves based on Latin stories, the

Reinardus and *Ysengrinus*, composed in Flanders around 1152 by Magister Nivardus, about whom nothing whatsoever is known apart from the fact that he lived in Ghent or Bruges. He strongly favoured the French language: the noble animals have French names, while the wolf and donkey have Flemish ones. To make the point clearer still, Nivardus at one point says: "Teutonicus miser et rudis est" (All that is Germanic is wretched and coarse).

It is supposed that Willem wrote *Van den Vos Reinaerde* to encourage Siger III, *châtelain* of the Counts' Castle in Ghent, who was unjustly deprived of his post around 1210 by Philip the Noble, Count of Namur and Regent of Flanders. The figure of the concupiscent and vacillating Noble the Lion seems to be based on Philip, who slavishly followed the King of France's orders and handed over two princesses as hostages to his master. Reinaert's castle is actually Siger III's country retreat at Destelbergen, which appears on later maps by the same name as Reinaert's lair, Mapertuus, meaning Hell's Gate. (The Ghent horror writer Jean Ray used the name in its French form as the title of his horror novel, Malpertuis, see p.91.)

The animals are thinly disguised discontented barons who plot against the Count of Flanders, but their conspiracy fails because of their own weaknesses. The Fox is accused of various crimes, such as adultery with the Wolf's wife, the attempted murder of the Hare and the theft of a sausage from the (small) Dog Courtois (who makes his complaint in French, which makes him a sort of proto-*franskiljon* or French-speaking Fleming). King Noble the Lion sends his emissaries to visit the Fox in his lair but Reinaert gets the better of his accusers by playing on their greed and gullible nature. As a gesture of contempt he sends back the dead body of the Rabbit, Couaert, to the King. In the end the Fox is condemned and goes into exile.

The Fox plays his cruel tricks on the Cock and the Wolf at the abbey of St. Peter at Elmare near Aardenburg (now in Dutch Flanders). He hides an imaginary treasure in the forest of Hulsterloo, or Hulst, in order to trick the Lion into setting him free (the supposed site has been renamed the Kriekeput after the place in the story).

The Flemish strongly identify with the subversive Reinaert while ignoring his more unpleasant traits. The popular café 't Vosken near the Cathedral of St. Bavo in Ghent at one time had wall paintings of scenes

in the story by Ghent painter Firmin de Vos, which have now been covered over and replaced with black and white photographs of the paintings underneath. Hulst in Dutch Flanders has also adopted Reinaert as its mascot. There is a 1935 statue of Reinaert wearing pilgrim's robes at the Gentpoort as well as a new statue of him preaching to six geese in the town centre.

The Tides of the Scheldt and Emile Verhaeren

The most attractive parts of East Flanders are around its main rivers, the Scheldt and the Leie. The Scheldt is tidal up to the lock system in Gentbrugge, to the east of Ghent. Between Dendermonde and Rupelmonde, where it meets the suburbs of Antwerp, some of the original floodplains survive, with bird sanctuaries and sailing facilities. From its source at Gouy in France the Scheldt flows through Valenciennes, through the Flemish city of Oudenaarde and past the attractive villages of Asper and Gavere until it meets with the Leie (French Lys) at Ghent. Rubens always included the god Scaldis (the

Latin name for Scheldt) in his allegorical paintings, along with triumphal arches and chariots, where the god appears as an old man leaning back on his amphora, which pours forth not only the river but also fortune and power. The stone for Ghent's Gothic buildings was floated down the Scheldt from Tournai and further south. Nowadays the flood-prone river threatens to take its revenge on those who tried to straighten it out against its will.

The novella by the Ghent-born writer Franz Hellens, *Les marées de l'Escaut* (The Tides of the Scheldt, 1953) links images of time and tide in which the tide is the factory workers' movement for justice in the late nineteenth century. The moods of the river rather explicitly reflect changes in society: "He had imagined that the workers' movement, or rather the absence of movement at the foundry, because that is all he noticed, would last no longer than the time of one tide." At Sint-Amands near Dendermonde, where the river bends towards the north, one feels the closeness of the sea:

> In this region, the Scheldt flows while forming large serpentine knots. At high tide, the water reaches the tops of the banks even though they are high; at low tide, the muddy banks are uncovered with a sticky black. The boat that jumps in the morning stays stuck in the afternoon in the rippled surface of this mud. When the wind comes from the east, the surface is covered with a sort of liquid eiderdown, while the west wind shakes it and breaks it up. On some days the river is a mirror broken into a thousand pieces. The storm turns the river into a branch of the sea. The waves beat its grassy sides like furies risen from hell. The sea appears close by, you hear strange groanings, as if huge chains were clashing and interlocking, tight enough to break.

Sint-Amands is the birthplace of the poet Emile Verhaeren (1855-1916), who is buried overlooking the river. A little way from the river, the Provinciaal Museum Emile Verhaeren contains an ingenious display, mainly consisting of mementoes of the poet. Given that Verhaeren wrote only in French, interest in his work among Flemish readers is distinctly limited. Verhaeren came from a wealthy French-speaking family and although he had trained as a lawyer he felt more drawn to literature. No one could doubt his intense attachment to his native land. His first published collection of poetry, *Les flamandes* (The Flemish Women, 1883) scandalized the local Catholic hierarchy with its provocative odes to voluptuous country girls. His mortified parents tried to buy up all the copies to destroy them. His next collection *Les moines* (The Monks, 1886), probably to their relief, dealt with more spiritual themes. Like many writers and painters in the 1890s, Verhaeren went through a Symbolist phase before returning to a more realist and Expressionist style at the end of his life. He moved to the Paris suburb of Saint-Cloud for good in 1898 while keeping a country retreat close to the French border in Wallonia.

Verhaeren identified the North as the source of European modernity and renewal, in opposition to the decadent South, represented by the French in particular. The hard workers of the North, he imagined, would become the new Nietzschean supermen. Verhaeren, along with Rodenbach and Maeterlinck, represented something innovative and exotic to French readers. Defining himself with Scandinavians and Germans as a "man of the North", it was in Germany that his work was most warmly received. Verhaeren had a considerable influence on the Austrian writer Stefan Zweig, who translated his poetry and wrote his biography, but the two fell out in 1914 when Zweig discovered that Verhaeren was fabricating German atrocities to increase support for the Allied cause. The two settled their differences just before Verhaeren's death.

Verhaeren was caught up in contradictory themes. On the one hand, the city offered the chance of aesthetic renewal, but he could not ignore the evils of industrialization and slums, which he deals with in his collection *Les villes tentaculaires* (Tentacular Cities, 1895). In this collection and in *Forces tumultueuses* (Tumultuous Forces) and *Les campagnes hallucinatoires* (Hallucinated Countryside) he is remembered both for his powerful social commentary and for a distinctive Expressionist style. The unfortunate poet was run over by a train in Rouen in 1916 while on a lecture tour to whip up support for occupied Belgium, and his ashes were finally brought back to Sint-Amands in 1927. One can still see Verhaeren's *passeur d'eau* (ferryman) at work:

The ferryman with the oars gripped in his hands,
Has wrestled for long against the stream,
A green reed between his teeth.

Alas, the one who called him from the other shore,
Over the waves, at the foot of the dikes,
He saw still further, vaguer in the mist.

Oostakker

Oostakker is a large village to the north-east of Ghent and a microcosm of Flemish culture. The Symbolist and mystical author Maurice Maeterlinck lived here, close to the canal that leads to Terneuzen, after his family had moved from the Peperstraat in Ghent. In his autobiography *Bulles bleues* (1948) he tells of his escapades along the canal (on one occasion he set out to cross it in a washtub) and of the bargees throwing coins to the children on the bank. Nearby was the pilgrimage place of Oostakker Lourdes, which the young Maeterlinck found interesting only as a place to buy gingerbread men. Later he was called on to officiate at a duel involving his friend, the poet Grégoire Le Roy, held in the woods at Oostakker (or Ostacker as he calls it). Maeterlinck had the sensible idea of removing the bullets from the pistols, with the result that there was a loud bang but no injuries. It was also while growing up in Oostakker that Maeterlinck first took an interest in beekeeping, from which sprang *La vie des abeilles* (*The Life of the Bee*, 1900), one of his most popular works. His ingenious father constructed modern wooden hives that could be used to centrifuge the honey:

> We were in a way brought up amidst bees. The hives were arranged at the end of our vegetable garden in a bed of wild pinks and melilots and, as soon as games left us with some moment of free time, we would go to visit those indefatigable workers. We had learned to move the combs like grains of coffee. We were rarely stung because we had acquired, at our own expense, the necessary experience, and the many stings had immunized us.

La vie des abeilles became a bestseller and was immediately translated into English, while Maeterlinck went on to write the scientifically accurate *La vie des termites* (*The Life of the White Ant*) and *La vie des fourmis* (*The Life of the Ant*). In the former he compares human society to that of termites and warns of the dangers of fascism and excessive regimentation. Maeterlinck became fabulously rich and moved to France in 1898, winning the Nobel Prize for Literature in 1911 for his Symbolist play, *The Bluebird* (see p.84). Leaving Symbolism behind after the First World War, Maeterlinck became more interested in making connections between science and religion, believing that human beings could discover spirituality through contemplation and silence, free of the need to practise an organized religion. His early work is static and pregnant with mystery. One critic termed his view of the world "a slight vertigo on the balcony of hypothesis". His final work, *Bulles bleues,* was written while he was in exile in Chelsea Village, New York, and looks back on his happy childhood in Ghent as a man at peace with himself and the world.

Flemish Catholics have no need to go all the way to the Basque Country to go on pilgrimage to Lourdes, as there is a Flemish version right on their doorstep, inside Ghent's city limits. This became a pilgrimage site after a wealthy family put up a statue of the Virgin Mary in the grounds of their private château in 1873. A workman named Pieter de Rudder had broken his leg in 1867 and the leg had started to rot away, so his doctors insisted that he should have it amputated. He would have none of it, however, and in 1875 went to pray to Our Lady at Oostakker, whereupon he got up from his wheelchair and started to walk. De Rudder died in 1899 and his leg bones were examined by doctors, who found that a new piece of bone had inexplicably grown where he had broken his leg. There is a basilica and a walking trail around various scenes of Christ's life. Our Lady has her grotto, with a statue of Bernadette Soubirou (from the original Lourdes in France) praying to her. A life-size statue of the Virgin Mary with light bulb halo completes the picture.

The strongly Catholic atmosphere in Oostakker made it an appropriate place for Flanders' leading writer Hugo Claus to locate his breakthrough collection of poetry, *De Oostakkerse gedichten* (Oostakker Poems). Its publication in 1955 was a liberating event for the Flemish intelligentsia and a declaration of war on the narrow-minded, hypocritical Catholic establishment. Claus' trademark is to use harsh, ugly images to touch the raw nerves of his readership as well as upsetting moral preconceptions with images of the peasants of Oostakker fornicating with gusto. Like Ted Hughes, Claus plunders myths and historical events to find ready-made material that he links to his usual themes of the Oedipus complex, incest and the revered mother:

"Do you think I'm making cow's eyes, then?"
"Big grey eyes and virile script."
"What the hell are you doing in the fields of Oostakker?"
"There are deaf-mute girls and I am blind."
"What would you do if I were an ugly hunchback?"
"I'd hate you. I could never love you again."

Sint-Niklaas: Santa Claus City

The town of Sint-Niklaas has turned its name to good use by having Santa Claus or Sinterklaas in residence in the run-up to Christmas. In the Netherlands and Belgium Sinterklaas has a politically incorrect assistant, Zwarte Piet or Black Peter, who carries his sack and hands out gifts or punishes naughty children (this does not actually happen because the presence of someone blacked up and in outlandish costume normally ensures that children behave themselves). Sinterklaas is believed to come on a steamer from Spain, as it says in the traditional song, *De stoomboot van Spanje,* although the original St. Nicolas came from Turkey. The story relates to the Spanish occupation, and Zwarte Piet is hence a Moor in this version. After disembarking (no one is quite sure where), Sinterklaas rides his white horse around Flanders dispensing biscuits and oranges.

Sinterklaas has recently kept open house on the town's Stationsstraat for a short time in November and December, and visitors can view his bathroom and bedroom. Christmas presents have traditionally been handed out on 6 December in Belgium and Holland, with Christmas a low-key affair and New Year more of a big party. Under Anglo-Saxon influence, however, Christmas is now gaining at the expense of St. Nicolas Day. Traditionally it was Zwarte Piet who came down the chimney with his donkeys, and to keep them happy children would put out clogs filled with carrots and turnips in the fireplace (children are expected to put a list of their resolutions for the following year in with the clog). At Sinterklaas' residence in Sint-Niklaas there is an exercise room for the Zwarte Pieten to practise crawling down chimneys and jumping over obstacles.

Presents were not guaranteed; before the big day itself locals dressed as Zwarte Piet would go round the village knocking on doors, shouting "Are there any naughty children here?" If no naughty children appeared, then a handful of sweets would be thrown into the house. As a teacher of morality, Zwarte Piet has long performed invaluable services but political correctness may soon see him off. In the area around Aalst it is St. Martin who brings presents on 10 November, leaving St. Nicolas with nothing to do.

St. Nicolas is also associated with *speculaas* or cinnamon biscuits. The recipe is simple enough: wheat flour, butter, eggs, spices and *cassonade* (brown sugar). The *cassonade* is the vital ingredient: a brown sugar with a delicate caramel flavour made from twice-heated beet syrup. Every baker uses his own mixture of spices, including cinnamon, ginger, cloves, nutmeg, cardamom, white pepper and vanilla. The flavours are developed by leaving the dough to stand overnight before baking. The spices may give *speculaas* its name, from the Latin word *species* for spices, while the name could also be derived from *speculator*, i.e. the one who sees everything, a reference to St. Nicolas' function as guardian of children's moral education. Some Flemings start their day with a *speculaas* inserted between slices of thickly buttered bread. For Sinterklaas on 6 December the biscuits are traditionally baked in wooden moulds in the shape of St. Nicolas, donkeys, flowers and the like.

Aalst and Louis-Paul Boon

Aalst, or Olsjt as the locals call it, is on the eastern end of what was historically Flanders and on the border between East Flanders and Flemish Brabant. The area east of the Scheldt up to the Brabant border was known as "imperial Flanders" in the Middle Ages. Count Baldwin IV of Flanders took it from the Holy Roman Emperor by force around 1000 AD. The Emperor acquiesced, so the Counts of Flanders became the servants of two masters, the French king and the Holy Roman Emperor. Flanders east of the Scheldt has more fertile soil than the area to the west, the result of deposits of rich loam during ancient times. Aalst is the onion growing capital of Belgium and locals are known by the nickname of *ajoin* (the local word for onion) or "onion-peelers", "onion-eaters" and so on. Some carnival-goers dress up as onions.

The writer Louis-Paul Boon is closely associated with Aalst. He was born there in 1912 and left school aged fourteen to train as an automobile painter like his father, but was thrown out of college for borrowing books from the Liberal Willemsfonds (see p.36). For a time he commuted to work in Brussels to paint automobiles while at the same time trying to train as an artist. He led a precarious existence until he won a major literary prize in 1942 with *De voorstad groeit* (The Suburbs are Growing), which deals with his trademark themes: the corruption of innocence, the evils of capitalism and the breakdown of human relations in the modern world.

Boon (the name literally means "Bean") came from a poverty-stricken family and identified strongly with the marginalized and downtrodden, empathizing with communism and socialism but unable to fit into any organized ideology. Behind his work is a rather typically Flemish preoccupation with truthfulness and morality and how to improve humanity—disguised Catholic themes that do not necessarily guarantee commercial success. Eventually he obtained a regular job from 1952 to 1972 writing a daily column called Boontjes (Little Beans) for the Ghent socialist newspaper *De Vooruit*. With these insubstantial pieces on his daily life, Boontje became a cheerful alter ego to the self-critical Boon. In 1953 he built his own refuge from the world, a modest bungalow he called Isengrimus after the wolf in the Reinaert saga at 4 Vogelenzang, near the Kluisbos outside Aalst. The house, which was designed by the poet-architect Albert Bontridder, is now in private hands and cannot be visited.

Boon was a revolutionary writer who broke with the old-fashioned simplistic styles of the pre-Second World War period. His classic novel is *Kapellekensbaan* (1953), of which there is an excellent translation, *Chapel Road*, by Adrienne Dixon. On the face of it, this could be termed a "difficult" novel as there are two main story lines printed in two fonts, one about a young girl called Ondine (the names are written in lower case) in the late nineteenth century and the other after the Second World War. By this device Boon is able to trace the history of the socialist movement from its origins to what he sees as its decline in the 1950s.

Interwoven with this narrative is a retelling of the medieval story of Reinaert the Fox. The style is reminiscent of *Ulysses,* but less complex, and for some it is the greatest novel every written in Dutch, while others find it too unconventional or difficult to define. With Aalst as its backdrop, Boon's novel is an exercise in the sub-conscious expressed in an earthy, colloquial language to which Flemish readers were not at all used in the 1950s. Many of the characters are identifiable Aalst figures: Ondine and her partner, Oscar, are based on Boon's childhood friends.

Aalst has recognized Boon's genius; the street running past the Kapel van Termuren has been renamed Kapellekensbaan. The sequel to *Kapellekensbaan* is *Zomer te Ter-Muren* (Summer in Ter-Muren), which has not been translated as yet. The chapel has a miraculous picture of the Virgin Mary on the wall (which is why she is called the Virgin on the Wall or Ter-Muren). The chapel is hard to find, but worth a visit. On the exterior is written:

> We greet you dear lady of Termuren
> We come to your little house
> Where lime trees along the walls
> Enclose the little chapel.

There was once a bronze statue of Ondine in the garden, but it was vandalized so often that it had to be housed indoors at the Stedelijk Museum (there is a replica at the Town Hall). The Aalst town museum (in the Oude Vismarkt) has Boon's writing desk and his typewriter, where his wife typed while Boon dictated. The Stedelijk Museum is remarkably extensive, with paintings by Valerius de Saedeleer (another Aalst son). Behind the museum, along the River Dender, clouds of steam swirl out from the Tate & Lyle sugar factory reminiscent of the era of nineteenth-century class struggle. The street called De Werf was once the edge of the notorious Chipka Island, an industrial zone recreated in the film *Daens* (1992).

Adolf Daens: Priest and Militant
The priest Adolf Daens (1839-1907) was one of Aalst's most famous figures. In 1893 men, women and children were working thirteen hours a day in the city's textile factories in atrocious conditions. At that point,

after working as a teacher and curate, Daens returned to his birthplace to help his brother with a Catholic workers' newspaper, in competition with *De Vooruit*, the socialist paper. Among an epidemic of fatal accidents factory owners were cutting wages and only employing women and children. After Daens had an article published on working conditions, a Committee of Inquiry came to visit—against the wishes of Charles Woeste, president of the Catholic Party—but none of its members could speak Flemish and so the workers were unable to tell them the truth. Nette, a younger worker, led a walkout after a young boy was crushed to death by a spinning machine; the cortège was attacked by mounted *gendarmes* with sabres, who stole the boy's body. Woeste then organized a campaign to discredit Daens, who had by now started a political party as an alternative to the socialists and the ruling Catholic Party. The local factory owners, the Church hierarchy and even King Leopold II conspired to persuade Pope Leo XIII to expel Daens from the priesthood. In the end, Daens became a full-time politician, and his party eventually transmuted into the Christelijke Volkspartij (CVP), which has now become the Christelijke Democraten en Vlaams (CD+V) in an attempt to draw votes from the Flemish nationalists. This story was made into the film *Daens* by Stijn Coninx, with Flanders' most popular actor Jan Decleir taking the part of Daens, and is a classic of Flemish cinema.

Sint-Martens-Latem School of Art

Latem means "village of serfs"—hardly appropriate for the present population of wealthy villa dwellers who like to live here because local taxes are low. The area consists of sandbanks or dunes deposited by the sea long ago, with coniferous forests and muddy tracks where the homes of the well-off are hidden behind trees. The uncontrolled building of luxury homes has turned Latem into a sprawling, big money ghetto, and not a place where one might get away from other people. Previously Sint-Martens-Latem enjoyed more positive international fame because of the "school" of artists who flourished here in the twentieth century. In reality, there was never any organized school as such; the artists who settled here came for the scenery and were influenced by the same trends.

The landscape movement started around 1850 as a reaction against the dehumanizing effects of big cities and industry, especially with Millet and Corot in the village of Barbizon in France where the Latem artists César and Xavier de Cock spent some time. The de Cocks often painted scenes on the Leie by Latem; the ancient farm, Het Tempelhof, behind the Sint-Martinus Church, appears in many of their paintings. The greatest star of Flemish landscape painting was Emile Claus (1849-1924), born at Sint-Baafs-Vijve into a flax-trading family. After studying at the Antwerp College of Art he went to North Africa (one of his paintings from Algeria is on display at the Museum van Deinze en de Leiestreek) and took part in the Paris Salons. Claus, who lived at Astene, was a master in capturing the changing effects of light and an exponent of a type of Belgian Impressionism known as Luminism. The Museum van Deinze en de Leiestreek has his *The Beet Harvest* (1913), an immense canvas that evocatively captures the winter cold with a woman blowing on her frozen hands while the sugar beets flash with psychedelic orange, red and purple.

The first artist to settle in Sint-Martens-Latem was Valerius De Saedeleer (1867-1941), who originated from Aalst. In his early years he painted conventional landscapes in an Impressionist style without great success. After many years of moving around Flanders he settled in Latem in 1898 and was joined there by the leading Ghent artists, Gustave van de Woestijne and George Minne. The Exhibition of Flemish Primitives in Bruges in 1902 had a decisive effect on De Saedeleer's direction as an artist as regards technique, while the French landscapist Emile Menard influenced his ideas about depth and meaning in landscape. His subsequent paintings present a unified vision of the Flemish countryside and its people. De Saedeleer considered himself a disciple of Brueghel and the Old Flemish Masters; his paintings of villages in the snow echo those of Pieter Brueghel the Elder, most of all *Hunters Returning in the Snow*. His paintings become more stylized and decorative after the First World War under the influence of Japanese art and Art Nouveau as he specialized increasingly in painting bare black trees against the snow in a calligraphic style.

Other painters in the first Latem wave made a similar journey. The vogue for imitating French Impressionists gave way to a more introverted and spiritual art under the influence of the Symbolist movement of the 1890s and a return to Christian devotion. The Symbolists favoured simpler lines, clarity and more deliberate layering of paint rather than the quick brushwork of the Impressionists. The Ghent sculptor George Minne (1866-1941) created a series known as *Kneeling Youths with a Fountain* around 1898, one of which stands by the Cathedral of St. Bavo in Ghent. Minne looked for the sculptural equivalent of Symbolist literature, and his figures were generally gloomy and introspective until 1908, when the Symbolist movement had run its course. From then he created figures in the realist style of the Brussels-born painter and sculptor Constantin Meunier. Gustave van de Woestijne (1881-1947) was one of a number who used local farm workers as models for monumental portraits with overtones of early Christian saints, or explicitly religious works with themes from the Bible. Sint-Martens-Latem became a mystical landscape to these artists, a place of contemplation far removed from superficial Impressionism.

The final representative of the first wave was Albert Servaes (1883-1966), a transitional figure who spanned the earlier and later generations of Latem artists and who is considered Belgium's greatest Expressionist painter. His house and studio have been transformed into a hotel, Het Torenhof, in the Baarle-Frankrijkstraat, Sint-Martens-Latem. Servaes built much of it himself between 1915 and 1917 in the style of a Romanesque monastery.

The second so-called Latem School included Constant Permeke (see Chapter Eight), Frits van den Berghe and Gustave de Smet (1877-1943). De Smet settled in Deurle, next to Latem, in 1929 after spending many years in Holland. He evolved from Expressionism to post-Cubism, specializing in scenes of village life and carnivals with influences from Henri Le Fauconnier and Georges Braque. His brother, Leon de Smet (1881-1966) was a follower of Emile Claus and painted landscapes of the Leie in an Impressionist style.

Many Latem artists left Belgium during the First World War and came into contact with French Cubism and German Expressionism in the Netherlands or in Britain. Permeke only lived in Latem between 1909 and 1912 and spent the war in England. Van den Berghe (1883-1939) was in Latem from 1910 to 1913 and painted in an Expressionist style. After the First World War his style becomes increasingly dark and pessimistic, while his original, poetic images are reminiscent of the work of Max Ernst. Van den Berghe developed an interest in automatic writing and painting, using accidental images found on pieces of wood.

In the latter part of his career he concentrated on drawing; his work in comic strips had an enormous influence on his successors. He also illustrated some works by Ghent horror writer Jean Ray, mainly Dutch comic strips.

The next generation of artists was far more diverse. Prominent among them is the figure of Roger Raveel, who lives at Machelen on the Leie, where a museum is dedicated to his work. After a period of abstract painting he developed the style he calls "De Nieuw Visie" (The New Vision) in parallel with Pop Art. Raveel works on the interrelationships between colours and shapes, taking everyday objects and the rural environment as a starting point. The simple colours, framing and narrative style have something in common with David Hockney. Raveel generated a school of followers in the area of the Leie, including Agnes Maes, Antoon De Clerck, Raoul de Keyser and Richard Smoens.

The main museums for the Latem School are in neighbouring Deurle: the Museum Gust De Smet at 1 Gustaaf De Smetlaan, the Stichting Mw.J. Dhondt-Dhaenens at 14 Museumlaan, and Museum Leon De Smet at 18 Museumlaan. These are not open every day. The Museum Gevaert-Minne, at 45 Kapitteldreef, reopens in 2007 after extensive restoration. The Museum van Deinze en de Leiestreek in nearby Deinze has a comprehensive collection.

The classical scenery along the Leie has largely been wiped out by the building of concrete banks to prevent flooding. Yet Sint-Martens-Latem still preserves some of the more picturesque stretches of water, such as the landing stage by the Meerstraat and further west by the Le Pêcheur restaurant. Here one might still recognize the landscape celebrated in Emile Claus' painting of cows fording the river.

Oudenaarde and the Flemish Ardennes

Running from Geraardsbergen on the border of the French-speaking province of Hainaut to Kruishoutem in the west is the area known as the Vlaamse Ardennen or Flemish Ardennes, a remnant of the great Ardennes forest that existed at the time of the Romans. While there are considerably fewer trees than in the main forest in Wallonia, the hills are a welcome change from the flatter landscapes to the north.

The city of Oudenaarde could be called the gateway to the Flemish Ardennes; it traces its origins back to the fortress of Ename, built in 974

Oudenaarde Town Hall

AD on the east bank of the Scheldt. The Battle of Oudenaarde was fought at the nearby village of Eine by the British, Dutch, Austrian and German allied forces against the French in 1708. Eine (see p.38) and the church of St. Eligius can be seen on the tapestry of the battle at Blenheim Palace, near Oxford. Also near Oudenaarde is the first church in Flanders in Scheldt Gothic style, the Church of the Virgin at Pamele, started in 1234 and completed in 1300. The church still has a horizontally extended Romanesque shape, but with the important innovation of an aisle that runs around the entire nave.

Oudenaarde has many interesting features, not least the town hall, a late example of Brabant Gothic built between 1526 and 1537 as a tribute to Emperor Charles V. This can only be visited with a guide. Oudenaarde was traditionally known for making ornate silver tableware and for its tapestry industry. The last weaver closed down in 1772, but recently the city has revived interest in tapestry by opening the Wandtapijtenmuseum and a tapestry repair workshop in the Huis de Lalaing. By the Kleine Markt in the Zakstraat is the house of Marguerite of Parma (1522-86), governor of the Netherlands and illegitimate daughter of Emperor Charles V and his mistress, Johanna van der Gheynst. There is a painting of the happy couple by Theodor Canneel (1817-92) in the Ghent Museum of Fine Arts.

Ename Church

On the other side of the Scheldt across the Ohio Bridge is the village of Ename, the original core of the town of Oudenaarde, with one of the best-preserved Romanesque churches in Flanders, Sint-Laurentius. After the Treaty of Verdun divided Charlemagne's empire into three in 843, the Scheldt formed the border between France and the Holy Roman Empire, with Ename in the latter. Around 1000 Ename was the largest fortress in the German Empire but in 1033 Baldwin IV of Flanders conquered it and in 1047 Baldwin V took over the entire area between the Scheldt and the Dender. The fortifications were demolished and the area demilitarized to stop the Holy Roman Emperor from taking it back.

The Church of Sint-Laurentius was started before 1000 and substantially added to over the years. The frescoes that are now its unique feature were whitewashed over in 974. The area around Oudenaarde was a Protestant stronghold in the time of the Iconoclasts. Protestants from

Ghent destroyed Oudenaarde's abbey in 1578 but Sint-Laurentius was left more or less intact until the task of restoring it to its original Romanesque shape started in 1907, with the replacement of all the brickwork with more authentic Doornik limestone. With the recent decline in church attendance, archeologists seized the opportunity to strip the church down to virtually what it was in the tenth century. All the original entrances have been restored and virtually every item of furniture removed. The Byzantine-style fresco of Christ Pantocrator high above the nave is unique in Flanders, a reminder of how all Flemish churches looked at the end of the first millennium. The extremely detailed explanations on computer screens in several languages make a visit here meaningful, even to the non-specialist.

The Belfry from Rue aux Laines.

Chapter Six
Bruges: Petrified Dreams

"City of waters, where the long weed flows
And swerves in shadowy streams and the lamp's light
Makes magical some corner of the night."
Laurence Binyon, "Bruges", 1919

Brugge has long been known to English-speakers by its French name, Bruges; the name, strangely, is accepted by the Flemish as the English for Brugge. The city gained its wealth by having the North Sea at its door, but time and nature isolated it and only the salt spray carried by the wind reminds us that we are but five miles from the coast. With the rise of tourism, Bruges has become what some have decried as a medieval theme park, overcrowded with visitors for much of the year. If Bruggelingen are not all pleased by the invasion of foreigners, they nevertheless do very well out of the tourist business and have done everything to attract visitors. This is a city of over a hundred hotels and even more restaurants, yet behind the theme park appearance lies a conservative backwater. The more ambitious young Bruggelingen leave for the bigger Flemish cities to study and never return. There is also something of Holland about Bruges; the French poet Paul Verlaine called it "a charming, small, Catholic Amsterdam". Its people have commerce in their blood, identifying with the great medieval trading city of Bruges, and much less so with the morbid imagery of Georges Rodenbach's novel *Bruges-la-morte* (Dead Bruges).

Bruges owes its appeal to its homogenous medieval appearance—and it is precisely an appearance, for much of the city was reconstructed in the nineteenth century. From 1850 the city's buildings were improved under the influence of British architects in a neo-Gothic style. The city centre is a more or less Baroque-free zone, with a purity of style lacking in most Flemish cities, and there are few places that can compete with Bruges for a concentrated cityscape of medieval-style streets and canals.

The city centre and the Begijnhof are a UNESCO World Heritage Site. In 2002 Bruges was European Capital of Culture, and the city fathers made a tentative move towards introducing some modern architecture into its centre. The pavilion by the Japanese architect Toyo Ito, which appears to float on water, has been allowed to remain near the original heart of the city, the Burg. Less fortuitously, the concert hall at 't Zand, has been cleverly disguised as a multi-storey car park. (The information centre In & Uit Brugge under the same roof offers free internet access.) The 40,000-ton building had to be built on 10,000 springs to protect the hall's acoustics from noises and vibrations from the nearby motorway and underground car park.

Bruges has been variously called the "City of Swans", the "Venice of the North" and the "City in the Shape of a Reliquary". Charles Baudelaire, never one to appreciate anything Belgian, called it a "mummified city", while others might describe it as sterile (its cleanliness and lack of litter are proverbial, even by West Flemish standards). Litter or not, Bruges receives so many visitors that it has arguably lost its mystique, but most tourists actually see very little, few of them straying outside the "golden triangle" between 't Zand, the Dijver and the Minnewater. Some parts of the town can be seen from a boat, which keeps the streets less crowded than they might otherwise be. The best time to visit is in winter after snow has fallen—something that rarely happens these days. Take away the tourists and Bruges looks a great deal more attractive, and a lot deader.

Early Days
Bruges' name comes from an Old Norse word, *bryga*, meaning a landing stage or quay. It was at the heart of Charlemagne's *Pagus Flandrensis*, a coastal plain between the Zwin and the Yser rivers. The estuary of the Zwin was created by sea flooding in the fourth century, giving Bruges a direct outlet to the North Sea, but it was not until the twelfth century, with more flooding, that the Zwin became large enough to take sea-going ships. Bruges was also conveniently located for overland trade. The surrounding landscape changed, with the building of sea dikes and canals creating conditions for new towns and a larger population. The first Count of Flanders, Baldwin Iron Arm, established his castle at Bruges in 864 on the site of the present-day Burg, and also brought the

relics of St. Donatian to the city so that the Church of St. Donatian became the most important religious institution in his realm. In 1127 Count Charles the Good was murdered while giving alms to a poor woman in the Church of St. Donatian, a particularly heinous crime. He had, it was rumoured, built up a vast fortune thanks to his competent management of the Flemish economy and thus attracted the attentions of robber knights. The killers were thrown from the church tower but never revealed the whereabouts of the treasure—if it every existed. Charles the Good was beatified, and there is a chapel dedicated to him in the St. Salvator Cathedral. The Basilica of the Holy Blood preserves a Horn of Damnation that was once sounded every year on the anniversary of Charles' death. The Church of St. Donatian was completely demolished in 1799 by the French, and the contents auctioned off on the saint's name day. A large section of the foundations and the tenth-century city wall can be seen in the basement of the Crowne Plaza Hotel across from the tourist office on the Burg.

Bruges' prosperity led to the rise of a newly wealthy class of patricians, the *poorters*, as well as tensions with the Count of Flanders. The Flemish counts owed a nominal allegiance to the French king and the patricians generally took the side of the French, while the artisan guilds wanted greater independence. In the fourteenth century Bruges was one of the largest cities in Europe, with a population of 50,000. Along with Ghent and Ypres, it was one of three Flemish cities allowed to manufacture and export high-quality woollen cloth. The weavers and dyers of Bruges, the so-called Blauwe Nagels or Blue Fingernails, took the lead in opposing French domination in 1302, led by Pieter de Coninck, head of the weavers' guild, and Jan Breydel, head of the butchers, whose statues stand in the centre of the Grote Markt. The great Flemish victory over the French, the Battle of the Golden Spurs, which took place outside Kortrijk, is celebrated every year in Flanders on 11 July (see p.5). Dante visited Bruges in the same year, and in his *Purgatory* he expresses the wish that the Italians could deal with the French in the same way: "If Douai, Ghent, Lille and Bruges could do this, then Italy's revenge could be as quick."

Bruges gained its wealth from the production of woollen cloth and stockings that were exported all over Europe, but the local supply of wool soon gave out and Bruges became reliant on imported English wool to keep its looms going. By the thirteenth century it was the leading trading city of northern Europe, with virtually all goods brought in by foreign vessels. Foreign merchants were organized into national fraternities or "Nations" under a governor who disciplined members, negotiated with local authorities and acted as an agent for their own government. The Nations had their buildings or *loges* around the Beursplein, which corresponds to the square on the Vlamingstraat a little beyond the theatre, and their own chapels in the Sint-Jacobskerk nearby (not always open). The Genoese Nation at 33 Vlamingstraat has changed considerably from the building of 1399, having acquired an incongruous bell-shaped gable, but the windows are still recognizably Gothic. The Venetians bought a house in 1379 at 37 Vlamingstraat, known as Ter Ouder Buerse, which has been replaced by a second-hand bookshop. The house called Ter Buerse at no. 35 derived its name from an inn displaying three purses (*beurs* in Flemish) where traders conducted business, and thus gave rise to the word "Bourse" or "Beurs", meaning stock exchange. The Florentine Nation has disappeared completely; all that is left is a plaque at 1 Academiestraat with a quote from Dante about the Flemish struggle to hold back the sea. William Caxton (c.1422-91) became governor of the English Nation of Merchant Adventurers from 1462. He learned the art of printing in Cologne in 1471-2 and set up a printing press in Bruges with a local calligrapher, Colard Mansion. The first book ever printed in English, *The History of Troy*, translated from French by Caxton, was apparently printed at the request of Margaret of York, sister of Edward IV of England, and wife of Charles the Bold, Duke of Burgundy, in 1474 or 1475. The following year Caxton returned to London to continue his printing business. Caxton was literally a one-man band; he first had to translate the books that he printed. In 1481 he published his translation of the Flemish epic, *Reynard the Fox*.

The Goddess of Luxury

When Philip IV, King of France, visited Bruges in 1301 his queen exclaimed: "I believed that I was the only queen here, but it seems that the Flemish in our prisons are all princes, because their wives are dressed like princesses and queens." In 1351 the burgomasters (mayors) of Ghent, Bruges and Ypres went to Paris to pay homage to King John II and were received with great pomp and distinction, but when they were invited to a festival they observed that their seats at table were not furnished with cushions, so to make known their displeasure at this lack of respect they folded their richly embroidered cloaks and sat on them. On rising from table, they left their cloaks behind them. When informed of this apparent forgetfulness, Simon van Aertrycke, burgomaster of Bruges, replied: "We Flemings are not in the habit of carrying away our cushions after dinner."

Pero Tafur, a Spanish traveller who visited in 1438, remarked on the wealth of the city:

It seems to me, however, and many agree with my opinion, that there is much more commercial activity in Bruges than in Venice. The reason is as follows. In the whole of the West there is no other great mercantile centre except Bruges, although England does some trade, and thither repair all the nations of the world, and they say that at times the number of ships sailing from the harbour of Bruges exceeds seven hundred a day. The inhabitants are extraordinarily industrious, possibly on account of the barrenness of the soil, since very little corn is grown, and no wine, nor is there water fit for drinking, nor any fruit. On this account the products of the whole world are brought here, so that they have everything in abundance, in exchange for the work of their hands.

Without doubt, the goddess of luxury has great power there, but it is not a place for poor men, who would be badly received. But anyone who has money, and wishes to spend it, will find in this town alone everything that the whole world produces. I saw there oranges and lemons from Castile, which seemed only just to have been gathered from the trees, fruits and wine from Greece, as abundant as in that country. I saw also confections and spices from Alexandria, and all the Levant, just as if one were there; first from the Black Sea, as if they had been produced in the district. Here was all Italy with its brocades, silks and armour, and everything which is made there; and, indeed, there is no part of the world whose products are not found here at their best.

Tafur put his finger on Flanders' vulnerability to changing economic circumstances. The region had to import ninety per cent of its grain from elsewhere in the fourteenth century and could quickly be brought to its knees by a blockade. Nor did everybody live in the lap of luxury:

> There was a great famine in the year of my visit. I departed to Sluys, which is the seaport of Bruges, and lodged with the captain. As I was in the church hearing Mass, a woman approached me and said that she had something to communicate to me in private which would be to my advantage. She took me to her home close by, and she there showed me two young girls and offered me the one who should please me most. Astounded, I enquired of her how she could bring herself to behave thus, whereupon she told me that she was almost dead with hunger, having had nothing to eat for many days except a few small fish, and that the two girls were likely to die of starvation.

Ships came down the Zwin from Sluis through Damme and into the River Reie. They then tied up along the Spiegelrei, now lined with classical style buildings. At the other end of the canal is the Herberghe Vlissinghe (at 2 Blekersstraat), an inn that has been in continuous use since 1515. The Herberghe Vlissinghe has long functioned as a cultural centre for Bruggelingen and has a very interesting interior. Looking back from the entrance (originally at the back of the inn) and imagining dozens of ships tied up along the Spiegelrei, one may have an idea of how Bruges looked when it was a great port. Smaller ships could go right up to the Markt and tied up next to the Waterhallen to sell their cargo. This building was twice replaced; the present white neo-Gothic Provinciaal Hof (Provincial Court) dates from 1878.

The Stadhuis and Brugse Vrije

The Burg was the original centre of Bruges; the castle and Church of St. Donatian have been replaced with a three-sided square. On the left is the former Landshuis van het Brugse Vrije, the administrative centre for the medieval province of "Free Bruges" or Brugse Vrije (corresponding to the province of West Flanders), whose symbol is a silver shield with a diagonal blue stripe. The building dates from 1727 and is an unusual example of French-influenced classicizing Baroque architecture. The Bruges tourist office is on the other side of the courtyard through the central archway. Around the courtyard are several sixteenth- and

seventeenth-century buildings that once housed the Vierschaar (Court of Assizes) and Aldermen's Chamber of the Brugse Vrije. This latter contains one of the major Renaissance artworks of the Low Countries, the Charles V Hearth, designed by the Bruges artist Lanceloot Blondeel in 1531 to commemorate Charles V's victory over the French at the Battle of Pavia. The hearth is decorated with 46 coats of arms and statues of Charles V's grandparents in order to demonstrate his ancestry. This complex can be reached by going through the doorway in the corner of the square.

Next to this doorway is a highly decorated building from 1534-7 known as the Burgerlijke Griffie (Clerk of the Court's offices), one of the first buildings in Flanders to be decorated in Renaissance style. The basic structure is purely Gothic. It was restored in the nineteenth century to repair the damage done by the French during the occupation of 1794-1814, and can only be viewed from the outside. To the right of the Griffie is the Stadhuis or Town Hall, the oldest Gothic town hall in Flanders, built between 1376 and 1421 and substantially restored in 1887 by Louis Delancenserie. The pendants with small wooden sculptures hanging from the ribbed wooden ceiling are partly original and partly nineteenth-century. These are no longer in their original locations and only an expert can see the difference, the newer pendants making use of more realistic perspective. The paintings around the walls showing the history of Bruges are from around 1900. They were intended to impress visitors and tie in with the building of the port of Zeebrugge (1895-1905), which it was hoped would reinvigorate sleepy Bruges.

The Holy Blood
Bruges' most precious relic is the Holy Blood, drops of blood and water wiped from the body of Christ by Joseph of Arimathea. According to legend, Count Diederik of Alsace brought the relic of the Holy Blood back from the Holy Land in 1150. More probably it was taken from Constantinople by Crusaders in 1203 after the Counts of Flanders briefly reigned over the Byzantine Empire. Count Diederik built a double chapel between 1134 and 1157, located next to the Town Hall or Stadhuis. The upper chapel was renamed the Basilica of the Holy Blood when it was used to house the relic from 1203. The basilica has been

rebuilt a number of times; the current version is in a rather over-decorated nineteenth-century neo-Gothic style. The lower chapel with the relics of St. Basil, however, is largely unchanged from the twelfth century and is Belgium's best-preserved Romanesque building. At around ten o'clock every morning (the time can vary) the relic of the Holy Blood is brought out for worshippers to kiss or touch. The blood is inside a piece of rock crystal and looks quite fresh. Until 1325 the blood liquefied every Friday at 6pm. When it stopped liquefying it was taken as a bad omen, although it took until the end of the following century for the city to decline.

The Procession of the Holy Blood is the high point of the Bruges festival calendar, a religious occasion when the shrine with the drops of Christ's blood is taken around the city. The ceremony takes place on Ascension Day, with a service in the morning in the basilica followed by high mass in the St. Salvator Cathedral in the afternoon. The procession starts out at noon, the first half depicting biblical scenes, while the second is more historical (and tourist-oriented), showing the entry of the Count of Flanders into Bruges with hundreds of costumed figures and magnificent floats. There is a good deal of emotion and shouting as the city's relics are displayed to the crowds. (For a good view it is essential to buy tickets for the stands well in advance.) There are also potential spiritual benefits: in 1310 Pope Clement V issued a bull absolving pilgrims of sin for five years and 200 days if they attended the procession in a pious manner, or if they visited the basilica within fourteen days of the procession.

Bruges has many other processions and festivals, and not only for the benefit of tourists. The Blindekensprocessie originated in the fourteenth century after the Battle of the Pevelenberg against the French. The wives of the soldiers promised the Virgin Mary that they would light a candle of a certain weight every year if their men were spared. Every year on 15 August a candle weighing 36 pounds is duly carried from the almshouse for the blind (hence Blindekens) between the Kammakerstraat and the Kreupelenstraat to the chapel of Onze Lieve Vrouw ter Potterie on the other side of the city. Every five years the city also holds the Gouden Boomstoet (Golden Tree Parade) to evoke the Burgundian period, the time of Bruges' greatest wealth—and to draw tourists. The Reiefeesten are similarly intended for visitors and are held every three or four years. There are also more genuine street festivals, such as the Feesten van de Verloren Hoek, celebrating the name day of St. Anna in August every year.

Almshouses and Beguinages

Beguines first appeared around 1190 in Liège as an order started by Lambert le Bègue (Lambert the Stammerer). These were groups of women (and also men) who wanted to lead a religious life but did not wish to take full holy orders, or who could not gain admission to a monastic order. The first beguines in Bruges were a group of women who went to live on the edge of the city by the Minnewater for their own safety in 1245 when their menfolk went off to the Crusades, while others later joined up because they had no prospect of marriage after their men were killed in the Holy Land. Living in their *beguinage* or *begijnhof*, they took vows of chastity, poverty and obedience to their *grootjuffrouw* or Grande Dame and wore habits with black and white hoods. They were meant to offer money when they joined; the poorest were instead allowed to offer herrings. Part of their devotions was directed towards a fictitious founder, St. Begga, the daughter of the Frankish king Pepin de Landes. The Catholic Church tolerated the beguines as long as they caused no trouble, but they were suspected of heresy in their early years. Part of the Begijnhof, with its calm poplar-filled grounds, has been opened up as a museum and can be visited at certain times of the day, every day of the week.

Beguines were suppressed during the religious troubles of the sixteenth century and again by Napoleon, who closed them down. By the 1920s there were too few of them, so the canon of the Begijnhof asked Benedictine nuns to take over. These fully ordained nuns, many of them from overseas, live at the back of the Begijnhof away from the public gaze, although they can be seen processing to church. The small white houses at the back of the Begijnhof are occupied by some forty single Bruges women. The last big colony of beguines was in Lier, but they too have all died out. In 2006 it seems that there was only one beguine left in the whole of Flanders, in Kortrijk. In front of the Begijnhof is the world-famous and picturesque Minnewater, a canalized lake that is home to many of the city's swans. Minnewater is often rendered in French as Lac d'Amour (Lake of Love) as the Dutch word

"The lofty gateway seems not to immure,
the bridge is going like-gladly to and fro;
in that old, open elm-court, though, secure
are one and all, and now no longer go
out of their little houses, save when wending
along that strip to church, for comprehending
better why so much love in them arose."

Rainer Maria Rilke, "Béguinage Sainte-Elisabeth, Bruges",
1907 (trans. J. B. Leishman)

minne means love, but another theory has it that the name derives from *manja,* a Germanic water sprite.

Flemish almshouses or *godshuizen* take two forms. Some were built by wealthy people within their estates as a sort of insurance policy for their entry into heaven, as the people who lived in them were required to pray for their rich patrons. The guilds also started almshouses to help the aged, widows and the disabled at a time when there were no old age pensions or social welfare. The residents were obliged to go to chapel, not to drink too much and generally to lead an exemplary life, in return for which they were supplied with coal and bread. The houses were very small; these days they have been knocked together to make more spacious accommodation. Since these houses belong to the city, tourists are allowed to sit in the gardens during the daytime. The best view of a traditional Bruges alleyway with almshouses is at the Vette Vispoort on the Moerstraat, near the Speelmanstraat.

Guido Gezelle

> *"Flemish is the sweetest language,*
> *as long as you do not treat her with violence."*

The great poet Guido Gezelle (1830-99) was born the son of a gardener at 64 Rolweg (or Rolleweg), now a museum and study centre, the Guido Gezellemuseum. A good view over the Rolweg can be had by climbing up the small hill on the Kruisvest, where the Sint-Janshuis Windmill is located. Gezelle's father was an observant man with a sharp wit and a devoted Catholic who tried to improve himself by following evening studies. After ordination as a priest Gezelle was sent in 1854 to teach commercial science, bookkeeping and chemistry (subjects he knew little about) at a seminary in Roeselare, and then became professor of poetry in 1857. He was popular with his students, many of them English, for his unconventional teaching methods, but came under suspicion from the Church authorities for his pro-Flemish views and original ideas. His superiors removed him from Roeselare and made him the sub-director of the English College in Bruges in 1859. In 1860 the English College closed down and he transferred to the English Seminary, where he was to teach philosophy. The seminary was funded by a wealthy English Catholic, John Sutton, to train British and Flemish missionaries to work in Britain and elsewhere. Gezelle and his sponsors believed that if Britain could be reconverted to Catholicism, then the rest of the world would follow, and although he wanted to go to England himself, he had to be content with training missionaries. His superiors, meanwhile, understood that Gezelle was more useful as a teacher than as a missionary, even if they had trouble handling a poet of world stature in their midst. After he translated Longfellow's *Hiawatha* into Dutch, he received a letter from Longfellow thanking him for his efforts, with the remark: "The only criticism I can venture to make upon it is, that occasionally you end a line with an accented syllable."

As a brilliant writer and satirist, Gezelle was encouraged by his superiors to write for Catholic journals started in opposition to the Flemish Liberal press. These writings became more extreme from 1864 during a period when the Catholic Church in Belgium was in conflict with the freemason-dominated Liberal government. Gezelle was a high-profile figure who attracted controversy, and so the Church authorities demoted him and made him the curate of the Church of St. Walburga in 1865, a Jesuit church on the Sint-Maartensplein built between 1619 and 1641. There is a plaque on the wall at nearby 5 Korte Ridderstraat where Gezelle lived between 1865 and 1872 (not 1865 to 1867, as it says on the plaque). Gezelle had more or less given up writing poetry from 1865 and life did not become any easier for him. An English family called Smith living nearby at 9 Hoornstraat dragged Gezelle into a scandal that forced him out of Bruges. The husband asked Gezelle for money, while Mrs. Smith was frequently at the priest's house, was rumoured to have given birth there and also presented Gezelle with a watch that she had not paid for. The watchmaker was a Liberal and demanded payment from Gezelle's superior. The anti-Catholic press made use of such rumours to discredit Gezelle, obliging his superiors to order him to leave Bruges.

Gezelle's health suffered, and he was grateful to be transferred in 1872 to the calmer environment of Kortrijk where he continued to work as a simple priest and started to write poetry again. Much of his best poetry dates from his later years in Kortrijk, while he also worked on his West Flemish dictionary, *Loquela*. His standing rose once more and he was showered with honours and knighted by Leopold I. In 1899 he was appointed spiritual director of the English Convent in the Carmersstraat, but he was too old to take on this heavy task and died within nine months.

Gezelle was on the one hand both a pious and modest figure, but also had a fanatical streak when it came to fighting for the causes he believed in, as well as being sensitive and highly-strung. The Antwerp novelist, Willem Elsschot, considered him "the greatest lyric poet since Virgil". Gezelle believed that West Flemish could serve as the basis for a Flemish literary language in conjunction with Medieval Dutch, but he used West Flemish words as and when it suited him, as well as importing older Flemish words where they sounded right. Preferring not to use the modern Dutch of the godless Calvinists in the Netherlands, the language he used is both anachronistic and highly individualistic; modern-day readers require notes to understand Gezelle's peculiar spelling and vocabulary. The basis of his poetry is the alliteration of the fairly harsh sounds of West Flemish, something that cannot easily be translated into another language. A number of English translations of his poetry exist. The leading translator of Flemish poetry, Paul Claes, contributed to the collection of thirty poems, *The Evening and the Rose* (1999). In the same year appeared *That Limpid Singer*, a more extensive bilingual collection edited by Paul Vincent. The most recent translations are the best; earlier efforts make Gezelle sound sentimental:

"Winter Midges"

The winter midges are
a-whirling, dancing dots,
as white as miller's meal,
as white as curdling clots.

They're flying high, in flood;
they're dropping deep, in ebb;
they're weaving, up and down,
their whitest winterweb.

Sint-Annawijk

To see a more authentic side of Bruges visitors should go to the lace-makers' quarter, the Sint-Annawijk, which includes Gezelle's birthplace in the Rolweg. At 85 Carmersstraat is the Engels Klooster (English Convent), with the striking rounded dome of the Kloosterkerk next door. This was started in 1629 by English Augustinian nuns and became a high-class finishing school for young Catholic ladies. It ceased to be an educational institution in 1972, and is now used to house seminaries and pilgrims, although the nuns will take visitors on a guided tour. The entrance is to the right of the church. This was where King Charles II worshipped during his exile in Bruges (1656-9). Further along the Carmersstraat at no. 174 are the extensive grounds and home of the Sint Sebastiaansgilde, the Guild of Archers, where members can practise firing at a round target or at the traditional *gaai* or wooden bird on a pole. This is a high-class social club more than anything else; Charles II was a member, as are Queen Elizabeth II and the current Charles, Prince of Wales. At the back of the grounds, under the entrance to the walled garden in the Rolweg, is the inscription "Den booghe can nyt altyd gespannen staen" (The bow cannot be drawn all the time), presumably an admonition to relax and have a drink. The tourist office can tell visitors when the museum is open.

Next to the Jeruzalemkerk and opposite the Kantwerkstersplaats is the Kantcentrum or Lace Centre at 3 Peperstraat, both a museum and a college. From time to time one of the trainee lace-makers will offer a demonstration of this traditional handicraft. Going north from the picturesque Kantwerkstersplaats (Lace-makers' Square), is the Balstraat, with the Museum voor Volkskunde (Folklore Museum) running along most of its length in a series of almshouses belonging to the Shoemakers' Guild. The museum has rooms illustrating different traditional professions and a small inn, "De Zwarte Kat". A little way further, on the corner of the Korte Speelmanstraat and the Carmersstraat, is a charming naïve crucifixion from 1760. The story goes that a woman called Anna was thrown into a well by a robber, but as it was winter the water was frozen over and she was able to climb out again. This was taken to be a miracle, and the unusual scene that now appears on the wall is kept freshly painted for all to admire. On the way to the town centre again is the unusual blue brick-paved Korte Sint-Janstraat, leading to the church where Guido Gezelle was christened and did his first communion, the Sint-Annakerk. There is a plaque on the wall.

The Jeruzalemkerk

Next to the Lace Centre at 1-3 Peperstraat is the Jeruzalemkerk, once the private chapel of the Adornes family, Genoese merchants who moved to Bruges in the fourteenth century. Peter and Jacob Adornes were given permission by Pope Martin V in 1427 to build a private church on the model of the Holy Sepulchre in Jerusalem. (Peter's son Anselm Adornes returned to Jerusalem in 1470 to check on the design.) Anselm died in the service of James III of Scotland in 1483, and his heart is buried here under the central tomb, while the heraldic Stewart unicorns are visible throughout the church. High above the nave is the Chapel of St. Catherine, at the top of fourteen steps directly under the tower. In between the steps is a representation of the Calvary, with skulls and bones and other symbols. The altar bears a reliquary with a piece of the True Cross. Below the Chapel of St. Catherine is the crypt, with the replica tomb of Jesus. The entrance has been deliberately made low, so that anyone going in to light a candle has to enter on their hands and knees. On the right is the macabre figure of the dead Christ behind a metal grille.

The Jeruzalemkerk is full of symbolism, pointing to its function as a place of preparation for the Apocalypse. On top of the wooden dome is half a toothed Catherine Wheel with a palm branch running through it, a symbol of the end of the world and the Last Judgment. Below this is the Maltese Cross, an emblem of the Knights Hospitallers to which Adornes belonged. Adornes' tomb is aligned to catch the sunrise in Jerusalem on Christmas Day—if it could reach all the way to Bruges. Behind this strange construction was the view that if Jerusalem was in the hands of the infidel, why not bring Jerusalem to Bruges, the city with the relic of the Holy Blood?

The Jeruzalemkerk passed to the Limburg-Stirum family by marriage and inheritance in 1856. The present owner, Count Henri de Limburg-Stirum, set up a non-profit organization to run the church, vzw Adornes. It is usually necessary to buy a ticket to enter the church from the Lace Centre next door.

Gruuthuse Museum

The Gruuthuse at 17 Dijver is now part of the Bruggemuseum, along with the Town Hall and the Archeological Museum at 36A Mariastraat, and houses the city's collection of antiquities and applied arts. The house was home to the Gruuthuse family from 1425 to 1596. The Gruuthuses controlled the right to sell *gruut* or *gruit* (grout), a mixture of dried flowers and plants that was added to beer before hops were introduced. In the fourteenth century beer with hops became increasingly popular as a result of imports, so the *gruutrecht* or tax on *gruit* was replaced with a tax on beer. Jan IV van Gruuthuse started to build his mansion around 1425, and his son Lodewijk completed it. When in 1471 Edward IV, King of England, was obliged to flee his country during the Wars of the Roses he stayed here. As a mark of gratitude he made Gruuthuse Count of Winchester. Lodewijk van Gruuthuse was also responsible for arranging the marriage of Mary of Burgundy and Maximilian of Austria, which led to the Spanish occupation. His son moved to France and took his priceless library with him, and this now forms one of the French Bibliothèque Nationale's greatest treasures.

The initiative to set up the museum came in part from some British residents, including the art historian James Weale who did much to restore Bruges' Gothic heritage. Weale (1838-1917) was a London antiquarian and art historian who lived in Bruges from 1855 to 1878. His main contribution was to publish definitive studies of the van Eyck brothers, Memling, Gerard David and others, and to raise appreciation of the Flemish Primitives. Another founder of the Gruuthuse Museum was William Brangwyn, the father of the artist Frank Brangwyn. The Gruuthuse's collection is varied, with tasteful pictures of doctors administering enemas, a dissection, the well-known terracotta bust of Charles V aged fifteen with a wooden hat, a vast collection of medieval furniture and household objects and, more seriously, an eighteenth-century guillotine near the entrance, used to execute the famous bandit Louis Bakelandt in 1803.

Lodewijk van Gruuthuse managed to persuade the city authorities to allow him to build a private chapel between his house and the Church of the Virgin Mary (Onze Lieve Vrouwekerk) so that his family could take part in services without having to leave their house. The Gruuthuse has a superb view over the Reie, the river passing through Bruges after which all the other wharves are named. On leaving the Gruuthuse's courtyard, the visitor can hardly miss the 350-foot Onze Lieve Vrouw tower, completed in 1440, reputedly the tallest brick building in the world. Many buildings in Bruges are of brick, since clay was more readily available than stone in these parts. Behind the Gruuthuse is the Sint-Bonifaciusbrug (Bridge of St. Bonifacius), dating from 1910, which gives one of the most picturesque panoramas of Bruges.

The Church of the Virgin Mary is made of Doornik stone in the Scheldegotiek (Scheldt or early Gothic style) found in the region between Doornik (Tournai) and Ghent and typified by corner towers, round pillars and carved capitals. The church is in a mixture of styles, the oldest part being the central aisle from the thirteenth century, and the general effect is rather like a Byzantine kasbah, with all kinds of surprising contrasts. The entire church was going to be remodelled in the style of the High Gothic north aisle, but the work was never completed because of lack of money. The south aisle has a *Madonna and Child* by Michelangelo from 1501-3, the only work by the artist to leave Italy during his lifetime. It was originally intended for the Duomo in Siena but a Bruges merchant was able to buy it. The Lanchalskapel has a Last Supper by the Bruges master Pieter Pourbus and a Christ on the Cross attributed to Anthony van Dyck. The most interesting feature of the church are the tombs of Charles the Bold and Mary of Burgundy and an exhibition of excavated medieval graves. Napoleon was so impressed on his visit that he donated 10,000 francs for the restoration of the church. It is rumoured, however, that the body is not of Charles the Bold, but an imposter sent by the French in 1553.

Groeninge Museum

To view the work of the Flemish Primitives one makes one's way to the nearby Groeninge Museum at 12 Dijver. This now comes under the umbrella organization "Fine Arts" along with the Arentshuis and the Forum at the top of the Concertgebouw. The Groeninge Museum has been remodelled in a very spare style, with stark white walls and bare metal flues (it has been unflatteringly compared to a cold meat store) and focuses on two world-class pictures. In the first room is the diptych by Gerard David (1460-1523), *The Judgement of Cambyses* and *The Flaying of Sisamnes*. Sisamnes was a corrupt judge in the time of the Persian

Empire, and the work was commissioned in 1498, perhaps as a warning to the Bruges magistrates.

The term Flemish Primitives is, of course, pejorative, referring as it does to the unwillingness of the Flemish to apply the rules of perspective in Italian Renaissance painting. It was coined by late nineteenth-century Belgian art historians who wanted to emphasize the national heritage of old Flemish art—even though many of its luminaries were not from Flanders. Van Eyck, after all, was born near the German border and was not Flemish in any historical sense. German art historians such as Max Friedländer and Erwin Panofsky preferred the term Early Netherlandish School, which emphasized the Germanic nature of this art (i.e. naturalism and realism) and downplayed the French and Italian influences.

The second room has the *Madonna with Canon van der Paele,* one of a small number of paintings definitely attributable to Jan van Eyck (1390-1441), whose greatest work is the *Adoration of the Lamb* in the Cathedral of St. Bavo, Ghent. Here one sees a typically unsparing portrait of a physically decrepit figure, the elderly van der Paele. On the other side of the Virgin is Bruges' patron saint, St. Donatian, in the blue brocade robes of a bishop, while van der Paele is protected by St. George. Van Eyck was long criticized for not idealizing his figures (aside from the Virgin and Child). Further on in the museum is the portrait of his wife, *Margaretha van Eyck,* who has a cunning, rather enigmatic air.

Jan van Eyck was born in Maaseik near Maastricht, the younger brother of the painter Hubert van Eyck. Although Jan van Eyck gave his brother credit as "the greatest painter who ever lived", he completely eclipsed him. The brothers trained under the miniaturists known as the Van Limburg brothers; the precision and technical mastery of their work is the culmination of a long tradition of Flemish miniatures.

Jan became a court artist and equerry to Philip the Good, Duke of Burgundy, in 1425 and moved to his court at Lille. It was a happy meeting and for eleven years van Eyck could work in an atmosphere of reciprocal admiration. He undertook diplomatic missions on the behalf of the duke, apparently to arrange marriages: to Spain in 1427, to Portugal and England in 1428, and maybe to Prague in 1436. His reputation spread to Italy and among the Italian community in the Netherlands, to whom he was known as "John of Bruges". Van Eyck's influence can be seen in Piero della Francesca's Montefeltro altarpiece from 1465 in the representation of the landscape stretching out into infinity. Another outcome of van Eyck's Italian connections is the well-known *Arnolfini Wedding* that can be admired in the National Gallery in London, painted for the Italian merchant Giovanni Arnolfini. There is extraordinary detail here, down to the nails in the floorboards and the texture of the hairs on the couple's dog. Jan van Eyck put himself into the picture with a small self-portrait in the metal mirror. Another work in the National Gallery, *Man in a Red Turban* is also thought by some to be a self-portrait of van Eyck. The leading contemporary Flemish poet Rik van Bastelaere wrote this on the *Arnolfini Wedding*:

> They circle slowly through the Gothic
> Of emptiness. A pair for the times
> Hands on top of each other.
>
> His hat is a monstrosity
> That does not obstruct death and the fall
> Of his clothes leaves his body a supposition.
>
> I would like to think that it
> Already was absent and perhaps,
> Entirely anonymous,
>
> Decayed into a hardstone church floor.

Van Eyck's great achievement was to push realism further than anyone had ever done before, while introducing new techniques for the representation of textures and light. His world is one of Burgundian splendour and the orderly world of the late Gothic, with man a courtly presence in the garden of nature.

The Groeninge Museum has works by other major Flemish Primitives, such as Petrus Christus and Dirk Bouts. The paintings are not all on display at the same time. There is also work here by Hugo van der Goes (?1435-1481), who originated from Ghent. He held a leading position in that city, organizing its decoration for the *joyeuses entrées* of the Duke of Burgundy and his wife in 1469 and 1472, as well as the decorations for the marriage of Charles the Bold to Margaret of York at Damme in 1468. His story ended less happily. He abandoned his career and entered the monastery of La Rouge Cloître at Auderghem near Brussels, but in 1481 he went mad and died soon after. Art historians have looked for signs of his impending madness in his paintings; all the figures look in different directions, for example, in the *Death of the Virgin* (1470) in the Groeninge Museum.

The final outstanding Flemish Primitive represented here is Roger van der Weyden, the greatest portrait-painter of his time, whose style is more dramatic and influenced by French models than that of van Eyck. He was born in Tournai in 1399 or 1400 and trained under another great Tournai painter, the Master of Flémalle. Van der Weyden married a woman from Brussels and moved there at some point in the 1420s, becoming court painter to the Duke of Burgundy. His original name was Roger de la Pasture, but as Flemish was still the main language in Brussels he translated his name to van der Weyden.

The Groeninge Museum has works by Bruges and other West Flemish painters continuing up to the present day, but these do not achieve the heights of their forebears. The Bruges-born neoclassicist Joseph-Benoît Suvée (1743-1807) became very popular in France. There is even a Magritte here, and some works by his follower Marcel Broodthaers as well as by twentieth-century Flemish artists Roger Raveel and Raoul de Keyser.

The Arentshuis at 16 Dijver is part of the same organization as the Groeninge Museum and is now used mainly for temporary exhibitions. The Arentshuis was started in 1936 by the English artist, Sir Frank Brangwyn (1867-1956), who was born in Bruges. In 1916 he published etchings of endangered Flemish monuments to help Belgium's war effort under the title of *Belgium*. He also illustrated the Flemish poet Emile Verhaeren's *Les campagnes hallucinatoires*.

The Hospitaalmuseum and Memling

What was formerly called the Memling Museum is now part of the Sint-Janshospitaal complex at 38 Mariastraat under the Hospitaalmuseum organization, which includes the Onze-Lieve-Vrouw-ter-Potterie museum of medicine. Hans Memling (or Memlinc) was born in Seligenstad in Germany at an unknown date. After his initial training as a painter he entered the workshop of Roger van der Weyden in Brussels around 1459. He moved to Bruges after the death of van der Weyden in 1464 and remained here for the rest of his days. After the death of Petrus Christus around 1472, Memling was Bruges' leading portraitist and one of its wealthiest citizens. The Sint-Janshospitaal commissioned him to paint the St. Catherine altarpiece for its chapel; many of his portraits were done for wealthy monks or nuns working in the hospital, hence these paintings have always been part of the hospital's collection. In his lifetime he enjoyed the reputation of being northern Europe's greatest artist, but he has since been overtaken by van Eyck. Memling's paintings are calm and homely, but he has less mastery of texture than van Eyck and does not achieve the same level of intensity.

British Visitors

After Waterloo numerous British tourists passed through Bruges on their way to visit the battlefield, and a colony of expatriates settled in Bruges as the cost of living was low and it was a pleasant place to live. Anthony Trollope's mother, Frances Trollope, stayed for a while when she fell on hard times. There was an English school and English bookshops and libraries, as well as the long-running convents. The British community had only one complaint: the Flemish practice of using dogs to draw small carts.

The British took great interest in restoring Bruges' Gothic architecture at a time when this style was not fashionable. They linked the Gothic revival to the promotion of Catholicism in England and were supported by the Belgian Catholic authorities in their plans. The main architects of this Gothicization project were Louis Delacenserie (also responsible for Antwerp Central Station) and Jean-Baptiste de Bethune, nicknamed "Jan Gotiek" (John Gothic). The English architects Thomas Harper King and William Brangwyn both worked on the rebuilding of the Basilica of the Holy Blood and other churches in Bruges. Another leading exponent of the neo-Gothic was John Steinmetz (1795-1883), an English architect who was on his way to Venice in 1819 but never got any further than Bruges. His collection of prints and drawings forms the basis of the Bruges city collection, the Steinmetzkabinet, now with some 20,000 pictures. This can only be visited by prior arrangement.

Bruges the Sleeping Beauty

"She was neither defunct nor moribund—just lethargic!"
Michel de Ghelderode, 1944

Like the Sleeping Beauty, Bruges slept for some three centuries, only to wake up with Georges Rodenbach's eccentric tourist guide, *Bruges-la-morte* (Dead Bruges), published in 1892. Bruges' economic decline was firstly due to changes in the physical landscape. The River Zwin retreated from the gates of Bruges back to the sea and gradually left the town high and dry from 1400 onwards. There were also political reasons for the city' downfall. After the death of the last Duke of Burgundy, Charles the Bold, at the Battle of Nancy in 1477 his daughter, Mary of Burgundy, was persuaded to marry the Habsburg Archduke Maximilian, but she died after falling from her horse in 1482. Maximilian was the regent during the minority of Mary's children, Philip and Marguerite, but had no right to succeed as Duke of Burgundy. In 1488 the Bruggelingen locked him up for fifteen days in the Craenenburg, a medieval mansion on the corner of the Grote Markt and the Sint-Amandstraat. While disorder reigned in Bruges after Maximilian's enforced stay, foreign merchants had been frightened off and their ships sailed up the Scheldt to Antwerp to unload rather than stopping at Sluis. Attempts were made to reopen the Zwin to shipping, but the Eighty Years' War against the Spanish (1568-1648) put paid to any hopes of an economic revival. Lack of economic activity during the following two centuries meant that Bruges was spared large-scale rebuilding, so that much of its original architecture survived, albeit hidden under later additions.

When Belgium became independent in 1830, half of Bruges' population was living from charity, hence the numerous almshouses. The rediscovery of the city by British tourists visiting Waterloo had a major impact on its eventual reawakening. The idea of a dead city and its crumbling medieval ruins appealed to Romantic poets. Wordsworth visited in 1820. In a collection of poems entitled *Memorials of a Tour on the Continent* (1822) he included two sonnets on Bruges:

Bruges I saw attired with golden light
(Streamed from the west) as with a robe of power:

*

The City one vast Temple—dedicate
To mutual respect in thought and deed;
To leisure, to forbearances sedate;
To social cares from jarring passions freed;
A nobler peace than that in deserts found!

The Halletoren and the Carillon

The Belfry of Bruges, or the Halletoren, was a lookout post and symbol of the city's freedoms. The main tower was built between 1280 and 1350, the octagonal crown in 1486. For those with a few pounds to lose, there are 366 steps to climb to the top. The tower leans over by about four feet. The poet Paul Verlaine climbed the steps to the first floor in 1893 and suffered a panic attack, refusing to go up or down. A major function of the belfry was to house the city's carillon or bells, used to regulate the working day and to warn of danger. The word carillon apparently originates from the Latin *quadri*, meaning "four" and referring to the four bells of the simple carillon. Those who played the bells were *quadrilones*, thus carillon, but to the Flemish a carillon is a *beiaard*, derived from the verb *beieren*, meaning to chime. Longfellow wrote the following on the Bruges carillon in 1826:

In the ancient town of Bruges,
In the quaint old Flemish city,
As the evening shades descended,
Low and loud and sweetly blended,
Low at times and loud at times,
And changing like a poet's rhymes
Rang the beautiful wild chimes
From the Belfry in the market
Of the ancient town of Bruges.

The Symbolist writer Georges Rodenbach, who is so closely associated with Bruges, also wrote a novel entitled *Le carillonneur* (The Carillon Player, 1897). Unlike *Bruges-la-morte*, this is not a morbid reflection on death but a rather more conventional work exploring the theme of the restoration of Bruges and the plan to build a new harbour,

Zeebrugge, to reopen Bruges' access to the sea. (The harbour was finally completed in 1907, but destroyed in both world wars and only came into its own from 1970.) Rodenbach was resolutely opposed to spending money on the harbour, and thought the city should buy up as many Flemish Primitives as possible instead. In *Le carilloneur* a certain Joris Borluut is appointed as the city's chief bell-ringer and also happens to be an architect specializing in restoring old houses. Borluut is thus a thinly disguised portrait of Bruges' neo-Gothic architect, Louis Delacenserie. In the story Borluut is dismissed from his post because of his hostility to the Zeebrugge project. One of the odder aspects of this novel is that the characters are pro-Flemish, and at one point the narrator even says, "In Flanders we must speak Flemish"—which shows that Rodenbach understood how the future would unfold. *Le carillonneur* did not gain the same attention as *Bruges-la-morte* and was not translated.

Georges Rodenbach and *Bruges-la-morte*

Bruges is even now a place that induces reverie, at least when tourists are not in the way. The nineteenth-century city was also a blank canvas onto which French-speaking writers could project their ideas, none more so than the Symbolist novelist Georges Rodenbach, who identified completely with Bruges. The city was his *âme sœur* or sister soul. His father was born at 6 Biskajersplein and introduced his son to the beauty of his birthplace. The Rodenbachs originated from Andernach in Germany and became wealthy from brewing beer in Roeselare (which they still do). Georges Rodenbach moved to Paris in 1888, working as a foreign correspondent for Belgian newspapers to make a living. The first edition of Rodenbach's *Bruges-la-morte* (Dead Bruges, 1892) resembled a tourist guide, with little text and liberal use of photographs. These were carefully taken early in the morning when there was hardly a living thing about, so the windows of the buildings look out like black, hollow eyes. The frontispiece was a drawing by Fernand Khnopff (1858-1921) of the Fair Ophelia floating in the water. Khnopff had many of the same preoccupations as Rodenbach. He spent part of his childhood in Bruges at 1 Langestraat (1860-6) but when he returned to Bruges as an adult he always remained inside a carriage and wore dark glasses, so that his image of the city would not be tainted by reality. Khnopff has left us more than thirty pastels with surreal scenes of Bruges. One of the most striking is

Une ville abandonnée (An Abandoned City, 1904), which shows the sea lapping at the foot of the Augustinian convent on the Woensdagmarkt, while the statue of Memling has disappeared. Khnopff was a fervent admirer of the English Pre-Raphaelites and inspired the early work of Gustav Klimt. He once reputedly said: "I have never seen and never will see the Memlings in Bruges."

When *Bruges-la-morte* became popular, Rodenbach had to write more text to expand it to a decent length. In the enlarged book the central character, the Englishman Hugues Viane, has moved to Bruges where he obsessively mourns his dead wife Ophelia. Rodenbach refers to the drowning of Ophelia in *Hamlet* and the words of the gravediggers at her funeral—"if the water come to [a man] and drown him, he drowns not himself"—to suggest that the waters of Bruges are also alive, even though Rodenbach's Ophelia dies a natural death. Bruges is the embodiment of Viane's own state of melancholy: "Bruges was his dead wife. And his dead wife was Bruges." One day, he emerges from the Church of the Virgin Mary and sees a woman who looks like his wife. She is Jane Scott, a French actress who is singing in Meyerbeer's *Robert le diable* at the city's theatre, the Stadsschouwburg. Scott does not take Viane's obsession with his wife seriously, and he eventually strangles her with his dead wife's hair as the Procession of the Holy Blood is passing under his window. Viane's house at 2 Rosenhoedkaai is now a foreign exchange bureau. The Rosenhoedkaai merited a sonnet from Rainer Maria Rilke: *Quai du rosaire.*

The Symbolists endeavoured to communicate with readers at a deeper level than through conventional poetry by using images and allusions to bring about a state of contemplation where they could connect with dream-like, meditative states and thus understand more profoundly the poet's own experience. Decadent Bruges was the perfect locale for this literary mysticism: a void where unusual states of mind could arise, a city on the edge of life and death.

The Flemish Symbolists, who wrote in French, may have had another reason for being interested in unreal states of mind. They did not speak the language of most of the population in Flanders, and so were in a way already cut off from real life. They were also rejecting the industrialization of society and the impoverished and unhealthy living conditions in the large Flemish cities. To the French, meanwhile, the

Symbolists were exotic Flemings who wrote in French, while they, in turn, had a great deal of influence on the Italian Symbolists or *crepusculari*, who for their part influenced Thomas Mann and his *Death in Venice*.

Bruges-la-Morte provoked strong reaction. A Frenchman, Arthur Martin, published a semi-factual novel in 1901: *Bruges la vivante: roman d'étude de mœurs bourgeoises* (Living Bruges: Study of Bourgeois Manners), including photographs, to try to prove that Bruges was a great deal livelier than was commonly thought. The Brussels French novelist, Dominique Rolin presents some personal reminiscences in *Bruges la vive* (Lively Bruges, 1990). Erwin Sels made a cartoon version of Rodenbach's classic: *Les villes tentaculaires: Bruges-la-morte* (1989).

Bruges-la-morte was not well received in Bruges itself. The city was trying hard to persuade the Belgian government to finance the new port at Zeebrugge rather than pandering to the decadent fantasies of morbid writers. One can well understand the resentment of the city fathers when they read lines like: "How melancholy is the grey of the streets of Bruges, where every day is like All Saints' Day!" Rodenbach was both decadent and a *fransquillon*—a French-speaking Fleming—so the city authorities refused to allow a statue of the author in Bruges, even one by Rodin. The statue of the reclining Rodenbach by Ghent sculptor George Minne eventually ended up next to the Church of St. Elisabeth in Ghent. A plaque to Rodenbach was put up in 1948 on De Roode Steen, 8 Jan Van Eyckplein (at his family's expense) to commemorate the fiftieth anniversary of his death (although Rodenbach had no personal connection with this house). It was taken down in 2002 and has not yet been replaced. Rodenbach died of appendicitis in 1898 and is buried in Père Lachaise cemetery in Paris.

Alchemists and Satanists
Bruges has served as backdrop for a great many other novels and cartoon strips. Of these the most successful is Marguerite Yourcenar's *L'œuvre au noir* (1968), translated by her companion Grace Frick as *The Abyss*. The hero is a city clerk and amateur alchemist called Zeno who copies forbidden manuscripts and is finally imprisoned by the Inquisition in a building that stood on the site of the present Town Hall. He cuts his wrists here in 1569 before he can be burned at the stake. At the start of

his career he has to swear an oath of allegiance to Our Lady with the Inkwell, the statue at the far left of the Town Hall. The fictional Zeno was born in 1510 and moves in the world of philosophers and politicians until he becomes a victim of the Counter-Reformation himself. He meets real historical figures such as the architect, Lanceloot Blondeel, who introduced Renaissance styles to Bruges.

Although Yourcenar had a distant cousin in Bruges, it seems that she spent little if any time there before writing *L'œuvre au noir*, which she had first started in 1921. This is a novel of ideas, concentrating the intellectual life of the time into one person, while the city of Bruges is a peripheral character. Its publication brought Yourcenar a wider audience and she started to spend much more time in Bruges, usually staying in room 302 of the Pandhotel in the Pandreitje so that she could enjoy the view of the Church of the Virgin Mary. She also became friendly with the owners of the De Reyghere bookshop on the corner of the Markt and the Steenstraat and spent hours sitting in front of the second storey watching the activities below. In 1971 Yourcenar retraced Zeno's steps all over Bruges and came upon a building from 1500 at the end of the Oude Zomerstraat (an unattractive dead-end), which she decided was Zeno's house.

Zeno was innocuous compared to the satanic priest Canon Docre in Joris-Karl Huysmans' *Là-bas* (1891), translated as *The Damned* (2001). Paris-born Huysmans (1848-1907) modelled Docre on Lodewijck van Haecke (1829-1912), the curate of the Chapel of the Holy Blood and a respected if somewhat unconventional figure who, Huysmans claimed, participated in black masses in Paris. (The author even believed that van Haecke had crosses tattooed on the soles of his feet, so that he could tread on them at every step.) No one in Bruges would comment on these allegations, but van Haecke was involved in at least one scandal. A certain Berthe de Courrière, who was known for seducing priests, was one day found naked on the sidewalk of the Smedenvest while her clothing was inside van Haecke's house. She was forced to undergo psychiatric treatment to cure her obsession with priests and subsequently wrote a book against contemporary psychiatrists, *Néron, prince de la science*. Huysmans took her as the model for Hyacinthe Chantelouve, the *femme fatale* of his novel. Van Haecke was investigated but never punished. He was also highly regarded as an exorcist and claimed to have attended black masses for research purposes. There is now a small park, the Pastoor van Haecke Plantsoen, off the Ezelstraat. Huysmans wrote a more conventional description of Bruges in *De tout* (1901). He became a Catholic lay brother, but believed to the end of his life that Bruges was full of satanists.

Bruges seems to stimulate writers to imagine what might be going on behind its antiseptic façade. Perhaps the only gay pornographic novel to be set in the city, *The Folding Star* (1994) by the British Booker Prize winner Alan Hollinghurst, is a tale of an English teacher who falls in love with one of his students but has to make do with a Moroccan he picks up in the (fictitious) Town Museum. Hollinghurst introduces a Symbolist artist, Edgard Orst (who seems to be a hybrid of Fernand Khnopff and Georges Rodenbach) and a figure based on Rodenbach's Jane Scott by the name of Jane Byron, a Scottish actress who drowns off Ostend in 1899.

Perhaps less controversially, Bruges is the setting for the sequence of historical novels about an ambitious fifteenth-century dyer's apprentice, the *House of Niccolò* series by Dorothy Dunnett. The English poet Marcus Cumberlege has lived in Bruges since 1972. With Owen Davies he is the author of the long poem "Bruges/Bruges" (1975). The city has also inspired many innocent comic strips such as *Yoko Tsuno: l'astrologue de Bruges* by Roger Leloup. The subject is dealt with in detail in *Bruges and Damme through Comic Strips* (2005) by Thibaut Vandorselaer.

"At Damme in Flanders"

A few miles north of Bruges is the little town of Damme, once the gateway to the city. Flooding in the early Middle Ages (especially in 1134) carved out a channel, the Sincfal or Zwin, from the North Sea to Damme and thus it became Bruges' port. Here sea-going ships had to transfer their cargoes to smaller inland vessels, which could continue along the River Reie to unload at Bruges itself. The city of Ghent dug its own canal, De Lieve, to Damme from 1251. But the Zwin soon started to silt up, and despite the efforts of the Bruges government larger ships were unloading further north at Sluis by 1400. The gradual decline of Damme and political troubles spelled the demise of Bruges as a world centre of commerce.

The drying up of the Zwin also left Damme high and dry, leaving it as a relic of the Middle Ages. It is hard to believe that this was once the most important wine market in Europe. Now it consists mainly of a street of superb medieval buildings and a great many second-hand bookshops. Along with the nearby village of Lissewege, this is one of the best-preserved medieval sites in Flanders. A new canal from Damme to Bruges was dug in 1810 on the orders of Napoleon. The landscape around it is now a protected area, and the footpath that runs along the dead-straight canal with its two rows of poplar trees offers spectacular perspectives on the approach to Bruges. A little to the north the tree-lined Afleidingskanaal van de Leie (Leie Diversion Canal) cuts at right angles across the Brugge-Sluis Kanaal and seems to take the walker away from contemporary Flanders into a more tranquil world.

"At Damme in Flanders" are the opening words of *La légende d'Ulenspiegel et de Lamme Goedzak*, the reworked tales of Thijl Uilenspiegel by Charles de Coster (see p.8). In the story Uilenspiegel is supposedly born in Damme in 1524, although in reality Thijl Uilenspiegel was from Kneitlingen in Lower Saxony, was believed to have been born in 1300 and died in Mölln in 1350. The oldest surviving edition of his stories dates from 1510. The word "Ulenspeghel" is said to mean "kiss my ass," although these days "Uilenspiegel" is interpreted as meaning "owl mirror", on the supposition that the wily Uilenspiegel held up a mirror to other people's hypocrisy and stupidity. The original Uilenspiegel was an unpleasant character who carried on a private war against respectable society, while in *La légende d'Ulenspiegel* he gains a new lease of life as a freedom fighter against the Spanish. De Coster spent his early years in Germany, and drew heavily on German folklore. While the original Uilenspiegel travelled far and wide in Germany, and even to Rome and Prague, de Coster's figure is placed against the background of the Spanish Terror of the sixteenth century. Like Don Quixote, Uilenspiegel has a sidekick, Lamme Goedzak, whose name approximates to "lame softy".

Jacob van Maerlant (1235-92), secretary to the town council, translated and added to a history of the world in 90,000 verses, the *Spiegel Historiael*, and is considered to be one of the founders of Dutch literature, for which he was rewarded with a statue next to the fine fifteenth-century town hall. It was said that the joker Thijl Uilenspiegel was buried under van Maerlant's gravestone, as people saw the image of

an owl and a mirror in the worn surface. The priest turned the gravestone upside down, and it was eventually sold to a stonemason in 1829, ending up in a graveyard in Sluis where it was broken up and lost from sight.

Chapter Seven
Ypres and the First World War

"We have no right to anything
But the old and withered earth
That is all in chaos
At the centre of God's glory."

Hedd Wyn, "The Black Spot", 1917

Belgium was recognized as a neutral country from 1839 (the end of its war with the Netherlands). This did not prevent Kaiser Wilhelm from informing Leopold II long before the outbreak of the First World War that Germany would cross Belgium on its way to France. The Schlieffen Plan for the invasion of France meant that German forces were bound to pass through Belgium on their way to the North Sea ports. The Belgian king was also told that he could expect a piece of French territory if he allowed the German army to cross his country. Both Great Britain and Germany were protectors of Belgian neutrality, and had to go to war if Belgium was attacked. When the Germans crossed the frontier on 4 August 1914, Great Britain duly declared war on Germany.

City of Cemeteries
The West Flemish town of Ieper is generally known to English speakers by its French name of Ypres. Entering through the Vauban fortifications, the visitor senses at once that this is a militarized town, even though the moats have been planted with willows and chestnuts and offer good fishing. The green is intense in the summer, and like the rest of West Flanders there is a very Dutch sense of tidiness and order, the hallmark of thrifty and hardworking people.

Perhaps in a bid to counterbalance the sombre nature of its history Ypres makes a great deal of its folkloric associations with cats. Until 1817 the Ieperlingen threw live cats from the belfry to ward off evil

spirits, and so earned the nickname of "Kattesmijters" (cat-throwers). This rather cruel ritual was enacted on the basis of an ancient Germanic belief that cats were the Devil's assistants. (It was said in justification that the cats landed on their feet and ran off, never to be caught again.) Another local story relates that Count Baldwin III threw cats from the church tower in 962 AD to prove to the superstitious Ieperlingen that the unfortunate animals did not have any supernatural powers. Since then the tourist industry has taken over, and the town has a Kattestoet (procession) every five years with elaborate floats on every imaginable cat-related theme. The high point takes place when the town jester throws velvet cats from the top of the belfry, while the crowd below tries to catch them.

There are 150 war cemeteries around Ypres looked after by the Commonwealth War Graves Commission, forming a marked contrast to the town's dark, gloomy Catholic burial places. The pure white headstones, ranged like so many perfect teeth, are so close together that you may wonder whether there could really be one body under each headstone. The effect is all the more powerful when one sees that each headstone has its own flowers or little plant, as if the living were trying to make amends to the soldiers for the horrible way in which they fought and died. Many combatants were officially too young to fight; the youngest were only fourteen and lied about their age to get into the army, as joining up was an adventure not to be missed.

Every Allied cemetery has certain standard features. Each has a monumental Cross of Sacrifice with a metal sword built into it. Officers and ranks all have the same type of plain white headstone carved with their regimental badge and whatever details are known about them. The stone used for the cemeteries and for the monumental Menin Gate (see below) is French white limestone. Most of the funding for the cemeteries run by the Commonwealth War Graves Commission comes from the United Kingdom. Tyne Cot, about six miles north of Ypres, has four full-time gardeners, and there are at least one hundred gardeners for the cemeteries as a whole, while a thick manual gives instructions on how the cemeteries are to be maintained. The grass must be mown to precisely the correct height—not one fraction of an inch too much or too little. Every grave has its flower or plant. As Marguerite Yourcenar put it in her *Notebooks (1942-1948)*:

Accept they are dead before their time.

Accept we have to forget them, because forgetting is in the nature of things.

Accept we remember them, because memory hides at the back of forgetting.

Even accept, but promising to do better the next time, and the next meeting, that we loved them unskillfully or too little.

Climbing the steps in the side of the Menin Gate one comes to the city ramparts walk and, to the right the Lille Gate and the Ramparts Cemetery, with 192 Allied graves including fourteen of the New Zealand Maori Batallion. In 1927 the Menin Gate was opened by King George V. English poet Siegfried Sassoon was there, and protested in "On Passing the New Menin Gate":

Who will remember, passing through this Gate,
the unheroic dead who fed the guns?
Who shall absolve the foulness of their fate, -
Those doomed, conscripted, unvictorious ones?

Crudely renewed, the Salient holds its own.
Paid are its dim defenders by this pomp;
Paid, with a pile of peace-complacent stone,
The armies who endured that sullen swamp.

Here was the world's worst wound. And here with pride
"Their name liveth for ever," the Gateway claims.
Was ever an immolation so belied
as these intolerably nameless names?
Well might the Dead who struggled in the slime
Rise and deride this sepulchre of crime.

Ypres was hit by six million shells in the course of the First World War, and nothing was left standing. Winston Churchill and others were keen to leave the city in ruins as a memorial to the dead, but the Ieperlingen disagreed and returned to rebuild their town once the war had ended. King Albert I had foreseen that Belgium's towns would have to be rebuilt and started a fund in 1917 for the purpose, with much of the money coming from German war reparations. The major buildings were only completed in the 1970s. A memorial was also required for the Allies, and this was built in the form of the Menin Gate, a massive archway covering the start of the Menin Road (Meensestraat) along which many soldiers marched to their deaths. The gate has inscribed on it the names of 55,000 Allied soldiers whose bodies were never found. The monument was originally intended to hold 60,000 names of the missing, but by the time it was built it became clear that there were far more than that number, so only those who died up until 15 August 1917 appear on the gate. The rest of the names are on the walls of the Tyne Cot cemetery at Zonnebeke. There are names from every corner of the British Empire; alongside Australians and Canadians are those from more exotic regiments from India with names such as "The 3rd Brahmans" and "The 1st Sikhs".

The Menin Gate was completed in 1927 and at 8 pm every evening since 1928 members of the Ypres fire brigade have sounded the Last Post. Several thousand people can stand under the Menin Gate, and the evening ceremony has become more elaborate over time as the names of soldiers who died on a particular day are read out. Alongside the Menin Gate, it was also felt that an English church was needed. St. George's Memorial Church was started in 1927 and completed two years later. The architect, Sir Reginald Blomfield, also designed the Menin Gate and many of the nearby military cemeteries. Next to the church is what was once the Etonian Memorial School, founded in memory of the 342 Old Etonians who were killed in the war. The school was evacuated in May 1940 and never reopened. St. George's Church, overloaded with brass plaques and regimental symbols in preference to aesthetic appeal, primarily serves to commemorate those who fell in battle. Services are held on Sundays in English.

The Ypres Salient

Ieper was always known as Ypres to the Great War generation, or "Wipers" to the British troops. The Salient was a bulge of territory that ran around the town, established in the first weeks of the war as the British held the line against the advancing Germans, with the Belgians holding the front along the River IJzer to the west running as far as the sea at Nieuwpoort. Ypres was particularly unlucky in its situation as it was overlooked by ridges on three sides from which the Germans could fire on the Allies emerging from the town. Yet Ypres was never captured by the Germans, even though they came close on many occasions.

There were three "battles of Ypres". The first was fought at the start of the war during the race to the sea in October 1914. The second was an offensive launched in 1915 by the Germans to take the Ypres Salient. The third was launched by the Allies on 31 July 1917 and culminated in the battle for Passchendaele (the village is now spelled Passendale in Dutch), a name that evokes terrible images of mud and death.

The third battle of Ypres started with a relative success. General Plumer, commanding Allied forces around Ypres, ordered tunnels to be dug at 24 locations under German positions on the Messines-Wijtschate ridge overlooking Ypres and planted 32 tons of high explosive under them. Nineteen of the mines were detonated at 3am on 7 June 1917. The sound of the explosion was so huge that it was heard in Dublin, the chandeliers rattled in Buckingham Palace and it was recorded in Switzerland as an earthquake. General Plumer commented: "We may not win the battle, but we will change the geography."

The Germans were taken completely by surprise and all the objectives of the day were achieved with ease. The Allies suffered "only" 10,000 casualties that day. The best place to see the effect of the explosions is at Spanbroekmolen (there was once a post-mill here) in the area between Wijtschate and the Kemmelberg. The explosion blew a hole over 150 yards wide and 50 feet deep in the German fortification. The crater soon filled up with water, and is now a protected nature reserve owned by the Toc H organization (see below), covered with water lilies and renamed the Pool of Peace on some maps. Four of the mines around Ploegsteert were not detonated as the area was no longer considered strategically important, and these mines may still explode. One mine exploded at Le Pélerin in the 1950s after it was struck by lightning; the only casualty was a cow that was blown into the air. Another tunnel was detected and flooded by the Germans.

The Allied success of the first day did not prevent the Battle of Passchendaele turning into another Battle of the Somme. The Allied supreme commander Field Marshal Haig had convinced Prime Minister Lloyd George that it was essential to break through the German lines and take Zeebrugge, where the German U-boats that were destroying Atlantic shipping were based. The main battle started on 31 July 1917 with the usual barrage of shells directed at the Germans. Yet the weather had the last say as unfortunately for the Allies, it was the wettest summer the area had ever seen. The landscape was already virtually denuded by explosions and turned into a vast sea of mud. All the medieval water defences had been destroyed by shelling, and there was nowhere for the water to run off. Many shells fell into the vast lake of mud and never exploded; it took superhuman efforts to bring out the wounded. Those who took shelter in craters drowned as the water rose about them.

These days the area around Ypres is lush farmland with rows of poplars and maize fields that obscure the view of the battlefield. This gentle topography was a serious problem to the Allies throughout the war. The Germans occupied relatively elevated ground (although the ridges were no more than 300 feet high) and could fire on the Allies as they came out along the Menin Road. The roundabout on the Menin Road one mile from the Menin Gate was known as Hellfire Corner since it offered a clear view to German gunners. The British tried to confuse the Germans by setting up models of trees and houses (without a great deal of success). Everything was shelled indiscriminately.

The Memorial Museum at Zonnebeke, a little to the south of Tyne Cot Cemetery in what was a medieval monastery and then a château in a country park, is essential for understanding the conditions in which soldiers fought and died.

Flanders Fields

Among the combatants were gifted young poets, most of whom had never published anything but who were so marked by what they saw that they had to write. The war generated great poetry and also took the lives of many promising writers. Some like Siegfried Sassoon (1886-1967) and Laurence Binyon (1869-1943) lived to a ripe old age, but most did not. There is certainly no better-known poem than "In Flanders Fields" by the Canadian doctor John McCrae (1872-1918). He started to write the poem on 2 May 1915 after seeing a close friend, Lieutenant Alexis Helmer, blown to pieces by a German shell. This was during the second battle of Ypres, and the location is close to the Essex Farm British

Military Cemetery. McCrae may well have been sitting watching the poppies between the graves when he wrote the poem. His commanding officer, Lieutenant-Colonel Morrison wrote:

> A couple of hundred yards away, there was the headquarters of an infantry regiment and on numerous occasions during the sixteen day battle, we saw how they crept out to bury their dead during lulls in the fighting. So the rows of crosses increased day by day, until in no time at all it had become quite a sizeable cemetery. Just as John described it, it was not uncommon early in the morning to hear the larks singing in the brief silences between the bursts of shells and the returning salvos of our own nearby guns.

Another version of events has it that McCrae threw the poem away and someone else picked it up and returned it to him. It first appeared in December 1915 in the English magazine, *Punch:*

> In Flanders fields the poppies blow
> Between the crosses, row on row,
> That mark our place; and in the sky
> The larks, still bravely singing, fly
> Scarce heard amid the guns below.
>
> We are the Dead. Short days ago
> We lived, felt dawn, saw sunset glow,
> Loved and were loved, and now we lie
> In Flanders fields.
>
> Take up our quarrel with the foe:
> To you from failing hands we throw
> The torch; be yours to hold it high.
> If ye break faith with us who die
> We shall not sleep, though poppies grow
> In Flanders fields.

The Flemish poet Hugo Claus offered another, more cynical version of the elegy in 1970 his poem of the same title:

The soil is richest here.
Even after all those years without manure
one could grow a dead man's leek here
to beat any market.

The tremulous English veterans have dwindled.
Each year they show to their dwindling friends:
Hill Sixty, Hill Sixty-One, Poelkappelle.

The combine harvesters in Flanders Fields describe
ever closer circles around the winding corridors
of hardened sand-bags, the bowels of death.

The butter of this region tastes of poppies.

The most idolized of all the Great War poets was Rupert Brooke
(1887-1915), who never saw action in Flanders but died of blood
poisoning on a hospital ship in the Aegean. His most popular poem,
"The Soldier", has a patriotic style that fitted the mood created by
Rudyard Kipling (1865-1936) and other more chauvinistic writers.

If I should die, think only this of me:
That there's some corner of a foreign field
That is forever England. There shall be
In that rich earth a richer dust concealed;
A dust whom England bore, shaped, made aware,
Gave, once, her flowers to love, her ways to roam,
A body of England's, breathing English air,
Washed by the rivers, blest by the suns of home.
And think, this heart, all evil shed away,
A pulse in the eternal mind, no less
Gives somewhere back the thoughts by England given;
Her sights and sounds; dreams happy as her day;
And laughter, learnt of friends; and gentleness,
In hearts at peace, under an English heaven.

Kipling's brand of patriotism was altogether more strident:

For all we have and are;
For all our children's fate,
Stand up and meet the war,
The Hun is at the gate!

The fourth stanza of Laurence Binyon's "For the Fallen", published on 21 September 1914 in *The Times*—adorns many war memorials:

They shall grow not old, as we that are left grow old:
Age shall not weary them, nor the years condemn.
At the going down of the sun and in the morning
We will remember them.

The poetry changed in tone as the war went on. Those who spent several years in the trenches became disillusioned or angry, like Siegfried Sassoon who recklessly got himself injured and then actively protested against the war when he was invalided back to England. In 1920 he published "Reconciliation":

When you are standing at your hero's grave,
Or near some homeless village where he died,
Remember, through your heart's rekindling pride,
The German soldiers who were loyal and brave.

Men fought like brutes; and hideous things were done;
And you have nourished hatred, harsh and blind.
But in that Golgotha perhaps you'll find
The mothers of the men who killed your son.

Much the same happened on the German side. There were poets such as Alfred Lichtenstein (1889-1914) and his "Homesick Warrior":

If I could lie in my own bed
In a white shirt.
I wish my beard was gone,
My head combed.

The conflict was also a breeding ground for Expressionist artists such as George Grosz, Max Beckmann and especially Otto Dix (1891-1969), the anti-war painter. He painted war scenes long afterwards, especially the 1932 triptych *Trench Warfare* and *Flanders* (1934). He had at first enthusiastically volunteered for the German Army and was wounded several times. His brutally objective art is still shocking; wounded men and blasted landscapes are painted with extreme intensity in which grotesque or monstrous imagery recalls Bosch and Brueghel. When the Nazis came to power in Germany, they put his paintings such as *The Trench* and *War Cripples* on display in an exhibition of "degenerate art" and then burned them.

The German dead were reburied at Vladslo cemetery, a few miles north of Ypres, after the Second World War. The cemetery contains the graves of thousands of men killed in the early days of the earlier war. German cemeteries differ from the British in that the soldiers' burial places are marked by black slabs laid flat on the ground. Among the graves is that of Peter Kollwitz, a student from Berlin who volunteered as soon as the war broke out. Two months later, in October 1914, he was killed aged nineteen in one of the war's first major campaigns. His mother, Käthe Kollwitz, a prominent German artist, sculptor, socialist, feminist and pacifist, was informed of her son's death and by December she had formed the idea of creating a memorial to him. In April 1931 her sculpture was dedicated, adjacent to her son's grave.

Passchendaele

The village's modern spelling is Passendale, meaning Easter Valley, and to the Flemish it is synonymous with a kind of cheese rather than with one of the most terrible chapters of the First World War. The attack on Passchendaele started on 4 October 1917 and was a massacre on both sides. At the cost of 245,000 casualties the Allies gained five miles of territory as they fought their way up a slope from outside Ypres to the present location of Tyne Cot cemetery. It is estimated that 35 soldiers died for every yard of territory that was gained. Passchendaele—a mere one square mile—was hit by a million shells. The name Tyne Cot was given to the three German pillboxes that are still to be seen in the cemetery; to the Northumbrian regiment they were reminiscent of their native Tyneside cottages. Passchendaele was finally taken on 6

November, but by then locals could no longer recognize their own village.

The battle for Passchendaele was an entirely misconceived operation; the Allies were fighting uphill and were outnumbered three to two by the Germans, whereas on paper they needed a three to one advantage to succeed. German tactics on the Western Front after the Battle of the Somme and Verdun were to defend the positions they held while waiting for reinforcements from the Eastern Front. Their defences consisted of six lines of trenches with barbed wire and pillboxes; there were light railway systems to bring up supplies and take away the wounded. German bunkers were better built than those of the Allies with six-foot thick walls of concrete. The German bunkers that still litter Flanders will last for eternity, while those built by the British are crumbling away.

Not surprisingly, much of the military hardware that was thrown around continues to turn up in the ground, with some 200 tons of shells—the "Iron Harvest"—dug up by farmers each year. These shells are in a corroded and unstable state and are a real threat to life and limb, so much so that farmers have insurance policies against exploding shells. The Flemish bomb-disposal service, meanwhile, blows up old ammunition every Thursday. More problematic are the unexploded gas shells, which have to be scanned first to see what they contain and are then deep-frozen and cut up into pieces before finally being disposed of at a special facility in Antwerp. The Germans tried various chemicals in the shells; the first type, chlorine, was effective when it took the Allies by surprise but it could waft back towards the attackers, and also tended to mix with water and mud to form hydrochloric acid. The Germans had most success with mustard gas, which appeared harmless at first but left hideous scars if it remained on the skin. The Allies had efficient gas masks, but the Germans then came up with the idea of firing tear gas first before firing the deadlier mustard gas. The British High Command's reaction was that using gas was "damned un-English", but they nevertheless also used it, but in smaller amounts than the Germans.

Bodies of soldiers are dug up all the time around Ypres. One builder digging the foundations for a warehouse at Boezinge in the 1970s ended up with a body count of 107 Allied and German soldiers. There are even some Flemish who spend their free time trying to locate them. The remains are generally no more than some bones and bits of uniform and personal items. No effort is spared to try to identify the bodies, but often all that is left now are regimental badges and pieces of jewellery. Once the necessary inquiries have been made, a funeral is held, and members of the dead man's regiment are invited—if it still exists.

Hedd Wyn

The Welsh poet Ellis Humphrey Evans, better known as Hedd Wyn (White Peace), was killed shortly after arriving in Flanders on 31 July 1917. His body was later moved to the nearby Artillery Wood Cemetery, also the last resting place of the Irish poet Francis Ledwidge, killed on the same day about a mile away. Evans, who until 1917 had been a shepherd as well as a poet, entered National Eisteddfods (poetry competitions) under the name of Hedd Wyn. In the face of hostility from officers in the Royal Welsh Fusiliers, he carried on writing in Welsh and sent in his entry for the 1917 National Eisteddfod. As he wrote in Welsh, the military censors were reluctant to allow his poems through. He won the competition with his poem "Yr Arwr" (The Hero) but had already been dead for six weeks. Instead of the normal chairing ceremony that greets an Eisteddfod winner, "his chair was draped in a black pall amidst death-like silence," reported the *Western Mail*. Evans only became known outside Wales at the end of the twentieth century thanks to a film of his life in Welsh, *Hedd Wyn*, which was nominated for an Oscar. He wrote of Flanders: "Heavy weather, heavy soul, heavy heart. That is an uncomfortable Trinity, isn't it? I never saw a land more beautiful in spite of the curse that has landed upon it. The trees are as beautiful as the dreams of old kings." His statue in his birthplace at Trawsfynydd bears the inscription Hedd Wyn had written for a friend who had died in the trenches:

Neither his sacrifice nor his dear countenance are forgotten,
though the Hun stained his fist of steel in his blood.

The Irish at Ypres

The role of Irish volunteers was quickly forgotten at the end of the First World War, yet 50,000 Irishmen died in the conflict. British generals had reservations about incorporating Catholic and Protestant militias into their forces, but leaders from both factions believed that Ireland had everything to gain from fighting for the Allied cause, given that Home Rule had already been granted in September 1914. Many Catholics enlisted to show solidarity with Belgium and to prove that Ireland was a nation state. The Catholic 16th Irish Division arrived at the Ypres Salient in September 1916 and fought alongside the Protestant 36th Ulster Division in the capture of Wijtschate on 7 June 1916 as part of the Battle of Messines Ridge.

Irish sacrifices in the war are commemorated by the Island of Ireland Peace Park, located near the N365 road from Ypres to Mesen (Messines), and inaugurated in 1998. The focal point of the park is a 110-foot round tower made of limestone brought from various locations in Ireland. The inside contains books of remembrance with the names of all the Irish dead and is only illuminated on the 11th hour of the 11th day of the 11th month. The Park stresses reconciliation and Irish unity and features nine stone tablets with prose, poetry and letters from Irish servicemen. Among the poets is Francis Ledwidge from Slane, County Meath, who is remembered in Seamus Heaney's "In Memoriam Francis Ledwidge" (1979):

> "To be called a British soldier while my country
> has no place among nations..." You were rent
> By shrapnel six weeks later. "I am sorry
> That party politics should divide our tents."

Ledwidge's own last lines, written nine days before he died were:

> Come often, friend, with welcome and surprise
> We'll greet you from the sea or from the town;
> Come when you like and whatever skies
> Above you smile or frown.

The Irish also volunteered in great numbers for the Royal Flying Corps. W.B. Yeats (1865-1939) recalled them in his "An Irish Airman Foresees His Death":

I know that I shall meet my fate
Somewhere among the clouds above:
Those that I fight I do not hate,
Those that I guard I do not love:

The Battle of the Lys and the End of the War

The madness of the Battle of Passchendaele gained the Allies some territory. The Germans also suffered great losses in men and materials, which they could less easily afford than the Allies who had American reinforcements on the way. The Germans took one last gamble, moving 700,000 troops from Russia to the Western Front for the Spring Offensive of 1918, which they hoped would win the war. In March and April the Allies lost all the territory they had captured the previous year and found themselves defending what was left of Ypres' city walls after the Germans had captured the strategic heights of Mount Kemmel or the Kemmelberg. The Kemmelberg has two summits, the Kemmeltop at 512 feet and the Monteberg at 433 feet. This is the second highest point in the Flemish Region after the Voeren in Limburg; from an observation tower on the top one can see the entire Westhoek area as far as the sea on one side and the French conurbation of Lille on the other. The Kemmelberg is carpeted with bluebells in the spring; it was made a nature reserve in 1979 to protect it from damage by sightseers.

The novelist Alan Sillitoe, who did not fight in either World War, gives a good description of the area as it looked before being bombarded in *The Widower's Son* (1976):

> The land was lush and green in the early light, flat till it hit the range of hills a bit south of west from where they were, which must have been Mount Kemmel, the way to its slopes dotted and clotted with woods, clumps and single trees which seemed to give off smoke in the still air. He picked out Dickebusch Church to the right.

The Germans never broke through to the sea and exhausted themselves in their effort to reach Paris. The Allies launched their counter-offensive to liberate Belgium on 28 September, with the Belgians under King Albert taking an active role, but it took until the end of the war to free Belgium.

Poperinge: Talbot House

With its comical name, the town of Poperinge was well known to Allied soldiers during the First World War as "Pops", a rest and recreation facility with cafés and black marketeers who made a tidy profit as British army stores turned up on the market at inflated prices. These days it is a typically quiet West Flemish town, with churches and houses in the characteristic yellow brick of this region. This is the centre of hop growing in Belgium, hence its title of the Hoppestad or Hop City (the surrounding area is the Hoppeland and there is even a Hop Museum). This is also the place to sample Hommelbier, a local beer with an excessively bitter hop flavour.

For anyone interested in the history of the Great War, Talbot House on the Gasthuisstraat (confusingly signposted as "Concert Hall") has a museum with a dormitory attached for those who wish to stay overnight. It was started in 1915 as a club for British soldiers by the Rev. Philip "Tubby" Clayton and Chaplain Neville Talbot, whose brother Gilbert had recently been killed at nearby Zillebeke. Commemorating the loss of a promising young life, Talbot House offered a sanctuary of spiritual calm to all ranks. Clayton's non-hierarchical approach and sense of humour made the place something special, with notices announcing "Pessimists—Way Out!" or "If you are in the habit of spitting on the carpet at home, please spit here." The expression Toc H is derived from signalers' code for Talbot House (TH became Toc H in Morse Code), and it was here that the international Toc H movement, stressing cooperation and reconciliation, found its inspiration.

Poperinge was known to Chaucer, who accompanied John of Gaunt on a diplomatic mission to Flanders in 1375. In the *Tale of Sir Thopas* we read:

And he was born in a far countrey,
In Flanders, all beyond the sea,
At Popering in the place;
His father was a man full free,
And of that country lord was he.

Of Bruges were his hosen brown;
His robe was of ciclatoun,
That coste many a jane.

Poperinge is also the home of Professor Dirk Frimout, a professor of electronics and Belgium's first man in space who gave rise to a new word in French, *frimoutiser*, meaning to orbit the earth. Frimout has started his own space education centre near Blankenberge. On a roundabout on the outskirts of Poperinge rests a rusted space capsule with the legend: "From Icarus to Frimout".

On the square some of the cafés that were once frequented by the British troops still stand. These had French names at the time. The Café de l'Espérance was dubbed "What 'Opes" by the soldiers and still bears a notice: "Officers Only". The landlord's daughter "Ginger", who was perhaps sixteen, was a favourite of the officers and was often mentioned in their diaries. Other local girls fell for dashing Allied soldiers, while some were prostitutes. The only available women on the Allied side were nurses, who became legends themselves; one nurse, Elsie Knocker, the "Angel of Pervyse", married the Belgian Baron 't Serclaes de Rattendael. The marriage seems not to have been a great success as it only receives one sentence in her memoirs, *Flanders and Other Fields* (1964).

The Flemish and the IJzerbedevaart

During the desperate fighting of October 1914 the Belgians opened the sluices on the River IJzer (or Yser) and so prevented the Germans from entirely overrunning Belgium. The corner of West Flanders behind the IJzer was never taken. King Albert I toured the front line in a plain black tunic, wearing neither braid nor signs of rank, while a popular drawing of the time had him standing next to a fallen soldier firing at the Germans. Albert was careful not to lose his army, keeping the troops behind the IJzer line and not taking part in the large Allied offensives. A Flemish soldier's song from the time expressed their feelings:

I wish the German Kaiser
An unhappy life,
A lot of pain in every tooth,
An abscess or seven,
I wish him the worst gout
In arms and legs.
And rheumatism too
In his feet and toes.

The chorus goes:

> I wish the Kaiser goitre as well,
> A big piece of iron in his head,
> I wish him sores all over his body,
> To smear with vitriol!

There are four verses in all, listing the common ailments of the day.

The IJzerfront was also the scene of the Frontbeweging or Front Movement, started in protest against a state that expected the Flemish to die for Belgium yet showed no respect towards Flemish language or culture. There was no question of mutiny, but the implications were still profound for the future of Flanders. Close to Diksmuide is the IJzertoren or IJzer Tower, a significant memorial to the Flemish who died in the war situated on a piece of land that had once been a notoriously dangerous spot opposite a German artillery battery, the IJzervlakte. The IJzertoren was built in 1925 as a protest against the Belgian War Graves Commission's decision to use 500 Flemish gravestones to make grit for roads. An annual pilgrimage had started in 1920 to the grave of the half-Irish artist Joe English (1888-1918) who had designed a gravestone specifically for Flemish soldiers in the shape of a Celtic cross with the characteristic AVV-VVK symbol, and the *blauwvoet* or fulmar (a kind of seagull), another Flemish nationalist symbol (see p.15). (AVV means Alles Voor Vlaanderen, Everything for Flanders, and VVK stands for Vlaanderen Voor Kristus, Flanders for Christ.) The theme of the IJzerbedevaart or "IJzer pilgrimage" was anti-militarism—the original slogan was "no more war"—but it was also a pro-Flemish event, which the authorities inevitably wanted to suppress.

The original IJzertoren was dynamited in 1946, probably by Belgian Army engineers in retribution for alleged Flemish collaboration with the Germans. The new version is 275 feet tall as opposed to the original 150 feet and has substantial buildings at its base holding a museum, while the previous edifice had large carvings of warriors on the four sides. As well as the AVV-VVK symbol the tower features the rising *blauwvoet* or fulmar. The AVV-VVK inscription on the top is not to everyone's taste, however, as it appears to exclude those who do not necessarily support the view that Flanders is entirely Catholic.

In the 1950s, when agitation for equal rights for the Flemish was at its height, the IJzerbedevaart (IJzer Pilgrimage) attracted up to 50,000 people, but these days as few as 5,000 attend. The rallies were frequently the occasion for pitched battles between the Flemish and mounted *gendarmes*, and the extreme right-wing Vlaams Belang (or Vlaams Blok as it was called) now organizes illegal parades outside the pilgrimage and enjoys clashes both with the police and more moderate nationalist groups. The paraphernalia of Flemish nationalism, including flags, symbols and songs, is easily confused with expressions of extreme right-wing opinion and is offensive to those who support the unitary Belgian state. Known as *belgicistes* to the Flemish, the unitary advocates are also sometimes guilty of causing uproar, such as when they flew a plane with a large banner proclaiming "Long Live Belgian Unity!" during the ceremonies in 2004.

Chapter Eight
The Coast and West Flanders

"Bury me in the dune, where you can hear the sea,
in the soft, pure sand, near the burnet and the elder."
Stefanie Verzele-Madeleyn, 1926

The Flemish national character has been less moulded than the Dutch by fear of flooding and by the need to organize sea defences and dig canals—except perhaps along the coast. Medieval monks laboured to reclaim the flooded land and made it into fertile polders, and, like the Dutch, the West Flemish organized *wateringen* or guilds to maintain the defences. The treacherously deep ditches by country roadsides are clear evidence of the work done to drain the muddy polders.

The West Flemish are sometimes called "the Dutch of Belgium", but their roots are even further north, as they are the descendants of the Menapii, a German-Celtic tribe who moved down here from Friesland in the early first millennium BC, and Saxons who were encouraged to settle here by the Romans. The Roman historian Tacitus called these coastal people "Ingvaeones". Their language was markedly different from that of the inland Flemish and still shows affinities with that of another coastal people, the English and, in particular, the Anglo-Saxons of Kent. West Flemish is the least comprehensible dialect as far as other Flemish are concerned. A house is a *hus,* just as it was in Anglo-Saxon, while the local word for "little" is *luttel.* The dialect of the Westhoek, the furthest corner of Flanders along the sea, is the closest form of Dutch to English. Ironically, the coast is the only part of Flanders where French is widely spoken by shopkeepers and hotel-owners, since in tourist resorts visitors expect to speak their own language, be it French, English or even German, and the locals do their best to meet their wishes.

The quadrant between Kortrijk, Roeselare, Tielt and Waregem is known as the Flemish Texas, as it reputedly has the largest concentration of millionaires in Belgium, and Kortrijk is the Flemish Dallas. Although

"Sands the colour of suntanned shoulders
Waves wash over waves."
        Stefanie Verzele-Madeleyn, "Homage to Ostend", 1934

many may now be prosperous, the West Flemish have been shaped by their past struggles to escape poverty, by the First World War, and by their close family bonds. Their recent economic success is based on small family businesses that can adapt quickly to meet market needs. The world's largest concentration of synthetic carpet factories is between Kortrijk and the French border. The textile towns along the (then) French-Flemish border were the most Calvinist during the Wars of Religion in the sixteenth century, and there is still something of a Protestant work ethic here. The contrast between the West Flemish and the more exuberant East Flemish is very striking. Although separated by only thirty miles, Ghent and Bruges are worlds apart. For much of their history the West Flemish lived in marshlands cut off from the rest of Belgium, reluctant to submit to any centralized power. The motto here is "Alles voor West Vlaanderen, voor Belgiekske nikske" (Everything for West Flanders, nothing for Belgium). The West Flemish are socially conservative and legendary hard workers; the Christian Democrat party commands more support here than anywhere else.

Seafarers and Superstitions

The people of the coast have long been courageous seafarers who undertook the hazardous journey from Dunkirk to the Iceland fishing fields in large numbers between 1619 and 1939; many never returned. An ex-trawler, the *Amandine*, standing in dry dock next to the Ostend railway station, houses an exhibition dedicated to the IJslandvaarders— or, more locally, the d'Ostensjhe Ieslandvisjherie. Fishermen were known to be extremely superstitious. At Ghyvelde near Bray-Dunes, so legend had it, there was once a witch, Babbe Roere, who could change into a Nekker, a water demon in the form of a crow, which would encourage fishermen to sail too far out to sea and drown. If a black bird was seen in the rigging, it was a sure sign that the boat would meet with misfortune. The baleful figure of Babbe Roere holding a crow is now one of the giants in the celebratory IJslandvaardersstoet in Koksijde and the Sint Maartens Ommegang (the procession around the town) on 10 November.

All fishermen feared the devil or "Roeschaard". An apprentice fisherman was always given a nickname so that if the devil came for him he could say he was not the person he was looking for. It was forbidden to bring certain objects such as a fish or a large loaf of bread on board a ship that was setting sail, as these would prolong the voyage. A broom was habitually tied to the masthead to frighten away devils. If the fisherman met any person dressed in black, a black animal or a pig on the way to his boat, this spelled disaster or a poor catch. Hearing a rooster or a cuckoo, on the other hand, was lucky, while meeting a shepherd and his flock or a prostitute was also a positive sign.

Consecrated objects from churches such as candles were taken on board for an Easter blessing. The first fish to be caught was always thrown back into the water, sometimes with its tail cut off, as an offering to the spirits of the sea. Fishing communities had their own chapels like that in the Visserskapelstraat in Heist, where the lifebuoys of dead fishermen are kept. The Sincfala Museum in the nearby Pannenstraat is the main folklore museum on the coast, and is housed in a disused school for fishermen. The Pannenstraat is one of the few places where traditional fishermen's cottages are still preserved.

The Virgin Mary also played an important part in local religious worship. A freshwater spring appeared at Dunkirk in 1603 when the city walls were being strengthened, and then a miraculous Virgin and Child were dug up. Every time the Virgin was moved elsewhere, she always returned to the spring, and thus eventually a shrine had to be built there to Notre Dame de la Fonteine. Other miraculous Virgins washed up onto the Flemish shoreline—those of Bredene, Meetkerke and Lombardsijde—had the same homing tendencies and refused to be moved from the places where they were found. Fishermen also frequently called on the Virgin Mary or other saints when they were in fear of their lives and promised to go on a pilgrimage or make offerings in exchange for being delivered safe home.

Two Sides of Ostend

In the early Roman era the coastline was about one mile further out than it is today. As it retreated, it left expanses of mud, which turned into salty grazing land or *schorren*. When the sea flooded in again in the twelfth century it carved out a new harbour. The present harbour was dug to the east of the original town in 1443. For this reason the town is called Oostende, the East End, however illogical it may seem. On the other side of the airport lies Westende.

Ostend is a city with a double identity: in the summer season an international resort but provincial and inward-looking the rest of the time. Some people come here in search of anonymity, and it is widely assumed that there are scandalous goings-on behind the walls of ostentatious villas—and sometimes these make it into the press. Wealthy retirees live cheek by jowl with petty criminals in a sort of down-market version of the French Riviera. We can still recognize the Ostend described by Michel de Ghelderode in *Choses et gens de chez nous* (Local People and Places, 1953):

> Let's say that this extreme town where in the past all bloods were mixed, appeared the least Belgian or, to be more precise, the least Flemish of our northern regions. The Ostender was always a complex person of murky origins, speaking an indescribable language with the most diverse resonances. He has only flimsy connections with the west Flemish loam, and is only moderately interested in the landscape that extends the horizon behind it. The typical character, immortalized by Ensor in *Pouilleux*, doesn't seem to be made of the heavy fertile soil, but rather the subtle sand of the beaches.

De Ghelderode is referring here to one of Ensor's most popular paintings, *Pouilleux, or Tramp Warming Himself by a Stove*, which was destroyed in 1940 by a German bomb (along with 400 other paintings in the Museum of Fine Arts). The Ensor Museum in Ostend has a life-size three-dimensional reconstruction.

Ostend is also the most English of Belgian towns. Many of the motley crew of seafarers and drifters who are washed up here and open a bar or hotel have come from over the Channel. One of the first was a certain William Haskett who set up a drinks tent on the beach in 1784. The English church on the Langestraat, inaugurated in 1865 to meet the demand for an Anglican place of worship, has a strikingly plain red exterior.

Ostend became fashionable in the nineteenth century when King Leopold II chose it for his holidays. He organized the construction of the Venetian colonnade or Venetiaanse Gaanderijen as well as many other buildings, all completed around 1905 in time to celebrate the 75th anniversary of Belgian independence. Leopold employed French architects only, but he asked them to make Ostend look as English as possible. The town also benefited from British tourists who visited Waterloo and then remained in Belgium because of low prices. Napoleon built two forts in the town, which the Duke of Wellington completed. One fort was razed and a racecourse, the Hippodrome, built in 1883 for the benefit of British tourists. But the real windfall for the coastal towns came in the form of the tram. Once the railway and the tram arrived, tourism could develop without hindrance and the presence of Leopold II set the seal on Ostend's success. The First World War in one sense damaged the town as a tourist resort, as the pre-war practice of wintering on the French Riviera and spending the summer on the Belgian coast ended. On the other hand, battlefield tourists usually passed through Ostend on their way to Ypres and the trenches (while there was a ferry service).

Arrivals

The "packet" steamer from Dover to Ostend was an institution for over 150 years until the ferry link ended in 1994. (It started again in 2004, but its future is uncertain.) Crossing times were unpredictable in the early days. Lord Byron took the ferry in 1816: "As a veteran I stomached the sea pretty well, till a damned 'Merchant of Bruges' capsized his breakfast close by me, and made me sick by contagion." He checked into his hotel and "fell on the chambermaid like a thunderbolt," according to his companion, Dr. Polidori.

On coming ashore, nothing could better the Orient Express for romance. This is how Graham Greene opens his spy novel, *Stamboul Train* (1932):

> The purser took the last landing-card in his hand and watched the passengers cross the grey wet quay, over a wilderness of rails and points, round the corners of abandoned trucks. They went with coat-collars turned up and hunched shoulders; on the tables in the long coaches lamps were lit and glowed through the train like a chain of blue beads. A giant crane swept and descended, and the clatter of the winch drowned for a moment the pervading sounds of water, water falling from the overcast sky, water washing against the sides of the channel steamer and quay. It was half past four in the afternoon.

D. H. Lawrence gives a long account of the departure of the train in *Women in Love* (1920), while Katherine Mansfield writes of the journey to Bruges in her short story of the same name (1910). Vladimir Nabokov noted the churning sensation as the ferry turns out to sea in his short story *Revenge* (1924): "Ostend, the stone wharf, the grey strand, the distant row of hotels, were all slowly rotating as they receded into the turquoise haze of an autumn day." French Symbolist poet Stéphane Mallarmé, on the other hand, developed an obsession with Ostend fisherwomen's stockings. On the train from Bruges to Brussels, where he was giving a poetry reading in February 1890, he wrote: "Went this morning to look at the sea at Ostend, but didn't have time to go on a shopping spree, because of the good pink woollen knitted stockings of the fisherwomen, which were impossible to find anywhere ready-made."

James Ensor: Painter and Eccentric

The painter James Ensor (1860-1949) was born in Ostend and lived there for most of his life. His father was an English businessman who had settled in Ostend, his mother a Belgian. Ensor was a rebel until he was made a baron, by which he time he had completely changed into an upstanding member of the Belgian establishment. Stefan Zweig thought him "a strange, very closed character", perhaps justifiably since Ensor compared himself to Jesus Christ and likened art critics to Pharisees. In his early career he was one of the leading Belgian Impressionists or *tachistes* (the term comes from the French *tache*, meaning a smear of paint), but he subsequently steered his own course and developed his own symbolic language without paying attention to French artistic movements.

In the early 1880s Ensor was still painting realistic portraits of local Ostend figures or bourgeois interiors. His painting from 1882, *Woman Eating Oysters,* which can be seen at the Antwerp Museum for Fine Arts, was considered so shocking that no one would exhibit it on account of the fact that there were two bottles of wine on the table and that the woman (actually Ensor's sister) was obviously enjoying her meal. From about this time he started to use lighter colours rather than the heavy dark shades commonly used by Belgian Impressionists at the time.

From the late 1880s Ensor moved into his avant-garde Expressionist style of painting masks and grotesque distortions of reality, his so-called "fantastic" or "masks" period. On occasion he added incongruous elements to conventional portraits that did not find a buyer. In 1888 he added a flowered hat to a self-portrait he had painted in 1883, the *Self-portrait with Flowered Hat*, considered the start of his Expressionist period (and a reference to Rubens' portraits of women with feathered hats). The following year he painted the *Old Lady with Masks*, a portrait of Dutch writer Neel Doff surrounded by a skull and grotesque masks representing her memories of life. Ensor also wrote comments on scenes in his paintings. In *Melancholy Fishwives* (1892), for example, two old ladies sit with a pot of coal and a cat between them while behind them three skeletons look through a mirror next to a placard reading "Death. They have eaten too many fish." Ensor's vast *Christ's Entry into Brussels* (1888-9), now in the J. P. Getty Museum in Malibu, brought him recognition from abroad and acceptance in his own country. Eventually he became a member of the Belgian establishment and was made a baron in 1929. At the same time he adopted Belgian nationality and renounced the British citizenship he had held all his life.

Ensor's house at Vlaanderenstraat has been more or less preserved as he left it and has a large number of oriental masks and other bric-a-brac. Anything that was not Belgian in his house was Chinese or Japanese (most of all masks). He had a ready supply as his mother sold Chinese souvenirs, while his sister had a Chinese husband. In the living room is his harmonium. Ensor was immensely proud of the (second-rate) music that he wrote for marching bands. Ostend had the first Rotary Club on the European continent, and Ensor wrote the *March of the Rotarians* for them. Later in life he lost interest in painting or even in meeting visitors. When the painter Kandinsky came to see him, Ensor informed him that he was a musician. He was also a highly original writer, interested in reconstructing French using mainly adjectives, many of them invented. He also spoke the local Ostend dialect fluently, as is proven by a recording of a radio interview that he gave in 1935, only rediscovered in 2003.

Ensor was delighted to be made a baron. He went to cafés every day in his top hat and tails to show off. When a bust was put up in the park, he would sit down next to it and inform passers-by that he was indeed the same person as the bust. Most of Ensor's best paintings are outside Belgium, especially in the United States, largely because his friend Emma

Lambotte (also an artist) sold her collection to American collectors. Ensor did much for Ostend by instituting an annual costumed ball in the Casino called Bal du Rat Mort (Dead Rat Ball), which he named after a café in Paris. As many as 2,500 people still take part.

Spilliaert and Permeke

Much more than Ensor, Léon Spilliaert (1881-1946) is the real painter of Ostend. His father ran a perfume shop on the Kapellestraat, and Spilliaert grew up during the heyday of the resort, the era of Leopold II's grand new buildings. A self-taught artist apart from a few months at the Academy in Bruges, he skirted around various artistic trends, melding Constructivism and Expressionism into a completely original vision. In some respects he could be called a pre-Surrealist; he has been compared to Edvard Munch, and, more improbably, to Picasso. Spilliaert's preferred media were watercolour on paper or pastel. The textures are flat, and the clearly defined shapes sometimes reminiscent of Japanese prints.

Spilliaert was an anxious, introverted character who had little social contact (although he had a family). As he suffered from a stomach ulcer he would wander around at night and painted lonely buildings reflected in pools of water, a reflection of his state of mind. Spilliaert had affinities with the Symbolists at the beginning of his career and illustrated Maeterlinck's *Serres chaudes*, but he did not remain bound to one style. The Musée des Beaux Arts in Brussels has a number of his paintings, some with simple abstract shapes, e.g. *Woman on the Dike* (1904), while others are more surreal. In Ostend work by Spilliaert, Permeke (see below) and Ensor can be seen at the Museum of Fine Arts or Stedelijk Museum, now housed in the former post office at 18A Hendrik Serruyslaan. The Provincial Museum of Modern Art at 11 Romestraat has a collection of modern Belgian artists, starting with the Expressionists and including Spilliaert.

The painter Constant Permeke (1886-1952) was a far more conventional character than Spilliaert or Ensor. He was born in Antwerp in 1886 and came to Ostend in 1894 when his father was appointed curator of the town museum. Permeke moved into Spilliaert's Ostend studio in 1909 after spending time among the first Sint-Martens-Latem school of painters (see p.113). Permeke made his name as a painter of angular and monumental portraits of workers, often lying exhausted on their backs in the sun or eating their lunch, and used browns and reds to suggest the connection between peasants and the earth. He started out with impressionistic seascapes, but his best-known work is central to the Flemish school of Expressionism with Cubist influences. While Permeke is regarded as the most significant Belgian painter of the twentieth century, Spilliaert is more original and varied. When Permeke became wealthier he built a large house in the village of Jabbeke, now close to a motorway and the Ostend-Bruges railway line. The house, built in 1923, is nothing more than a rectangular box with a vast painter's studio. To complete the effect of straight lines, Permeke designed a sunken garden surrounded by rows of pollarded willows.

Michel de Ghelderode and the Dunes

The Brussels-born playwright Michel de Ghelderode (1898-1962) considered himself Flemish in every respect, but could not speak or write Dutch, claiming that it was only by accident that he wrote in French. He was of Flemish ancestry, his real name being Adhémar Mertens, but he had been sent to a French school, entirely usual at the time. His parents were native speakers of Dutch but always spoke French to him, so with some justification he felt cheated of his rightful language. In the 1930s he actively supported equal rights for the Flemish and even voted for the ultra-right VNV party. Most of his early plays were first performed in Dutch translation by Flemish theatre groups. De Ghelderode considered everything Belgian to be mediocre and stupid, while Flanders was a fantasy land into which he could escape from his dull existence as an archivist in Schaarbeek Town Hall in Brussels. As he said: "I am not Belgian and I don't belong to Belgium. I belong to Flanders and anyone who disagrees can eat their own shit." During the Second World War he supported the German occupation, which he believed would lead to political independence for Flanders, and so lost his job after liberation in 1944. Yet when he applied for membership of the Belgian Academy in 1952 he claimed that he had always written in French and did not know a word of Dutch. Known in his lifetime as the Belgian Shakespeare, de Ghelderode was an immensely popular playwright in the 1950s and would most likely have won the Nobel Prize for Literature if he had lived a few more years. These days he has largely been forgotten outside

Belgium; his texts are difficult to understand in French, with a large part consisting of in-jokes and dialect words.

De Ghelderode was a great admirer of James Ensor, and was also conspicuously influenced by Brueghel and Hieronymus Bosch. The characters in his *Voyage autour de ma Flandre: tel que le fit aux anciens jours Messer Kwiebe-Kwiebus philosophe des dunes* (Journey around My Flanders: as Done in Ancient Times by Sir Kwiebe-Kiebus the Philosopher of the Dunes, 1947) are taken out of Brueghel paintings and start to talk to each other. Kwiebus is supposed to have been Charles V's former drinking companion and is a well-known character in Flanders. He lives in a hut in the dunes and offers some pertinent remarks on the Flemish mentality:

> Kwiebus crossed the arid polders and discerned on the horizon a town whose distinguishing feature was to be bristling with church steeples. And all these steeples, the bells sounded without respite making a shattering carillon. The philosopher entered the town, which was otherwise like all other towns, except that it was divided up into 100 well-defined districts each with its own church steeple and its own bell. Kwiebus went from district to district, and noticed that the inhabitants of one district did not want to know anything about the inhabitant of the others. On every town square the crowd exclaimed with pride: "Isn't our bell unique; is there a bell that is equal to it for its precision, tone, size, form, noise?"... After going round the town and hearing 100 different bells, Kwiebus concluded that these lovers of bell-ringing could only hear one sound because they had only ever heard one bell.

There is a play on words here, because the French expression *esprit du clocher* (church bell-tower mentality) means a lack of interest in anything outside one's own village.

During the revolt against the Spaniards Ostend was the only town not to be taken from the Protestants. The Duke of Parma came with his army in 1587, took one look and gave up. Finally Albert and Isabella (daughter of Philip II) laid siege to the town in 1600, but it still took four years to capture it. The Siege of Ostend also gave a new word to the French language—*isabelle*—the colour of Isabella's shirt, which she vowed not to wash until Ostend was taken. De Ghelderode and his translator David Willinger made it rhyme in his play, *The Siege of Ostend* (1933):

THE OSTENDISH ARTILLERY AND CHORAL SOCIETY:
The Chemyse of Isabella
Got to have quite a smell-a,
And it's been that way for a while,
Never seen a chemyse so vile.

THE WHOLE SPANISH ARMY:
Who in the world could think
A chemyse could make such a stink.

De Ghelderode drew on a pantomime written by James Ensor in 1920, *The Gamut of Love,* for some of his characters and succeeds in flattering the painter throughout the play. Ensor had published a eulogy to de Ghelderode in 1932, so the playwright was simply returning the favour. Ensor has a role as the leader of the Protestant defenders of Ostend, Sir Jaime, and there are many references to his paintings.

Marvin Gaye in Ostend

Marvin Gaye, the American soul singer, arrived in Ostend in February 1981 from London, close to self-destruction from cocaine abuse. Freddy Cousaert, a Flemish nightclub owner and promoter, had been courting him, and Gaye agreed to let him set up a concert tour in Europe. Cousaert accommodated Gaye and his girlfriend in an apartment on the 5th floor of 77 Zeedijk overlooking the sea. Gaye stopped taking drugs and took up jogging, cycling and punching the bag at a local boxing club. For a while he became a part of Cousaert's family, eating with them at their bed and breakfast in Ostend. On arriving in Ostend, Gaye recalled:

Mostly it was the air that made me happy. It was incredibly clean, strong air. I didn't realize it, but I'd been choking to death on English pollution. There was an energy about Ostend I found stimulating. The tempo was right, a little slow, but still hard-working.

Ostend Kursaal Casino and the Albert I Promenade

Gaye had a taste for prostitutes and even came close to marrying one in Ostend. He moved over to CBS Records, whose staff kept a close eye on his rehabilitation. Cousaert also bought him a racing bike, which he would pedal up and down the sea-front, sometimes as much as 25 miles a day. He hung out with black American basketball players, who had been hired by a local businessman for his basketball team, the Sun R.

Gaye had a four-track home recording studio with him and a drum machine; he could play all the instruments he needed to create basic demo tracks. He also hired a lead guitarist in the shape of Danny Bossaer, who now runs the café De Tijd on the corner of the Koningstraat. Bossaer went on to become a member of a backing band for visiting American artists, the Atlantic Rhythm Machine. Virtually every evening Gaye would go to De Bistro (no longer in existence), a café owned by Jan Van Snick, as well as Jan's Café, near the Casino.

Gaye wrote some songs with the help of local musicians. The most famous, *Sexual Healing*, was the work of several people and led to a protracted legal action after Gaye's death. The track was originally an instrumental by Odell Brown, Gaye's bass player, recorded in December 1981 and left incomplete because Gaye could not come up with any lyrics. In March 1982 the journalist David Ritz appeared in Ostend and started spending time with Gaye. Gaye showed him some sado-masochist magazines, to which Ritz reacted by telling him: "Man, you need some sexual healing," thus giving Gaye the words for his song and the title of his album. Gaye did not credit Ritz, leading to a court case in the US that dragged on until after Gaye was dead and Ritz was finally awarded royalties. Ritz was clever enough to record the whole writing process on cassette, but there are those who believe that he had no right to claim to have written the lyrics. The album was recorded at Studio Katy in Ohaine near Waterloo, run by Marc Aryan, an Armenian pop star and entrepreneur. The last stop on Gaye's European tour was the Casino-Kursaal of Ostend, a show that was broadcast live on Belgian radio. The Casino has now decided to make the most of its Marvin Gaye connections, with a bronze statue playing the piano, and videos and songs every evening.

Gaye disliked father figures, and his relationship with Freddy Cousaert deteriorated. At one stage, Interpol came to Cousaert's house looking for Gaye, who was called as a witness to the murder of a drug dealer in Copenhagen. In the end the Belgian Ministry of Justice left him alone and even gave him a telephone number to call if the police bothered him again. In a state of cocaine-induced paranoia Gaye imagined that Cousaert was stealing money from him, so left Ostend and bought a 21-room house in Moere near Torhout. In September 1982 he went back to the US. The *Sexual Healing* album was a success and he could pay off his creditors, but he fell back into his old drug-taking habits. He was shot dead by his father Marvin Sr., a fundamentalist minister, on 1 April 1984.

Stijn Streuvels and *The Flaxfield*

Stijn Streuvels was the pseudonym of Frank Lateur (1871-1969), a pioneer of Flemish literature and the great-nephew of the West Flemish poet, Guido Gezelle. He was a poor student, was taken out of school and on Gezelle's advice became a baker's apprentice in Avelgem, a village in the far eastern corner of West Flanders, not far from the Scheldt. He taught himself several languages and started work as a translator and novelist on the side. In 1888-9 he was apprenticed to the Van Mullem patisserie opposite the Stadsschouwburg (Municipal Theatre) in Bruges. He looked out over the theatre from the top floor of the patisserie, but it took him two years to find the courage to go to a performance.

In 1902 Streuvels wrote his major work *Langs de wegen* (translated as *The Long Road*), which earned him the Belgian State Prize for Dutch literature in 1905. That year he gave up baking and went to live at Het Lijsternest, a house in Ingooigem, a little north of Avelgem close to the border with East Flanders where he spent the remainder of his life. By an unlucky chance, the house was built on clay and the walls are cracking, with the foundations due to be entirely renewed. Even so, there are attractive walks nearby over the hilly countryside, and the view from Streuvels' study is a protected site and cannot be changed. The house was left just as it was when Streuvels died. On his 90th birthday he received 35,000 birthday cards, and he replied to every one of them with a signed photograph.

Streuvels is not much read these days, as his language is peppered with regionalisms, and readers sometimes need notes to understand it. As a result, he is mostly filed away under "Flemish classic" and ignored. Generations of Flemish schoolchildren have been forced to read *De vlaschaard* (translated as *The Flaxfield*) and lost interest in him. Streuvels is too didactic for modern tastes, and too obviously trying to interest the non-reading Flemish in literature. While he succeeded in making a mythical landscape out of his surroundings and the everyday life of his neighbours, he is now judged to be too unsophisticated.

The Flemish countryside that Streuvels describes has in many places been lost. His classic *De teleurgang van de Waterhoek* (The Downfall of the Waterhoek, 1927) concerns the rebellion of a village against plans to build a bridge across the Scheldt near Avelgem. It was made into a film entitled *Mira* in 1971; the bridge used in the film is across the River Durme in Hamme in East Flanders and has been renamed the Mirabrug and is now a tourist attraction. The film makes much of the affair between Mira and an engineer played by the ubiquitous Antwerp actor Jan Decleir. The screenplay is by Hugo Claus. Streuvels wrote a great deal about his youth in Avelgem:

The trip to the Kluisberg with my sister, in company with a number of her friends. I felt uncomfortable, shy, embarrassed with those girls, kept myself apart, was clumsy, but felt a certain pleasure within. There was something valuable that remained from the paths that we had passed; I kept thinking with pleasure of the crossing with the boat over the Scheldt; the visit to the farm where we picked berries in the garden; our stay on the Kluisberg itself, the walk between the pines, where the girls had picked flowers, sung songs; all of that had hung around me like a dream.

Peter Benoit and Flemish Music

The Flemish composer Peter Benoit was born into a poor family in Harelbeke, near Kortrijk, in 1834 and died in Antwerp in 1901. The house of his birth at 55 Marktstraat is now a museum. After studying at the Brussels Conservatory and winning the Prix de Rome he travelled widely through Germany and France, returning to Belgium for good in 1863 and eventually settling in Antwerp in 1867. Here he was appointed director of the Vlaamsche Muziekschool (Flemish Music School), a radical type of institution where Dutch was used in lessons. His pro-Flemish views brought him into conflict with the authorities, but eventually in 1898 his music school received the title "Royal". While he started out as an innovative and daring composer, from 1877 he decided to limit himself to writing music for the masses, drawing on folk songs of the "Flemish music movement" of the nineteenth century. His works include an oratorio dedicated to the River Scheldt, a cantata to the River Leie and another cantata to Cornelis Sneyssens, the Ghent standard-bearer who died at the Battle of Gavere in 1452. His services to education eventually outweighed his artistic significance.

On the face of it Flanders has produced few great composers, and yet during the lifetime of Emperor Charles V (1500-55), the Franco-Flemish school of polyphony dominated the European music scene. Johannes Ockeghem (c.1420-97) is well known to lovers of polyphonic music for his motets and masses. It is assumed that he was born near Dendermonde, as his name is taken from the village of Okegem. Most of his career was spent in the service of the French court. Josquin Desprez (from Cambrai near the Belgian border) studied with Ockeghem in Paris. Josquin's pupil Nicolas Gombert (1490?-1560?), who originated from near Lille, was ranked as one of the greatest composers of his age; his style of imitative fugue influenced many of his contemporaries. Unfortunately he was sent to the galleys in 1540 for raping one of Charles V's choirboys, but regained the Emperor's favour with some pieces of music written specially to gain his release. The West Fleming Adriaen Willaert (1480?-1562) was master of the Chapel of St. Mark, Venice from 1527 to his death. He was followed by the Mechelen-born composer Cipriano de Rore (1516?-1565).

Art on the Coast
The best-known artist on the Flemish coast apart from Ensor is Paul Delvaux (1897-1994), a Surrealist who originated from near Huy in the province of Namur. His house at Sint-Idesbald near the French border has been turned into a museum and is open for much of the year (except in the winter). Surrealism in Belgium is very much identified with the Walloons or French-speakers, and the philosophical ideas popular with painters such as Magritte and other Bruxellois art theorists who more or less discovered Surrealism at the same time as the French have never had much of a following among Flemish artists. Delvaux was rather a marginal figure to the Surrealist mainstream. He developed his own personal style of dreamscapes, with wide-eyed pale nudes and trains in nocturnal stations creating a sense of menace that reflected the anxious war-torn times that he lived through.

Rather more typical of coastal art are *marines* or seascapes, which were much in vogue around 1900. The doyen of Belgian seascape painters was Louis Artan (1837-90), a Dutchman who modelled his works on Joseph Turner's in his semi-abstract attempt to capture the moods of sea and sky.

While the coastal environment has suffered from unregulated building, there is a great deal of money available to promote art in the wealthier resorts, most of all in Knokke. There are some seventy art galleries in this town, of which about fifteen are devoted to modern art. The presence of free-spending art lovers attracts artists from other countries to set up shop, while Knokke has engaged the New York architect Stephen Holl to rebuild and extend its casino, which has a set of murals by Magritte. On the Rubensplein the entrances to the underground car park run through the pedestals of statues by the German

Antony Gormley—Beaufort 2003

sculptor Franz West. Many other resorts have outdoor sculptures, such as the British artist Barry Flanagan's work in the nature reserve, Het Zwin. In 2003 all the coastal towns participated in an outdoor art exhibition, "2003 Beaufort". The Antwerp artist Jan Fabre placed a 23-foot-long bronze turtle on the beach at Nieuwpoort, with himself on top. The English artist Antony Gormley put images of himself on the beach at De Panne, which disappeared under water at high tide. A similar outdoor and indoor exhibition was held in 2006 as "Beaufort 2006".

Cycling Nationalists
The Belgian national sport is officially archery, but in reality it is cycling. The sport has traditionally been monopolized by the Flemish (and especially the West Flemish), but the golden age of Belgian cycle is long gone, with fewer successful riders and endless doping scandals. On a local level, however, the idealism remains. The success of Flemish riders before and after the Second World War played a major part in building up Flemish pride and showing the rest of the world what the Flemish

could do. This movement was termed *wielerflamingantism* or "cycling Flemish nationalism". The years before the war were the era of "les Flandriens"—the nickname for Flemish migrant workers in Northern France—and the greatest of them was certainly Albéric Schotte (1919-2004) from Kanegem in West Flanders, known as "IJzeren Briek" or "Iron Brick".

Flemish riders had to be tough, as many races were run on cobblestones (*kassei*). To avoid this uneven surface the cyclists rode on the gravel cycle track by the side of the road—a challenge that was almost as difficult. Their lot was to "keep riding until you don't know what village you're from," as Briek Schotte put it. Potholes, puddles, tram rails, sub-zero temperatures and howling North Sea gales were everyday obstacles. Schotte won De Ronde van Vlaanderen (Tour of Flanders) twice and was world champion twice. There is now a statue of him on his bicycle padlocked to the church railings in his native village of Kanegem, close to the town of Tielt. The most popular riders among the media were those who could give a good interview, and in the usual Flemish style many were also good linguists. Schotte learned French and Italian so as not to appear foolish when he was riding abroad.

Since commercial sponsorship came into professional cycling, the young men entering the sport have been organized into teams. Cyclists eat together, sleep in dormitories and follow orders to let their team-mates win if necessary. They eat a strict diet and have to be in bed by 9 pm. Starting out as impressionable teenagers, they are supposed to receive a moral (at least in the early days) as well as sporting education. Drugs have entered the sport, however, along with greater pressure from sponsors, and these make an honest trainer's life very difficult. The concoction known as *le pot belge* (Belgian drink) has become internationally notorious and consists of heroin, cocaine, amphetamines and caffeine (and possibly other substances). Cycling is a particularly arduous sport because of the strain placed on the heart; from time to time cyclists literally drop dead after over-exerting themselves. Doctors found that the Flemish cyclist Rik van Steenbergen had the largest heart ever observed in a human being, with a capacity of 1700 cc, but he never won the Tour de France. These days team doctors try to make cyclists who show signs of an irregular heartbeat or fainting episodes retire before they die at an early age.

A bumpy ride on cobblestones

Eddy Merckx's Rear End

Belgian rider Eddy Merckx won more races than Lance Armstrong and has a metro station named after him in Brussels. He comes from the linguistic border in Flemish Brabant—the village of Meensel-Kiezegem—but was educated in French-medium schools in Brussels. Since he spent his entire career working with Flemish teams he became fluent in standard Dutch, but still managed to cause offence by holding his wedding ceremony in French. His grim determination to win at all costs earned him the nickname of "the Cannibal". The Flemish public never entirely took him to their hearts; he had after all taken the place of their great hero, Rik Van Looy.

The Antwerp thriller writer Stan Lauryssens published his account of the golden age of Flemish cycling, *De Flandriens*, in 1973, but the book did not sell. One of the photos showed Eddy Merckx pulling his trousers down, so the publishers came up with the idea of distributing posters of the mooning Merckx to every café in Flanders to try to boost sales. The posters ended up in café toilets, where they were useful for witty graffiti. Merckx took the publishers to court and had the books with the offending photograph pulped, but he also indirectly ensured the book's success. Notwithstanding this episode, Merckx probably does have a sense of humour: he called his son (also a professional cyclist) Axel.

Church of St. Charles Borromeo, 1620

Chapter Nine
Antwerp: City of Rubens

"For you Antwerp, so many of those nymphs and long white veils that cover your beguines;
Antwerp, your heavy missals cannot prevent Satan from parting the lace,
When beauties kneel in the nave on velvet benches."

Amédée Achard, *La cape et l'épée*, 1835

Antwerp looks out to sea, conscious of its dual identity as a provincial and an international city. From 1500 until the Spanish Fury of 1576 Antwerp was the world's cultural capital and greatest port, something that Antwerpers remember. The city is known as the "Metropool" or *Métropole des Arts* from a time when making and selling art was big business. It was said that there were more painters than bakers at the time, and many artists came from elsewhere to make their careers.

Sir Thomas More (1478-1535) opens his political science fiction novel *Utopia* (1516) in Antwerp:

Henry VIII, the unconquered King of England, a prince adorned with all the virtues that become a great monarch, having some differences of no small consequence with Charles, the most serene Prince of Castile, sent me into Flanders, as his ambassador, for treating and composing matters between them.

After we had several times met without coming to an agreement, they went to Brussels for some days to know the Prince's pleasure. And since our business would admit it, I went to Antwerp. While I was there, among many that visited me, there was one that was more acceptable to me than any other, Peter Giles, born at Antwerp, who is a man of great honour, and of a good rank in his town, though less than he deserves; for I do not know if there be anywhere to be found a more learned and a better bred young man: for as he is both a very worthy and a very knowing person, so he is so civil to all men, so

193

particularly kind to his friends, and so full of candour and affection,
that there is not perhaps above one or two anywhere to be found that
are in all respects so perfect a friend.

There is a painting of More's friend, Pieter Gilles, in Antwerp's Royal
Museum of Fine Arts (KMSKA). In recent years More's role in the
murder of William Tyndale, the translator of the Bible, has become
better known. The Protestant Tyndale had taken refuge in a safe house
in Antwerp but, hungry, was lured out with the promise of a meal by
More's agent, Harry Phillips. Tyndale was put to death at the prison of
Vilvoorde north of Brussels in 1535 some months after More lost his
head at the Tower of London.

Antwerp (Anvers in Franch) is not part of Flanders in a historical
sense, but rather belongs to Brabant. It is widely said that "Antwerp is
not Belgium," and while this is arguably true of almost anywhere in
Belgium, it is particularly the case with Antwerp. Antwerpers, for their
part, tend to consider their city as an independent state with its own
unique identity. The right bank of the Scheldt was the frontier between
the Holy Roman Empire and French territory from the time of
Charlemagne's death in 814 AD. Note that there is no bridge across
the Scheldt here—although there are tunnels. Antwerp was a small
port and part of the Marquisate of Antwerp until it was conquered by
the Duke of Brabant in 1106. The city came into its own after the
decline of Bruges and Ghent at the end of the fifteenth century, but its
heyday was short-lived. In 1566 the Iconoclasts destroyed the interiors
of the churches and in 1576 the Spanish garrison mutinied and killed
3,000 citizens. In 1585 the population fell virtually overnight from
85,000 to 42,000 with the expulsion of the Protestants. The Dutch
then imposed exorbitant tolls on shipping sailing up the Scheldt to
Antwerp, until Napoleon arrived in 1800. Willem I helped Antwerp by
extending the harbour, but the Belgians had to go on paying tolls to
the Dutch until 1863, when the Belgian government paid the Dutch a
huge sum in compensation to open the Scheldt. The result was a
doubling of the population and an immense influx of immigrants. The
German and Hanseatic trading families came back after a 300-year
absence.

Antwerp's Origins

At the time of Julius Caesar, in 51 BC to be precise, there was, we are told, a giant called Druon Antigon who terrorized the city of Antwerp. According to some versions of events, he was a seventeen-foot-tall Russian. Demanding half the cargo from all ships sailing up the Scheldt, he straddled the river and took the goods from those who refused, then chopped off the boatman's right hand and threw it into the Scheldt for the fish to eat. But one day a young fisherman named Silvius Brabo took him on; the giant had a cuirass and helmet, the young man only some rope and a sharp knife. The giant encouraged Silvius to fight and in so doing his legs were caught up in the rope and he fell into the river. With his knife Silvius cut off the giant's hand. Caesar rewarded him by giving him in marriage his cousin Silviana, sister of the future Emperor Augustus, and made him Duke of Brabant and King of Tongeren. The city's name is thus derived from the word *Handwerpen* (hand-throwing), even if a more popular explanation these days is that it comes from *aan 't werf* (on the quayside). The most likely origin, however, is the word *aanwerp*, referring to the piece of land jutting out into the Scheldt where Het Steen (see below) now stands. In front of the Stadhuis or Town Hall is a gruesome statue by the Antwerp sculptor Jef Lambeaux (1852-1908) of local legend Silvius Brabo holding Druon Antigon's hand spouting water. The typical local Antwerp biscuits are *handjes* or "little hands".

Antwerpers have never been reluctant to invest in their city, and it sometimes seems that there is no limit to the money available for restoring the old or for new projects. The Stadhuis or Town Hall was built between 1560 and 1564 under the direction of Cornelis Floris de Vriendt with assistance from Italian artists and architects. The original plan for a new town hall, drawn up in 1540, was for a late Gothic style, but twenty years later times had changed and the Renaissance was in vogue. The Stadhuis retains a typical Flemish feature, namely the tower in the centre reminiscent of the traditional belfort or belfry in many Flemish towns. The Flemish developed their own style of Renaissance architecture with more colourful decorations, while retaining elements of the Gothic. The Renaissance was associated with rationalism and Protestantism in the North and soon gave way in Flanders to the Baroque, which was more in keeping with the thinking of the Catholic Counter-Reformation. The Stadhuis is perhaps the only building in

Belgium that is faced with marble, a stone that does not resist the weather well. The ostentatious style of the Town Hall was intended to remind the nearby guilds who was in charge.

Sinjoren and *Pagadders*

Antwerpers have a reputation for arrogance in the rest of Belgium, hence their nickname *sinjoren* (lords), from the Spanish *señores*. The Flemish accused Antwerpers of imitating the haughty Spanish in the sixteenth century, but Antwerpers tend to view their supposed superiority complex as a joke. The trials of numerous wars and occupations have not reduced their self-confidence, or it could be that material excess and a penchant for cockiness are defence mechanisms against the memory of past wars as well as future threats.

The city has certainly always been open to foreign influences, and Antwerpers inhabit a world of motion in which ships from around the globe constantly arrive and leave. Many traders came from the Baltic, Scandinavia or Germany and stayed here. There is also a strong Spanish imprint, and not only in the gold decoration on the buildings. As Emmanuel de Bom puts it in *De psychologie van den Antwerpenaar* (Psychology of the Antwerper, 1929):

> Basically, he is broad, jolly, sensual, jovial. Some foreigners judge the Antwerper wrongly, when on the basis of certain exterior appearances, they consider him cautious, suspicious, envious. His nature is lyrical, decorative, childlike. His lordliness is nothing other than a certain panache, learned from his contacts with the Spanish, with Don Quixote.

De Bom paints the *sinjoor* as a perpetual *nouveau riche* or *baron stokvis* (dried fish baron) who can be either crudely materialistic or has genuine nobility. This is a city of live and let live, where the general style is lighter and edgier than in the rest of Belgium (perhaps like Holland without Calvinism). The streets and cemeteries have more cheerful names than those of other Flemish towns. *Sinjoren* are also born sceptics and the most litigious of all Flemish. Where other Belgians might tolerate offences, the *sinjoor* keeps a lawyer on a retainer and goes to court.

Another type of Antwerper (but not a pure one and considered shorter in stature) is a *pagadder,* a ruffian whose name derives from the Spanish *pagador,* meaning a paymaster in the Spanish Army. The offspring of outsiders are *pagadderkes,* so if one or both of your parents is not Antwerp-born, then you are a *pagadder* and not a *sinjoor.* In the past there were forty *pagaddertorens* or lookout towers in the city, where boys were paid to watch for ships arriving on the Scheldt. Trading vessels sometimes stayed away for more than a year, and when their rich cargoes approached the city they brought relief and wealth to the merchants who had invested in them. These days only four of these towers remain, and an entirely new one was erected on the Steenplein next to the river in 2002. One of the original towers is at 9 Heiligegeeststraat and another inside the Rockoxhuis at 12 Keizersstraat.

Long before the Spanish arrived in Antwerp the Vikings—or maybe even earlier peoples—worshipped a fertility god with an outsize phallus, whose remains can be seen embedded in the entrance to Het Steen, the fortress that has stood guard over the city since the Dark Ages. The original name is lost to posterity but the demi-god was known as "Semini" in the sixteenth century when Antwerp ladies came to request his help in procreating (all Antwerpers are thus "Semini's Children"). The Jesuits deprived him of his most important attribute in 1587, while acid rain did the rest. What remains is hardly recognizable as a deity. Some Antwerpers still exclaim "Semini's kinderen!" or even "Godjumenas!" (a deformation of "God! Semini!") when riled, while the Semini cult has been revived by modern pagans who use a stylized logo for the annual Semini festival. Newly married couples eat *seminikoek,* a light, sweet biscuit with sesame seeds and a representation of Semini in marzipan. At the base of the steps leading to Het Steen is a statue (1963) of two drunks looking up at the giant Antwerp bogeyman, the Lange Wapper.

Het Steen (literally stone, as it was among the first non-wooden buildings) was first erected in 1200-25, and then substantially reconstructed in 1520 by Charles V. For many years the castle was a prison and it retains its menacing air as a place where many Protestants were tortured and then put to death. The Christ on the Cross, with his back turned to the street, unintentionally suggests what might happen to you if you step out of line. Nowadays it houses the National Navigational Museum.

The Lange Wapper and Het Steen

Antwerp and Diamonds

Antwerp is first and foremost a trading city, the undisputed international diamond capital with 90 per cent of the world's uncut diamonds passing through. The diamond trade was traditionally in the hands of the Jews, but trading in lower quality diamonds has lately been the preserve of the Indian community and much of the less skilled work is now done in India. The area around the Central Station is packed with workshops where diamonds worth billions are discreetly cut. Quality is overseen by the Hoge Raad van de Diamant or High Council for Diamonds; there are tours for sightseers. The business is run within closed communities of Jews and Indians and is very much based on trust. Dealers are invited to "viewings"; if they buy nothing on three occasions then they are not invited back. When a deal is made, both Jews and non-Jews seal it by saying *Mazel u bracha* ("luck and blessing" in Hebrew), which has the status of a written agreement. Tourists can visit the Diamond Museum on the Koningin Astridplein, immediately visible from the entrance to the Central Station. There have been a couple of spectacular robberies, carried out with inside help. The local writer Jef Geeraerts uses the diamond quarter as a backdrop for his thriller, *Diamant* (1982), which takes place partly in the Schupstraat.

Antwerp has the last *shtetl* or Jewish ghetto in Europe, concentrated around the Pelikaanstraat. There are still streets full of kosher shops such as the quietly affluent Lange Leemstraat and Belgiëlei, or the more down-market Korte Kievitstraat near the Central Station with its "Heimishe Shop" and Hebrew notices. Some high-class families speak French, a complete anachronism in Belgium's least French city. These are descendants of Eastern European Jews who had already learnt French before they came to Antwerp or who chose to use French when they arrived before the First World War. There are some 16,000 Jews in Antwerp, of whom 6,000 are strict Hasidim. The Orthodox Jewish men wear satin greatcoats and fur hats or black fedoras, and their wives Eastern European clothing from a hundred years ago. They like to take the air around the Stadspark and spend their holidays in Knokke on the coast. But the Jewish community is moving out of the city centre to the suburbs, in particular Wilrijk, Mortsel and Edingen, where they can live less conspicuously.

The Schipperskwartier and the Rietdijk: Red-Light Delight
Over the centuries the red-light area of Antwerp has shifted around the city, as the authorities closed down or demolished streets with too many brothels. In the Middle Ages the main area of amorous operations was De Blijde Hoek (Happy Corner) at the southern end of the Nationale Straat in the Sint Andries quarter. In the seventeenth century the red-light area transferred to the Rietdijk, named after a dike with reeds. The Rietdijk became internationally famous as the place to have a certain sort of fun in Antwerp; the Haringvliet or Canal aux Harengs was the most notorious street and was often mentioned in French literature. When ships arrived at the Bonapartedok or Willemdok to the north of the Rietdijk, the local businesses sent "runners" on board to persuade crews to visit the whorehouses. On the streets there were *aanklampsters* and *loksters*, women whose job was to get hold of sailors and make them spend their money. Some establishments such as the Cristal Palace had extraordinarily sophisticated facilities. The local writer Georges Eekhoud

gives a detailed study of the situation in his novel *La Nouvelle Carthage* (1888). The red-light areas of Brussels and Antwerp were sufficiently notorious for an English author using the name of William Stuart (real name Lord Monroe) to publish the novel *Clarissa* in 1882, warning English girls against being lured into Belgian brothels. The author used court records of cases that were heard in 1874-7 in Antwerp and Brussels.

The French became acquainted with the Rietdijk during the Napoleonic era. Between 1794 and 1815 French writers and painters had been able to admire Rubens' paintings in the Louvre, but after the Battle of Waterloo many Flemish paintings had to be returned to their homeland, so there was no alternative but to visit Belgium. French visitors of this period are credited with encouraging local writers to use Dutch rather than to persist in their efforts to use French. Charles Baudelaire, who came here between 1861 and 1863, was of the same opinion. With an influx of tourists, it became necessary to widen the Scheldt and to straighten out its banks as well as to clean up the city in time for the Universal Exhibition of 1885. Respectable promenades along the Zuiderterras and Noorderterras were built where the old quays had once stood; the only remnant of the Rietdijk is the Burggracht, the ditch around Het Steen, the city castle. By the 1930s the name Rietdijk had been completely forgotten and is now only known to historians. The prostitutes who "worked the dike" may have given us the English slang word for a lesbian, perhaps taken home by American sailors.

These days the red-light area is around Sint-Paulusstraat and Sint-Paulusplaats, north of the Groenplaats and closer to the docks of Het Eilandje. The whole of the Schipperskwartier has been drastically redeveloped, with the docks themselves moved further downstream, and the northern end of the Schipperskwartier now has many warehouses converted into lofts. Housing laws have been used to close down most of the brothels, while more drastic measures became necessary in the 1990s following the arrival of the Albanian mafia after the Kosovo war. The open gangsterism around the Falconplein had to be reduced, but there have been some distinctly unusual consequences. The police now have an office on the top floor of the ultra-modern boutique-style brothel called the Villa Tinto on the Verversrui, which has space for 102 prostitutes. The presence of closed-circuit cameras puts off customers, so there is a new type of prostitution based around the "night shops" that have recently appeared all over Flanders. Most Belgian clients, in any case, prefer to go to the brothels that are clearly advertised with neon signs by the side of old turnpikes.

Antwerp has also taken steps against gay prostitution in the notorious "Vaselinestraatje" or Van Schoonhovenstraat near the Central Station by using the same tactics of rebuilding and closing off the street. Yet this remains the centre of the gay scene in Antwerp, albeit more subdued than before. At 97 Pacificatiestraat there is a gay nightclub, L'Envers d'Anvers (the backside of Antwerp) and an annual competition for the prettiest transvestite: Miss Lanvers Danvers.

Puppets and the Vleeshuis

The *poesje* (from the Italian Pulcinella) or Antwerp puppet theatre once thrived in the working-class district around the Schipperskwartier and the Vleeshuis. The slums left after the bombing of the Second World War were torn down in the 1960s and 1970s and replaced with new and attractive low-cost housing, but also with more expensive accommodation that was out of the reach of the original population. The legendary Antwerp flamenco guitarist and folk singer Wannes van de Velde sings of the *poesje* and his sadness at the disappearance of the Schipperskwartier.

The Vleeshuis or Butchers' Hall is the oldest public building in Antwerp, dating from 1501-4. It was quite appropriately built in "bacon" style, with strips of red and white brick. It currently houses a collection of applied arts; in the future it will only have a musical instrument collection, while the rest of the exhibits will go to the new Museum Aan de Stroom (due to open in 2008). The Sint-Pauluskerk next door has a remarkable display of works by major painters, including Rubens, van Dyck, Teniers, Jordaens and many other Antwerp artists. The church was badly damaged by fire in 1968. All the local residents, including the prostitutes, turned out in the middle of night to save its treasures, an event that has gone down in local folklore.

Puppet plays were mainly put on in cellars called *poesjenellenkelder* or sometimes in attics. Texts were taken from medieval tales or historical incidents, and these underground theatres were wild places. Puppets would at the least provocation bash each other over the head, while the puppeteers were also experts in making their characters fly off the stage after a mighty punch. The life and soul of the performance was always De Neus (Nose), along with De Schele (Bent) and Kop (Head). There was even a net in front of the stage to ward off the apple cores and nut shells thrown by the audience. De Neus has his statue next to the Lange Vlierstraat on the Nationalestraat, on the unofficial Neusplein.

There are different types of puppets: those controlled with rods are *stangpoppen* or *dubbelstangpoppen* and those operated with wires or string are *draadpoppen*. The main permanent puppet theatre is the Poppenschouwburg Van Campen, based in the Sint-Nicolaasplaats off the Lange Nieuwstraat. The revived Poesje next door to the Vleeshuis only puts on performances on request. There is also the hybrid Figurentheater Froe Froe, which mixes actors with puppets, animals and monsters.

Peter-Paul Rubens

Rubens (1577-1640) was far more than just a painter; he was an important figurehead of the Counter-Reformation and spent many years in the service of the Spanish as a diplomat. He embodied the revival of Antwerp after the catastrophes of the Iconoclast period and by the same token his death meant the end of a glorious artistic era. After Belgium became independent in 1830, Rubens became a national hero and symbol of renewed Belgian pride. He is ubiquitous in present-day Antwerp.

Rubens' life reflected the troubled times in which he grew up. His family were wealthy Antwerp patricians. His father, Jan Rubens, ran a pharmacy but his Protestant sympathies forced him to leave for the safety of Germany in 1576. Rubens was born in Siegen in 1577 and spent his early years in Cologne, returning to his ancestral city in 1589. His mother intended him to become a diplomat or scholar, but he went to work as an apprentice painter. From 1600 to 1608 he lived in Italy and absorbed the influence of the great Renaissance painters, also coming into contact with the Jesuits, who would later commission much of his work. He could have remained in Rome, like many Flemish artists, but chose instead to return to Antwerp as conditions were more favourable than before. The Twelve Year Truce had been declared between the Spanish and the Dutch in 1609, and in the same year Rubens was appointed court painter by the art-loving rulers of the Spanish Netherlands (as we should call Belgium at this time), the popular Archduke Albert and Archduchess Isabella.

This was a time when many works of art were being commissioned to replace those destroyed by Protestants in the Iconoclast Fury. The Catholic Church started a charm offensive to win back the hearts and minds of the people, many of whom still had Protestant sympathies. The Baroque style was promoted by St. Ignatius of Loyola and the Jesuits, the shock troops of the Counter-Reformation in Belgium, and is characterized by the use of swirling lines to pull the viewer into a painting or sculpture. The theatrical energy of the Baroque matched the traditional vitality of Flemish art, which had in any case always catered to a liking for excessive decoration. Rubens developed the vogue for painting sensual ruddy figures, combining pagan mythology with Christian devotion. He received numerous commissions from wealthy patrons, and is credited with producing some 2,500 paintings between 1608 and 1640 with the help of his assistants.

In 1620 Rubens was given the task of designing the Jesuit Church of St. Charles Borromeo, now on the Hendrik Conscienceplein. Not only did he act as an interior designer, but he was also commissioned to create 39 religious paintings with the help of Anthony van Dyck and a few others. St. Charles Borromeo and other Baroque churches are intended to represent heaven on earth on the lines of the Santa Susanna in Rome, built in 1603 by Carlo Moderno. No expense was spared in using the costliest white marble and most lavish decoration. The altar and pulpit are close to the worshippers, with confession boxes along the walls. In contrast to the Gothic style, which is all soaring lines pointing to heaven, the Baroque places man at the centre of the universe, making use of horizontal rather than vertical planes, and making paintings the focal point for religious devotion. Baroque churches were intended to give a feeling of intimacy and involvement, even if that is not how modern worshippers might see it. Unfortunately, St. Charles Borromeo was gutted by fire in 1718, but some parts such as the Houtappel Chapel with original designs by Rubens still remain.

In 1610 Rubens bought a house in the Antwerp theatre district on the Wapper, now the Rubenshuis, which he had rebuilt to look more like an Italian *palazzo*. Opposite a traditional brick Flemish house he built a

Baroque studio with high windows to accommodate his vast paintings. He accumulated an immense collection of classical sculptures and paintings; everywhere he went he copied Old Masters and used these as models for his works. Rubens considered himself a humanist scholar and saw no conflict between ancient pagan culture and Christianity. For Rubens painting was also a business; he became successful by hard work rather than because he was a born genius.

As a loyal servant of the Catholic state he was rewarded with high aristocratic status and entrusted with diplomatic missions between the Spanish and English. He hoped to bring harmony between Catholics and Protestants, but by 1635 he was disillusioned with his role as a public figure and retired to a country estate near Mechelen, Het Steen (of which there is a painting in the National Gallery in London). His death in 1640 marked the end of a golden age for Antwerp; for the next 200 years the city was more of a backwater, cut off from the sea by the Dutch blockade and without the artistic driving force of a Rubens or van Dyck.

There are some fifty paintings by Rubens on view in Antwerp, as well as numerous sketches and engravings. The Antwerp Museum of Fine Arts (KMSKA) has the largest number. There are other major collections in the Rockoxhuis and the Museum Mayer Van Der Bergh. The Church of St. Paul should also not be missed, as it is the only place in Antwerp where paintings by the three great Antwerp masters, Rubens, van Dyck and Jacob Jordaens, can be seen under one roof. There are also four Rubens masterpieces in the cathedral: the *Raising of the Cross* and *Descent from the Cross*, commissioned by the Guild of Arquebusiers, as well as *The Assumption* and the *Resurrection*. Rubens became more daring with his technique over the years, and one can trace an evolution from the Titian-influenced *Raising of the Cross* through the *Descent from the Cross* (which both use diagonals to create energy), culminating with the turbulent energy of *The Assumption*, an example of Rubens' use of a spiral framework typical of his mature style.

Rubens has long been pilloried for his excessive style, yet he is a pivotal figure in Western art, as he reinvented the influences of the Italians in a more forceful northern European style, liberating painting from the restrictions of the Renaissance and opening the way for every school of art that followed. Rubens combines classical sculptural figures with the vitality of Flemish peasants in his nudes, a movement taken up by the nineteenth-century French artists, most of all Renoir. In his more abstract work he developed a vision of energy or organic chaos and so showed the path followed by the early English Impressionist Joseph Turner. His more expressionist side was taking up by Goya and El Greco, and reappears with the Flemish Expressionist Ensor in the nineteenth century (see p.177). The rapid, spontaneous brushstrokes in his preliminary studies also prefigured the work of the French Impressionists who came 250 years later. These preliminary studies are often far more representative of Rubens' intentions than the completed paintings, which had to be toned down for his sponsors, or were simply spoiled by his assistants.

Rubens expresses the "infinite movement" of the Baroque, when music was on the verge of becoming a dominant art form. His use of intense colour was also revolutionary, especially the reds in the faces of his figures, which one sees echoed in Van Gogh. To Rubens there was nothing more prodigious than the human being, however low he might fall. Behind the Baroque there is also a constant fear of death; man battles the forces of the universe and, if only temporarily, wins.

Past English visitors were often unappreciative of Baroque excess and much preferred the more restrained Anthony van Dyck, who was considered an honorary Englishman from the time he started to work for the English court. The British Pre-Raphaelites detested Rubens. Dante Gabriel Rossetti wrote:

"Messieurs, le Dieu des peintres": We felt odd:
'Twas Rubens, sculptured. A mean florid church
Was the next thing we saw, from vane to porch
His drivel. The museum: as we trod
Its step, his bust held us at bay. The clod
Has slosh by miles along the wall within.
... To the Cathedral. Here too the vile snob
Has fouled in every corner.
There is a monument we pass.
"Messieurs, you tread upon the grave
Of the great Rubens." "Well, that's one good job!
What time this evening is the train for Ghent?"

Lord Byron visiting Antwerp in 1816 confessed that he knew nothing about Flemish art, but still he thought that Rubens was "the most glaring, flaring, staring harlotry imposter that ever passed a trick upon the senses of mankind."

Anthony van Dyck

Antoon van Dijck (1599-1641), or Anthony van Dyck as he became, is often thought of as English, but he was an Antwerper through and through. He was born in Den Berendans (the Bear House) on the Grote Markt (where his descendants run an ice cream shop) but left the same year for the Korte Nieuwstraat. His father was a cloth merchant, and van Dyck had a remarkable ability to paint all kinds of textures of cloth. (It was said that he became a great artist because his mother did embroidery while she was pregnant.) Van Dyck was apprenticed at the age of ten to the painter Hendrik van Baelen and at fifteen to Rubens; by the age of seventeen he was Rubens' chief assistant and already a mature painter. The Rubenshuis has a portrait of him by Rubens from that time, in which we see a confident, even arrogant figure, already a complete master of his art.

At the age of 21 van Dyck went to England as court painter to Charles I, but gave up after five months and returned home. He then went to Italy for six years where he discovered the Mediterranean colours of the great Italian masters such as Titian and Veronese, as well as making his reputation as one of the leading painters of his age. On his return to Antwerp he became court painter to the Archduchess Isabella, ruler of the Spanish Netherlands. Charles I invited him back to London in 1632 and he died there in 1641. He is buried in the choir of St. Paul's Cathedral, but the grave was destroyed in the Great Fire of London in 1666. Van Dyck transformed the art of portraiture in Britain. He is mostly remembered for his portraits of Charles I and other figures caught up in the English Civil War. His great talent was to communicate character and subtle emotions in paint; in this skill he has probably never been equalled. There is a statue of him at the crossing of the Meir and the Jezusstraat.

Around the Grote Markt

Tourists are naturally drawn to the pedestrian-only streets such as the

Hoogstraat and Vlaeykensgang, while Antwerpers mainly frequent the cafés and restaurants south of the Nationalestraat, near the Museum of Fine Arts. Most visitors avoid the rather unattractive area around the railway station and head straight for the spacious Groenplaats, and then the cathedral. The Cathedral of the Virgin Mary (Onze Lieve Vrouw Kathedraal) has the tallest church tower in the Low Countries at 403 feet, three feet higher than that of the Church of the Virgin Mary in Bruges. Work began on the cathedral in 1352, but was delayed for fifty years by a Flemish occupation. The foundations of the North Tower were laid in 1420, but lack of funds meant that no further work could be done until 1475. The building of the tower took until 1521, and the result is a magnificent example of High Gothic architecture (see p.xii). With the split between Holland and Belgium in 1585, Antwerp became a frontier city, its high cathedral tower clearly visible to the Protestants on the other side of the Scheldt. The Virgin Mary is the patron saint of Antwerp and 121 Virgins were put up on street corners and house frontages to promote the Catholic Church. Neighbourhoods still take pride in having the best-maintained Virgin.

The entrance arch holds some fascinating secrets. There are four saints to the left and right of the central doorway. On the far left, St. Norbert tramples the arch-heretic Tanchelm or Tanchelijn, who started his own sect in 1115 and built the first Onze Lieve Vrouw church. Tanchelm had 3,000 followers, wore a gold robe and officially married the Virgin Mary. His fame was such that he is mentioned in Wolfram von Eschenbach's *Parzifal* from 1200. His story is also the basis for a classic play by the Dutch writer, Harry Mulisch. It took someone of the calibre of St. Norbert to rid Antwerp of Tanchelm, who was soon murdered by a priest.

Sitting over the Virgin Mary is the Archangel Michael, the subject of a well-known poem by the Antwerp writer, Maurice Gilliams, "Sterven in Antwerpen" (Death in Antwerp):

The stone angel on the Cathedral
Lifts his scales at midnight for the faint-hearted
The army of lice cracks. Cats piss
In crooked draftless alleys.

Gilliams is known for his morbidly pessimistic style; he has been called the "Flemish Marcel Proust".

On the left of the frontage is an ornate wrought iron well, reputedly built by the painter Quentin Metsys with nothing more than a hammer. Metsys (or Matsys) was a simple apprentice locksmith who was born in Leuven around 1460. Opposite his smithy he often saw the daughter of the painter Pieter de Vos at the window and asked for her hand in marriage, but the painter told him that he would only marry his daughter off to another painter. Metsys gave up being a locksmith and studied painting, and after three years was able to present de Vos with three paintings of his daughter. De Vos realized that Metsys was a genius and agreed to the marriage. His greatest work, *Christ in the Tomb*, painted around 1509 as part of a triptych, is in the Antwerp Museum of Fine Arts. The inscription on the well in archaic script reads: "Quentin Metsys made me. Love turned a blacksmith into a painter." Metsys is a transitional figure between the Flemish Primitives and the Renaissance, whose satirical paintings have something in common with the more distorted images of the Italian Mannerists, a style that began around the time that Metsys died in 1530. A fine example is his *Ugly Duchess* in the National Gallery in London, which served as the model for Sir John Tenniel's Duchess in *Alice in Wonderland*. Metsys combines the precision of the Flemish Primitives Memling and Dirk Bouts, and the more dramatic expressiveness of the figures in Rogier van der Weyden's work.

The Groenplaats, where most visitors start their tour of Antwerp, was originally the Groen Kerkhof or "Green Cemetery". It was recently redesigned by bOb van Reeth, Flanders' leading architect; the statue in the middle is of Rubens. The leading contemporary Flemish writer Hugo Claus, who has lived in Antwerp on and off since 1975 (in 2006 he was living in Paardenmarkt, north of the centre), composed the following "Rhymes for a Traveller in Antwerp":

> The sun is an Antwerp planet,
> The Earth ends at the Scheldt.
> Cyclones lie down on the Groenplaats.
> Of all mighty cities to fall,
> Antwerp will fall last,
> Autochthonous to the last.

A day out at the Zoo and the Zuid.
Steam from French fries and sausages.
The café spreads like a cabin
The café dies of thirst.

The cathedral stands ready
Like a slate rocket
Full of Gothic instruments,
Stalactites, pinnacles, niches
Full of holy happenings.
Ready? Count down. Now, into the blue!
In the cathedral's shadow
We read our newspaper about earthly love and pain
And eat the most radioactive croquette on the planet.

Two blocks south of the Groenplaats is the Boerentoren (nowadays called the KBC Toren after the bank which occupies it), whose construction was financed by the Flemish farmers' cooperative or Boerenbond in 1929-32. This was the first (rather modest) skyscraper in Europe. The entrance is flanked by four monumental figures in art deco style. Many locals are not enamoured of it, but then they do not have a reputation for being easily satisfied. Tom Lanoye, who was appointed city poet by the Antwerp City Council in 2003—one city councillor called this "the peak of surrealism"—imagines the KBC Toren falling in love with the cathedral:

why do I hang around here PLOMP
lost angles in your
slender shadow side
lace in stone
—too small as a tower
too young to be your lover

accept me, TAKE me
see me STANDING
start to see me day and night
your BEAUTY before me. Oh

Unrequited love: the cathedral and KBC Toren

look then LOVE me
surrender don't HOLD back...

In 2005 Lanoye was replaced by half-Palestinian but Antwerp-born Ramsey Nasr, whose appointment did not please the Jewish community, given his anti-Zionist utterances. The post carries an annual salary of US$6,000.

Literature and Theatre in Antwerp

From the beginning literary activity revolved around the *rederijkerskamers* or chambers of rhetoric, clubs for writers which have carried on since the Middle Ages without interruption except for a few years when they had to close down under the Spanish in the sixteenth century, and again under the French rule of Napoleon. Dutch literature has its origins in Flanders, first in Bruges and then in Antwerp. With the separation of the Netherlands in 1585, the leading writers of Brabant moved north and the language of southern Brabant became the basis for literary Dutch. As such, it is ironic that Dutch publishers in the Netherlands for a long time considered Dutch written in Belgium to be incorrect and employed editors to correct Flemish writers—something not always appreciated by those whose work was "improved". Since the start of commercial television in Flanders in 1988 Belgian Dutch has evolved a new standard language, so-called *verkavelingsvlaams* (housing estate Flemish) or *schoon vlaams* (pure Flemish). Flemish writers are in any case much more careful about their language use these days and are respected rather than ridiculed by the Dutch.

Antwerp quite reasonably considers itself Belgium's leading literary centre, a claim reinforced when it was made World Book City by UNESCO, an event that ran during 2004 and 2005. Antwerp has more theatre groups than Brussels or Rotterdam, cities with twice the population. The quality and stability of these groups stem directly from the centuries-old tradition of the chambers of rhetoric. On the Lange Nieuwstraat near the Sint-Katelijnevest, for example, is the Sint-Nicolaasplaats, an inner courtyard housing De Violieren Rederijkershuis and the Noordteater. De Violieren won the sixth Landjuweel or competition between some twenty Brabant chambers of rhetoric in 1541, and so had to put on the last one in 1561. The Juweel (jewel) was the first prize in the competition. A Welsh merchant, Richard Clough, has left us a description of the magnificent procession that preceded the competition:

> But principally of all came Brussels; which methinks was a dream. In fine, I do judge to be there, 600 horsemen, all in crimson satin, and 130 wagons... hats of red; trimmed as the rest, with white feathers; white satin doublets, and white buskins; great girdles of gold Taffeta, with their swords accordingly.
>
> I would to God that some of our gentlemen and noblemen of England had seen this (I mean them that think the world is made of oatmeal) and then it would make them to think that there are other as we are, and so provide for the time to come; for they that can do this, can do more.

The chambers of rhetoric were temporarily suppressed after 1566 as hotbeds of resistance to Spanish rule. Theatrical and literary activities continued after the leading lights had moved north, but declined in quality. The most important Flemish poet of the Counter-Reformation was Anna Bijns (1493-1575), who blasted Protestants, Jews and heretics in brilliant verse. She was a nun all her life and a schoolmistress in the Keizerstraat. Her birthplace at 46 Grote Markt is now a restaurant. The tradition of writing plays in local dialect went on until the French occupation of 1797, and has recently been revived.

The Antwerp theatre scene was dominated by visiting French companies in the nineteenth century. The first professional Dutch company, the Nationaal Toneel, started up in 1853. The French opera, Le Royal, was housed in the Bourla Theatre, but there was no home-grown company and only foreign performers. This was an affront to the growing number of supporters of the Flemish Movement in Antwerp, and they started the Dutch-language De Opera on the Frankrijklei from 1908. The French opera finally went bankrupt in 1930. The Nationaal Toneel became the Koninklijke Vlaamse Schouwburg and is now called Het Toneelhuis, with its permanent home in the magnificent Bourla Theatre (1829-34) on the Komedieplaats, named after its architect Pieter Bourla. The café is worth a visit, even if one never goes to a play there. The Bourla's director Luk Perceval left in 2005 to take up the same position at the Schaubühne in Berlin.

Contemporary Flemish theatre is appreciated abroad, especially the Antwerp-based group, TG Stan or Stan (short for Stop Thinking About Names), which emerged from a group of rebellious students at the Antwerp Conservatory from 1989. TG Stan breaks all the rules of conventional theatre. Sometimes the actors call each other by their real names during performances, leave the lights on or do not bother to rehearse at all. Their innovative approach and ability to perform in French and English have made them into international stars and a permanent fixture at French theatre festivals.

Antwerp also has commercial, unsubsidized, theatre. The largest venue is the Stadsschouwburg near the Rubenshuis, which puts on large-scale productions and musicals in Dutch and English. There is also the local Echt Antwaarps Theatre (Real Antwerp Theatre) in the nearby Arenbergstraat, which puts on works in local Antwerp dialect. The area between the Komedieplaats and the Theaterplein could be called the Broadway or West End of Antwerp, with its high concentration of theatres. The Vlaamse Opera (Flanders Opera) has its premises at the Koninklijke Vlaamse Opera building on the Frankrijklei and also performs in Ghent. Until the late 1980s operas were sung in Dutch translation, but it has since become the policy to sing them in the original language and use sub-titles, thus enabling foreign singers to work here.

Typesetting and Paul Van Ostaijen
At its peak Antwerp was the publishing capital of Europe. Nowadays, the printer Christophe Plantin (1520-89), who dates from that golden age, is surprisingly still at home on every computer around the world, thanks to the typeface or font named after him. Born in France, he migrated to Antwerp in 1548 and started his printing works in 1572. He moved to the present-day site of the Plantin-Moretus Museum at 22 Vrijdagmarkt in 1576. Soon he was employing eighty staff and printing the works of great humanists such as Vesalius, Ortelius and Justus Lipsius. Plantin was official printer to the King of Spain, but still managed to retain a degree of freedom to print works by Protestants without upsetting his Catholic masters. The most contentious work that he published was the anti-Protestant poetry of Anna Bijns. The printing business passed to the Moretus family on Plantin's death in 1589, and continued uninterrupted until 1876, when it was sold to the city of Antwerp with all the original equipment intact. Here one can easily imagine great scholars labouring on epoch-making publications such as the *Biblia Polyglotta*, a Bible in four languages. Plantin did not invent printing as such, but was the first to print books on a large scale. The Plantin-Moretus Museum has portraits of the Moretus family by Rubens as well as priceless incunabula from the fifteenth century, the dawn of the printing revolution.

Antwerp also prides itself on being the home of the world's first regular newspaper. Abraham Verhoeven (1575-1652) was given permission by Archduke Albert and Archduchess Isabella in 1605 to publish a "gazette" or newssheet to be known as *Nieuwe Tydinghen*, literally "New Tidings". This began as an irregular single-page sheet in Dutch, sometimes in French or Latin, under strict censorship and appearing about every eight days, depending on how much news there was. Verhoeven had foreign correspondents; otherwise he did all the work himself. From 1620 his newspaper appeared more frequently, numbered and dated. Verhoeven was cautious enough to end his reports with the words: "If it is true, only time will tell." His original premises at 6 Lombardenvest are marked with a plaque; there was a newspaper museum here between 1987 and 2002.

Antwerp's great typographical tradition also lay behind a revolutionary new style of poetry from the First World War, started by Paul van Ostaijen (1896-1928). His moody statue can be seen at the Pottenbrug on the Minderbroedersrui, close to the Letterenhuis, the archive of Flemish literature and culture. Van Ostaijen remained in Antwerp during the war working for the Town Hall while involved in the Flemish Activist movement, which hoped to gain some advantage for its cause under the German occupation. To most Antwerpers, van Ostaijen was an eccentric who dressed in the style of the 1830s and was involved in various amusing incidents. In 1917, for instance, the French-speaking Cardinal Mercier, a sworn enemy of the Flemish cause, was in Antwerp, and van Ostaijen and a group of activists had agreed simultaneously to shout out "Down with the Cardinal!" But at the crucial moment his "friends" deliberately kept quiet, and van Ostaijen alone was arrested and sentenced to a term in prison. He fled Antwerp in November 1918 and stayed in Berlin until 1921, where he came into contact with the revolutionary Spartacists and avant-garde artists and writers. He set down his experiences of wartime Antwerp in the Dada-inspired poetry collection *Bezette stad* (Occupied City, 1921), which uses visually arresting typography to objectivize the images the writer has experienced. Van Ostaijen was influenced by the sculptor Oscar Jespers in the layout of this work, which represented a complete break with the Romantic and realist styles of Flemish poetry at the time. He became a major literary critic and a figure of world stature, but died of tuberculosis before his influence was recognized outside Belgium.

Hendrik Conscience and the Sint-Andrieskwartier
The Austrians divided Antwerp into 32 quarters in the eighteenth century, and by far the poorest was the Sint-Andrieskwartier or Fourth Quarter, dubbed the Parish of Misery by local writer John Wilms (1893-1978). There is now little left to recall the fetid alleyways and colourful characters of yesteryear. The building of the Nationalestraat from 1877 onwards finally wiped out most of the district's unhealthy slums.

The defining monument here is the Sint-Andrieskerk (Church of St. Andrew), where Rubens' children were christened. In 2001 the priest of Sint-Andries had the idea of asking leading local fashion designer Ann Demeulemeester to create a new outfit for the statue of the Madonna in the church. The result was a transparent, clingy white dress with black braids and a collar of dove's feathers. Our Lady of Help and Victory, as she is called, is a svelte marble figure with a carved linen robe, while most Flemish madonnas are just wooden skittle-shaped sticks with a head on top. Her wardrobe mostly consists of eighteenth-century damask and brocade, with a Spanish mantle fixed to her head with a crown. The Sint-Andries madonna has since gone back to her more conservative dress, with only photos to remind us of when she was the height of fashion. The church is only open on certain days and for services.

The literary renaissance of Belgian Dutch after independence started out from the Sint-Andrieskwartier. The pioneer of this movement, Hendrik Conscience, was born at 30 Pomp Straat close to the Sint-Andrieskerk in 1812. (The present-day house is not original, although there is a plaque on the wall.) At the time of his birth there was virtually no original Dutch literature being written in Antwerp, or even in Flanders, even if Flemish literature revived somewhat from 1834 with the publication by Jan Frans Willems of *Reinaert de Vos* and other medieval classics. Conscience wrote numerous novels, some of them set in Antwerp, but the only work for which he is remembered now is *De leeuw van Vlaanderen* (The Lion of Flanders, 1838), the tale of Robert of Bethune and his father, Guy of Dampierre, Count of Flanders, and the defeat of the French at the Battle of the Golden Spurs in 1302. Largely a romantic fantasy, *De leeuw van Vlaanderen* was immensely popular and was written with the intention of reawakening interest in reading among the Flemish working class, and encouraging pride in their great medieval past. It is perhaps ironic that a present-day publisher found it necessary to translate this work into modern Dutch when republishing it, as the original is not easily comprehensible to a modern audience, even though it was only written in 1838. During his lifetime Conscience was appointed tutor in Dutch to the King of Belgium's children.

Willem Elsschot and the *Will o'the Wisp*
Willem Elsschot (1888-1960) is considered by some critics as the finest
Dutch prose stylist of the twentieth century. Elsschot (real name Alfons
de Ridder) started a career as a businessman, first going to work in Paris
and then Rotterdam, and eventually became director of an advertising
company in Antwerp. His experience of duping companies into paying
for articles about them in bogus magazines was a source for his classic
Lijmen (Soft Soap, 1923). His first literary success, *Villa des Roses* (1913),
is set in a Paris boarding house, bringing together characters from various
northern European countries. The men are all out to seduce the maid,
Louise, and one—a German named Grünewald—succeeds. By the time
Louise finds that she is pregnant, Grünewald has moved on to another
boarding house and she is obliged to go back to her village in the
countryside. The film of *Villa des Roses* won the Best Feature award at the
Hollywood Film Festival of 2001.

Elsschot observed relations between the sexes with a grim humour.
The poem "Het huwelijk" (Marriage), written in 1910, has a husband
contemplating murdering his wife with a meat cleaver:

> But he did not kill her, because laws stand between
> Dreams and deeds, as well as practical objections,
> And also melancholy, that no one can explain,
> That creeps up on you as you're going to bed.

The poem was not, apparently, about Elsschot's own marriage, but that
of an uncle.

Kaas (*Cheese*, 1938) is one of a series of satires on business life. The
first, *Lijmen*, concerns a swindler in Brussels called Boorman who sets up
a fictitious trade journal, and his victim, Frans Laarmans, who reappears
in the sequel *Het been* (*The Leg*), also of 1938. In between appeared *Kaas*,
compared by some critics with *Diary of a Nobody* and *Three Men in a
Boat*. The trilogy deals with social divisions and the hopeless attempts of
the perennial loser Laarmans to better himself. In *Kaas* he gives up his
job as a clerk with an Antwerp shipping company to start a cheese
importing business under the name of General Antwerp Food Products
Agency. He has no experience of running a business, and when 10,000
Edam cheeses are delivered to his house, he spends his time looking for

a desk and typewriter to type invoices. The statue of Elsschot on the Mechelseplein has a little figure on its back, who is Laarmans. Boorman and Laarmans are Elsschot's sub-personalities, one a trickster, the other a pathetic victim.

Elsschot's most admired work is *Het dwaallicht* (*Will o'the Wisp*), a meditation on the elusive nature of experience. In this story, Laarmans meets three Afghan sailors who are in search of a young Antwerp woman by the name of Maria van Dam, who came on board their ship and left her address with them. Laarmans is inclined to leave them to their fate but then takes pity on them and accompanies them around the back streets of Antwerp looking for the mysterious Maria. The sailors are approached by a pimp and end up in a police station, while the mysterious Maria is nowhere to be found. Finally Laarmans comes to an address that appears to be the right one, and finds a mother breastfeeding her baby. The elusive Maria is evidently the Virgin Mary. Elsschot's classic trilogy has been translated under the title *Three Novels* (1965).

There is a plaque on the wall of 21 Lemméstraat, where Elsschot lived from 1919. The café where he spent much of his time, the Quinten Matsijs at 17 Moriaanstraat, organizes monthly tours of places associated with him, and other artistic tours. He is buried in the Schoonselhof cemetery along with other leading Antwerp writers.

The Red Star Line and Het Eilandje

Antwerp was the gateway for many European emigrants to America, including Bob Hope and Albert Einstein. Between 1880 and 1935 some three million people left from the Rijnkaai on the Red Star Line. The original wharf is being restored and opened in 2006 as a museum with a tie-up to the Ellis Island museum in New York. It is estimated that up to thirty million Americans are descended from emigrants who left from Antwerp. Poverty or a sense of adventure drove many Flemish to migrate to the New World, with large-scale emigration starting after the Flemish potato famine of 1845. In the early days the Belgian government deliberately sent ex-convicts and beggars to the US, saddling Belgians with a negative image there.

Those who were leaving Belgium behind were—at least until the First World War—mainly illiterate farmers and the desperately poor, who became an easy target for unscrupulous shipping agents. Some were robbed before they could even board a ship. A common trick was to promise emigrants work in Canada, or board and lodging until they found a job. On arrival in Quebec after a long and trying crossing, the immigrants were then left to their fate. Without work they were soon penniless and obliged to ask for help from local Belgian charities. For many it was a matter of entering the United States illegally, being smuggled on a train from Windsor, Ontario to Detroit, one of the centres of the Flemish community in North America. They would then find themselves on the streets and somehow had to make their way back to Antwerp. The Antwerp poet Karel van den Oever (1879-1926) wrote the following verses on an imaginary East European migrant:

> From an old village,
> Camel-brown as the steppe—
> From Plocka
> Came Dinska Bronska.
> Her headscarf was Prussian blue
> And her hair flaxen yellow.
>
> O Dinska Bronska
> You are leaving for Canada
> The rusty steamer awaits on the quay
> You read in a Red Star Line almanac
> That Canada has more attractions than Plocka;
> It must be a lot better in Canada!

The artist Eugeen van Mieghem (1875-1930) devoted himself to depicting the real lives of emigrants and port workers. He was himself the son of a café owner and worked in the docks after he was thrown out of the Antwerp Academy of Fine Arts. His work can be seen at the Eugeen van Mieghem Museum on the Beatrijslaan, on the other side of the Scheldt. This collection will move in 2008 to the Museum Aan de Stroom (MAS), now being built on the site of the Hanzehuis at the Hanzestedenplaats near the Oostendekaai. The building will be 204 feet tall and is intended to represent several warehouses piled on top of each other. The MAS will also house the current collections at the Vleeshuis, the Nationaal Scheepvaartmuseum (Navigational Museum) in Het

Steen, and the Volkskundemuseum (Museum of Folklore). The area of Het Eilandje, where the MAS is located was used from the sixteenth century for warehousing but is now being redeveloped with expensive apartments and a yachting marina. It was once literally a small island, surrounded by drawbridges that could be raised to cut it off from the rest of the world.

ModeNatie: Flemish Fashion

Many visitors are surprised to find that Antwerp is one of the world's leading fashion cities, rivalling London and Paris since 1988 when a group of designers known as the Antwerp Six emerged. One thing is certain: Antwerp women are the best dressed in Belgium—a reflection of the city's prosperity and taste for display. The Antwerp Six trained at the Koninklijke Academie voor Schone Kunsten in Antwerp and made their breakthrough with their Paris show of 1988. The big names include Dirk Bikkembergs (who moved to Milan), Ann Demeulemeester (who has her store at Het Zuid), Walter Van Beirendonck (who dresses U2 and Antwerp's garbage collectors), Dries Van Noten and many others with outlets close to the ModeMuseum.

The ModeNatie is the name of the building housing several fashion institutions: the Flanders Fashion Institute, the Fashion Library and the ModeMuseum with both permanent (ground floor) and temporary (first floor) collections. The term *natie* or "nation" is very typical of Antwerp and first appears in a document around 1434. A *natie* was an organization of manufacturers or traders, such as the Katoennatie or "Cotton Nation". The humble workers, the ordinary stevedores and dockworkers also had their own *naties* or unions. The ModeNatie building, located between the Drukkerijstraat and Nationalestraat, looks rather like a car park from the outside and could easily be overlooked, but the internal construction is highly innovative, with a huge amount of hardwood used to face the internal stairwell. The main exhibition can be visited free of charge.

The Underdog of Flanders

Antwerp's cathedral has inspired many writers, not least the English Victorian bestseller Ouida or Louisa de la Ramée (1839-1908), author of the sentimental classic, *A Dog of Flanders* (1872). While the book is virtually unknown in the West, the story is hugely popular in Japan—where it probably amounts to the sum total of Japanese knowledge about Flanders. Japanese visitors make sure to have their photo taken with the statue of the book's hero Nello (or Nero to the Japanese) and his dog in Hoboken, on the corner of the Kioskplaats and the Kapelstraat. The story symbolizes loyalty and perhaps reminds Japanese tourists of the statue of the faithful dog Hachiko, the most famous landmark in Tokyo. Opposite the entrance to the cathedral is a black rectangular slab with a Japanese inscription to Nello and Patrasche, and a suggestion to tourists to go to Hoboken.

In the novel the boy Nello lives with his grandfather in a mud hut, where they survive on the "occasional crust and leaves of cabbage". The two of them rely for this meagre subsistence on a dog, Patrasche, who draws a milk cart. (It seems that Ouida, who was living in Brussels at the time that she wrote *A Dog of Flanders*, took the name for the dog from the Brussels slang word *patraque*, meaning "sick".) Nello gets into the habit of going into the Cathedral of the Virgin and leaves the dog waiting outside for hours on end. The little boy is obsessed by the idea of seeing two Rubens masterpieces that are only shown to those who can pay with a silver coin: the *Elevation of the Cross* (1610) and the *Descent from the Cross* (1612). Nello then enters a drawing into an annual competition for under-eighteens and hopes to win a large amount of money. He and the dog are meanwhile evicted from their mud hut for not paying the rent, and Nello's only chance of survival is hence to win the prize—but predictably enough, it goes to someone else. On Christmas Eve Nello and Patrasche finally get into the cathedral by night and see the two great paintings for a moment in a sudden illuminating beam of moonlight. The following morning the people of Antwerp find both dog and boy in the crypt of the church, dead for the sake of art.

Zurenborg and Art Nouveau
Antwerp has the greatest concentration of Art Nouveau architecture in Belgium (although Brussels has more in numerical terms) in a small area of the Zurenborg district north of Berchem railway station. Zurenborg, meaning "Sour Hill", was subject to regular flooding until the sixteenth century (hence making the land sour) and was left uninhabited, but then in 1570 property developer by the name of Michel van der Heyden had

the land drained and its level raised. The renowned street of eclectic Art Nouveau houses, the Cogels-Osylei, named after Senator Cogels and a Baron Osy, runs from close to Berchem Station towards the Draakplaats, with its extraordinary neo-Renaissance tram shed. The area has the most ostentatious and colourful houses of any Belgian city. They have been bought up by wealthy Dutch immigrants and are now extremely pricey.

The popular Flemish novelist Kristien Hemmerechts lives in Zurenborg at 65 Cogels-Osylei, one of the most elaborate houses on the street. Her husband Herman de Coninck (1944-97) was probably the most popular Flemish poet of the last century. Hemmerechts has written about her life with de Coninck and her widowhood in *Taal zonder mij* (Language without Me, 1998). Hemmerechts writes both in English and in Dutch and is mainly known for her psychological studies of family life. After de Coninck suddenly died in Lisbon in 1997 some of his poetry was displayed on the train viaduct at the Draakplaats.

Antwerp Central Station

Antwerp boasts the most impressive railway station in Belgium, if not the largest. The entrance hall is on a gigantic scale and the bar lavishly decorated with gold. This palace of steam was designed and built by Louis Delacenserie between 1894 and 1905 at the behest of King Leopold II. Delacenserie also restored many of Bruges' Gothic monuments. In 2006 an underground railway station opened for high-speed trains to pass under the city and then on to the Netherlands. The city considered it so important that the new train should go right through Antwerp rather than pass it by that it decided to spend US$8 billion to make sure it did so. The BBC used this neo-Baroque masterpiece for its *Poirot* series and put up a large sign saying "Gare de Bruxelles"—a station no more real than Agatha Christie's notorious Walloon detective himself. The Belgian detective comes down the steps and exclaims: "How wonderful to be in Brussels again!"

Turning right out of the station, we see the Antwerp Zoo, founded in 1848 and one of Europe's major zoological gardens. Perhaps its most attractive aspect is its eclectic architecture, with varied styles of animal enclosures including the lion cages in which suspected collaborators were locked up at the end of the Second World War. Note the statue of a man on a dromedary on top of the building on the left of the entrance.

Beneath is the Grand Café Paon Royal, a restaurant that figures in Willem Elsschot's *Tsjip* and *De leeuwentemmer* (The Lion Tamer), semi-autobiographical works dealing with the marriage of his daughter to a Pole and the difficulties he and his daughter had in bringing his grandson, Jan Maniewski or Tsjip, back from Poland. When Tsjip finally gets off the train from Poland Elsschot takes him to the Paon Royal: "We went into the Paon Royal were he had drunk his first grenadine. He went to fetch the straw to drink through, which the waiter had forgotten, from the counter, because he still knew where they were kept." Jan Maniewski still gives talks and guided tours relating to his grandfather.

Museum of Fine Arts and the Antwerp School

The highly fashionable quarter of Het Zuid is, quite logically, at the southern end of the Nationalestraat, in an area of imposing nineteenth-century mansions. Close to the Lambermontplaats is the KMSKA or Museum of Fine Arts, built on the site of a Spanish fortress in 1872. Het Zuid went into decline after the Second World War, as even its wealthy inhabitants found their houses too expensive to maintain. The area became an immigrant ghetto, property prices fell, and so many writers and artists moved in, making Het Zuid the centre of the city's literary life. Different cafés have alternated as the most fashionable. Until the death of Herman de Coninck in 1997, De Nieuwe Linde or the Entrepôt du Congo were best-known, but this role has since been taken over by Café Hopper on the Leopold De Waelstraat.

The KMSKA is one of Belgium's finest art museums, with a collection ranging from the Italian Renaissance to the early twentieth century. While its official name is Koninklijke Museum voor Schone Kunsten Antwerpen (Royal Museum of Fine Arts Antwerp), pro-Flemish Antwerpers generally drop the word "Royal" and prefer to call it the Museum voor Schone Kunsten Antwerpen or MSKA. The richness of the collection owes everything to the foresight of the pioneer art collector and Antwerp burgomaster Florent van Ertborn (1784-1840), who understood the value of Renaissance paintings before anyone else and left 141 paintings to the city's new museum. The KMSKA has the largest collections of drawings and paintings by James Ensor and Rik Wouters, but perhaps not their best works.

The legacy left by van Ertborn in 1841 enabled the museum to acquire major works from the fifteenth century, but there is only one van Eyck, a sketch of *St. Barbara and the Madonna at the Fountain*. Works by foreign fifteenth-century masters include the *Madonna* by the Frenchman Jean Fouquet and the *Crucifixion* by the Italian Antonello da Messina, which are among the most important paintings in the museum's collection. The KMSKA has the *Altar of the Sacraments* from the studio of Rogier van der Weyden (1400-64) and the *Madonna of the Cherries* by Joos van Cleve, who worked in Antwerp from 1511. There is also the *Flight into Egypt* by the pioneer landscape artist Joachim Patinier or Patinir (1485-1524), who was active in Antwerp from 1510.

An Antwerp School of painters is deemed to have existed from about 1470, the time that the city began to take over from Bruges as the economic centre of the Low Countries. The Brueghel family is represented by *St. George's Fair* and *Census at Bethlehem* by Pieter Breughel the Younger (1564-1638) and *The Homage of the Kings* by Jan Brueghel the Elder (1568-1638), and many more works by these two artists that are not on display. The KMSKA has no paintings by Pieter Brueghel the Elder, something of a sore point with Antwerpers, although there are three paintings by Brueghel the Elder in the Musée des Beaux Arts in Brussels. His descendant David Teniers III (1630-85) founded the Antwerp Academy of Fine Arts in 1663, where van Gogh studied for nine months in 1885.

Those who are looking for works by Rubens will find them at the Rubenshuis (see above). Antwerpers are particularly fond of Jacob Jordaens (1593-1678), who took over the mantle of Rubens after his death, going further than his predecessor with his voluptuous nudes where he used coarser brushstrokes and cruder forms—but less cellulite. His style reflects the ascendancy of the Flemish Baroque, while also having more of an appeal to the common people. Jordaens worked in the Netherlands and England and secretly converted to Protestantism, but did not travel to Italy and was less influenced by Italian models. With his death Flanders ceased to produce innovative artists until well into the nineteenth century.

MuHKA and Panamarenko
The Museum of Modern Art in Antwerpen or MuHKA houses works from after 1970. The building is a disused 1920s grain silo on the

Leuvenstraat whose ochre-coloured exterior seems to have been lifted from the Great Mosque of Marrakesh. MuHKA has permanent and temporary exhibitions on its six floors with a Keith Haring mural in the cafeteria. In 2000 MuHKA displayed the notorious digesting machine, the Cloaca, designed by Wim Delvoye. His great ambition was always to sell excrement to the public and he achieved this aim with the Cloaca, where the idea is to feed food in one end and to package what comes out at the other and sell it at an exorbitant price. The Cloaca is made up of a series of Perspex and metal chambers where different acids and ox bile are used to create the necessary output. There are three different versions touring the world.

MuHKA also holds many works by the improbably named Panamarenko, one of Flanders' most widely recognized artists, although the only one permanently on display is his Prova Car, a sort of rusty sports car. He rejected his classical training at the Antwerp Academy and after a pop art phase developed an interest in aerodynamics. Born in Antwerp in 1940 as Henri van Herreweghe, he changed his name to Panamarenko after he heard the name on the radio. He builds potential flying machines, sometimes thirty feet across, with wings and engines that would like to fly but somehow never actually get off the ground. To display and store his earth-bound creations he has taken over a disused electricity generator shed in the Karel Geertsstraat in Borgerhout, which he calls the Antwerpse Luchtschipbouw Panamarenko Deurne or Antwerp Airship Building, not far from Antwerp's Deurne Airport. Panamarenko's works are not all huge by any means; there are also insects or birds with diaphanous wings mounted on rods. He works on the boundaries of science and art, stimulating dreams and celebrating the beauty of flight. His works are also arguably meditations on failure, since none of them flies, but to Panamarenko they are just there to entertain. The Antwerpse Luchtschipbouw is open to visitors between Wednesdays and Saturdays in the afternoon, longer hours from May to August. His statue of a man with airplane engines strapped to his back, officially called Pepto Bismo, can be seen in the open air on the Sint-Jansplein near the Italiëlei. Locals have rechristened this hopeful aeronaut De Vliegenier or "Flyer".

224

Chapter Ten
Brussels, Leuven and Mechelen

"O golden Breughelland, that never knows a care,
Fill all your children with delight.
O long-lost paradise, where are you now?"
  Michel de Ghelderode and György Ligeti, *Le Grand Macabre,* 1955

The City Changes Language
The very idea of Brussels as a Flemish city requires some explanation, since historically Brussels was part of Brabant and not of Flanders. Yet Brussels is now the capital of the federal state of Belgium, and hence of Flanders. The Dukes of Brabant, who ruled Brussels from 1005 were vassals of the German emperor and generally used Dutch as their official language. Matters gradually changed with the arrival in the fifteenth century of the Dukes of Burgundy, who preferred French. This process was accelerated by frequent French invasions in the eighteenth century and the occupation by France from 1794 to 1814. Once French was established as the language of officialdom, the immigrants who moved to Brussels in the nineteenth century mostly adopted it. There is therefore a class of French-speaker in Brussels with entirely different roots from those of the Walloons or original French speakers of Belgium. A further class of French-speaker is the *fransquillon* or *franskiljon,* a Dutch-speaker who gives up his or her language in favour of French. Until the start of the twentieth century the majority of the population spoke some form of Dutch dialect as their first language but many had to speak French as well in order to make a living and improve their social status. Brussels officially became a bilingual city in 1935, but by this time many Dutch-speakers claimed to speak French as their first language. The Frenchification of the city was a *fait accompli* by the 1950s.

The original Bruxellois call themselves *zinnekes*—mongrel dogs, fit only to be drowned in the River Zinneke—or *ketjes,* from the Brussels Flemish for "little scamp". The original Brussels Flemish dialect has a low

Tintin on the Stoofstraat

status, and is only spoken by the elderly. There are organizations such as De Academie van het Brussels which attempt to keep it alive by teaching it, but it appears that Brussels Flemish has reached a terminal stage in its decline. There is also a new type of Dutch-speaker in Brussels, the Flemish yuppie or newcomer who works for a big company or government body and often commutes from elsewhere. This new group has its own social circles and cultural venues in the capital and inevitably loses touch with roots in Flanders.

The large amounts of money available from the Flemish regional government for cultural subsidies have encouraged the setting up of numerous organizations in Brussels specifically for Dutch-speakers. The Flemish Community Commission, which is responsible for culture in the Flemish region, has extensive office buildings in the capital's centre. Another bastion of Flemish culture is the Vlaams-Nederlands Huis (Flemish-Dutch House) at 6 Leopoldstraat, a body set up by the Dutch and Flemish governments in 2004, whose job it is to promote Dutch culture. There is a Flemish cultural centre at De Markten at 5 Oude Graanmarkt 5, which promotes theatre performances and runs Dutch classes.

The present linguistic situation is unstable, with many French-speakers moving out to the surrounding municipalities that are officially Dutch-speaking, while more Dutch-speakers are moving into the city centre. The recent economic success of the Flemish region has led many French speakers to send their children to Dutch medium schools, in the hope of giving them a career advantage. At the last count perhaps some fifteen per cent of the population of Brussels proper, that is the nineteen *communes*, spoke Dutch but it is no longer possible to organize an official linguistic census because the question is deemed too sensitive.

Cartoon Capital
Brussels Flemish has found its way to the far corners of the globe, through the *oeuvre* of Hergé (1907-83), creator of Tintin. Hergé evidently learned this colourful dialect from his grandmother and used it to create imaginary languages like Syldavian (in *King Ottokar's Sceptre*) and Arumbaya (in *The Broken Ear*). Certain words also turn up in *The Land of Black Gold,* such as the name of the town Wadesdah (from Flemish for "What's that?"). Tintinologists have worked for many years

to reconstruct all the original Flemish words (although some of these do not appear in the English versions), notably Frédéric Soumois in *Dossier Tintin* (1987).

French-speaking Belgian cartoonists strongly influenced the development of comic strip art in France and the USA after the Second World War, but the most productive cartoonists in terms of sheer quantity (if not always quality) have generally been Flemish. Marc Sleen, who has been associated for over sixty years with the Ghent newspaper *De Gentenaar,* holds the world record for the number of cartoon albums (over 200) produced by one cartoonist. Sleen, whose real surname is Neels, created his immortal character Nero in 1944. Nero is a fat, middle-aged Gentenaar with anarchic tendencies who also happens to have some laurel leaves sprouting behind his ears. The connection with the Roman Emperor Nero is entirely obscure, but the device gives him a certain universality. The characters generally have wildly improbable traits and travel around the world becoming involved with the events of the day. At the end of every story Nero arrives home in Ghent to be greeted by his wife with a pile of steaming waffles. Sleen has long lived in the Brussels suburb of Hoeilaart, which now claims to be "home to Nero". There is a bronze statue of Nero outside the Nerocafé at 1 Albert Biesmanlaan. Middelkerke near Ostend has put up statues of Nero and several other Flemish comic strips heroes along the sea front.

Nero's direct competitor over the years has been Lambik (named after the Brussels beer) in the *Suske en Wiske* series created by Willy Vandersteen and his successors. The series has been translated into twenty languages and sold 160 million copies worldwide, but is perhaps less imaginative than the *Nero* series. The third great post-war Flemish cartoonist, Jef Nys, has also produced over 200 albums with various assistants and sold 50 million copies almost entirely in Belgium. His archetypal character is Jommeke, a young boy with a thatch of blond hair.

Brussels is indisputably the cartoon capital of Belgium. The subject has been dealt with in English by Thibaut Vandorselaer in his *Brussels through Comic Strips* (2004). The sides of 29 houses have been painted with scenes from the great Belgian cartoonists, with new ones added every year. Tintin is to be seen on the Stoofstraat (Rue de l'Etuve), while Nero is in the historical heart of Brussels on the Sint-Goriksplein (Place

St. Géry). There is also the Centre Belge de la Bande Dessinée (Belgian Centre for Comic Strip Art) located at 20 Rue des Sables near the centre of Brussels, housing an extensive exhibition of cartoon exhibits and a vast library. The building is a converted Art Nouveau department store designed by the architect Victor Horta (1861-1947), who started out life as the son of a humble Ghent shoemaker.

Brussels and Theatre

The Flemish theatre scene is inextricably linked with the Flemish Movement, which began in earnest around 1850. Many leaders of the movement were writers who believed that they should first persuade their own people to read Dutch so that they would value their own heritage. The tradition of chambers of rhetoric has persisted since the late Middle Ages (see p.211), with numerous small prizes being offered for plays. The first professional companies were in Antwerp (1853), Ghent (1871) and Brussels (1873). These three companies are still at the heart of Flemish theatre. Brussels' KVS or Koninklijke Vlaamse Schowburg (Royal Flemish Theatre) was virtually the only official Flemish cultural centre in the city for a century. In 1975 the Flemish Community passed a decree creating three main repertory companies (Antwerp, Ghent and Brussels), each with 20-25 professional actors and required to mount at least eight productions per season. The KVS now has premises in the Lakensesteenweg and the Arduinkaai. Not far away is the Kaaitheater arts centre on Sainctelettesquare, a thriving enterprise whose origins lie in a short-lived attempt to start up Dutch theatre in Brussels in the 1930s. There has been a year-round programme here only since 1987. The Kaaitheater also hosts occasional performances by the Brussels Flemish dialect theatre group, the Brussels Volkstejoêter.

The revival of Flemish theatre started with Cyriel Buysse (1859-1932), who specialized in darkly humorous plays about family life influenced by the Frenchman Georges Feydeau and other European playwrights. He wrote in dialect and his most highly regarded plays *De plaatsvervangende vrederechter* (The Deputy Justice of the Peace, 1895) and *Het gezin van Paemel* (The Paemel Family, 1903) are still popular. Buysse also launched the review *Van nu en straks* (From Now On), which lasted from 1893 to 1902 and more or less determined the course of Flemish literature for the next fifty years. At this time Flemish writers adopted the slogan "Let us be ourselves," meaning in essence "let us not be like the French." August Vermeylen, the leading intellectual behind the Flemish Movement at the time, coined the well-known phrase: "We wish to be Flemings in order to be good Europeans."

By far the most significant figure in Flemish theatre in the twentieth century was Herman Teirlinck (1879-1967), who initiated a tradition of monumental and more adventurous drama with productions of Greek tragedies and works of his own influenced by Wagner and the idealistic tradition of Maeterlinck. He was the son of Isidore Teirlinck, who wrote a notorious exposé of the poverty of the Flemish underclass, *Arm Vlaanderen* (Poor Flanders), as well as works on folklore and plants. Herman Teirlinck was born and spent his life in the industrial Brussels *commune* of Molenbeek. He started out writing in French but switched to Dutch early in his career and was able to make a living from writing novels in instalments for Dutch language magazines. In the lengthy *Het ivooren aapje* (The Little Ivory Monkey, 1909) Teirlinck tries to observe cosmopolitan Brussels society at all levels. His main legacy is as a theatre producer.

Brussels and Belgium have become known for two choreographers, Anne Teresa de Keersmaeker and Wim Vandekeybus. De Keersmaeker (who originates from Mechelen) trained with Maurice Béjart at the Muntschouwburg from 1978 and started her company, Rosas, in 1983. She has been the resident choreographer at the Muntschouwburg since 1993. Her work combines the main trends in modern dance with music and other art forms. Vandekeybus started as a protégé of the Antwerp theatre director and artist, Jan Fabre, and also works as a film director. In 1987 his first performed piece "What the Body Does Not Remember" became an international success and won him the prestigious New York Bessie Award in 1988. His company is Ultima Vez.

Brueghel in Brussels
Pieter Brueghel the Elder, born somewhere near Antwerp about 1526, came to Brussels six years before he died, following his marriage to the twenty-year-old daughter of his teacher, the well-known painter Pieter Coecke van Aalst. His father-in-law only consented to the marriage on condition that the couple moved to Brussels because of Brueghel's reputation as a playboy and heavy drinker, hence his nickname "The

Droll". There is a cryptic painting from 1562 of two monkeys chained to a wall, with the port of Antwerp visible through an archway, which has been interpreted as an allusion to Brueghel's impending loss of freedom. Brueghel's wife, Mayken, bore him three children, Pieter Brueghel the Younger (1564-1637), Jan Brueghel (1568-1625), known as "Velours" or "Velvet", and a daughter, Maria. Brueghel probably lived and worked in the step-gabled house at 132 Rue Haute (which was certainly owned by his granddaughter), in the colourful Marolles district, and was married and buried in the Eglise de la Chapelle at the end of the same street in 1569. The inscription on his tomb reads: "Petro Bruegelis Exactissimae Industriae Artis Venustissimae Pictoris".

Brueghel the Elder spent most of his career doing drawings, and his precise renditions of the architecture and artefacts of his time are a valuable source of information to historians. He travelled to Italy in 1552 to study landscape drawing and only applied himself to painting in 1559, ten years before his death. Brueghel largely ignored contemporary art, taking the maxim that an artist should learn from nature rather than from other artists. His work is both an accurate portrayal of the life of the ordinary people of his time, and prophetic in many ways, which accounts for his continued popularity. His paintings of marriages and feasts appear to express joy but if we look more closely we see the suffering and helplessness of humanity masked by frivolity. Brueghel lived through a time when the Spanish Inquisition was becoming increasingly active and when mass murder was being carried out in the name of religion. He was also clearly influenced by Hieronymus Bosch in some of his more surreal works, which include scenes of torture and executions. Yet his attitude towards religion is far from clear. One can see, for example, the dead body of a Catholic murdered by Protestants in the lower left corner of his *Fall of Icarus* (see below). It seems that Brueghel simply reproduced what he saw around him, without taking an explicit position. There is a moralizing aspect to many of his works, but also fatalism and perhaps the suggestion that the Church and religion had little to offer to the masses. The peasants are rooted in the landscape like the houses and trees, but behind all the activity is a feeling of perplexity, impending death and ultimately, silence.

Brueghel's great achievement was in his crowd paintings, with each character expressing individual emotions suggested by a few spare lines using thin tempera diluted with water. His *Tower of Babel,* based on his visit to the Colosseum in Rome, is another prophetic work, a comment on the dehumanizing effect of large cities and the dangers of mass hysteria. His landscapes combine his native Flemish Brabant with incongruous mountains or rocks joined by streams of water that suggest constant movement. Brueghel did not use conventional perspective but rather combines paradoxical elements to create a filmic effect. The painter himself seems to be suspended in the air, with the horizon near the top of the painting, increasing the sense of space and depth.

Only forty of Pieter Brueghel the Elder's works have survived, while his son, Pieter Brueghel the Younger—or rather his workshop— produced some 4,000 copies of works by his father and others. The original *Fall of Icarus* by Brueghel the Elder is in the Musée des Beaux Arts, while a copy made by his son can be seen at the Musée Alice et David van Buuren in Ukkel. This was the painting that inspired W. H. Auden's poem "Musée des Beaux Arts", written in December 1938.

Vlaams Brabant and the Pajottenland

Flemish Brabant or Vlaams Brabant is the landscape of Brueghel, a region of dark earth and fertile fields. Brueghel found inspiration in the countryside around Dilbeek, now a suburb of Brussels, which reappears in his paintings of the harvest and village feasts. In his late masterpiece, *The Parable of the Blind* (1568) we see the church of Sint-Anna-Pede in the background, a metaphor for an institution that is unable to prevent the six blind men from falling one by one into a lake. It is worth bearing in mind that this was painted in the same year as the execution of the Counts Egmont and Horn in Brussels. There is now an open-air Bruegelmuseum in Sint-Anna-Pede with reproductions of his local landscapes.

Vlaams Brabant is the newest province in Belgium, created in the federalization process in 1993; Brabant was previously one province with two languages. Vlaams Brabant completely surrounds Brussels, an important fact to remember, and the strip between Brussels and French-speaking Brabant Wallon consists of *communes à facilités,* where French-speakers are given special dispensations by the Dutch-speaking administration. In reality, the French-speakers are becoming the majority in these communes but are under pressure to communicate in Dutch with the authorities. In 2005 there were bitter arguments about whether French-speakers in the officially Dutch-speaking Halle and Vilvoorde should have the right to vote in Brussels elections.

The western half of Vlaams Brabant is the Pajottenland, a name derived from *patriotten*, the Patriots who fell in the Belgian Revolution of 1830, while the eastern half is called the Hageland, or land of hedges. Brabant is an area of gently rolling hills and rich farmland with few large towns; Brabanters are reputedly expansive, jovial and religious but also clannish and politically conservative. They even call their region "the Tuscany of the North" as a retort to Bruges' claim to be the Venice of the North. Nor is the title entirely misplaced. One thing that is unambiguously true is that Vlaams Brabant produces some of the world's greatest beers, with Leuven the headquarters of the world's largest brewing conglomerate, InBev.

Zichem in the Hageland is the setting for the film *De Witte van Sichem* (The Blond Boy of Zichem), based on the popular series of books by Ernest Claes (1885-1968) about the "white" boy's struggle against injustice and brutality after the First World War. The film begins with sunrise around Zichem and the local priest taking a swig of communion wine while "De Witte" wakes up in his miserable hovel. The boy finds salvation in reading the books of Hendrik Conscience, but his passion for reading leads him to steal or beg money to buy more books, while—paradoxically—he also finds serenity in the nearby Abbey of Averbode. De Witte is clearly Claes himself, who was born in a modest house by the road leading from Zichem to the pilgrimage place of Averbode. He lived in Brussels from 1913 on account of his work at the Belgian parliament. The director of *De Witte van Sichem*, Robbe de Hert, has had one of the most successful careers in Flemish film, coming from the same left-anarchist school of thought as Louis-Paul Boon, who had a small part in his short film *De Bom* (The Bomb, 1969). *De Witte van Sichem* won several prizes, but then disappeared without trace.

Leuven or Louvain?

The home of Belgium's most internationally reputed university is a city with two names. Leuven means "lions" in the local dialect (which has resemblances to German) but in the English-speaking world it is still often referred to by its French name, Louvain. This has become an anachronism since the University of Leuven ceased to use French in the 1960s. The people of Leuven are traditionally known as Peetermannen after their cathedral, St. Peter's, and there is a long-standing rivalry between the Peetermannen and the Guild of St. Lawrence in Brussels. The dispute began when Duke John III of Brabant rewarded the Guild of St. Lawrence for fighting off some Peetermannen in 1308 by allowing them to plant a May Tree, the Meiboom, on the eve of St. Lawrence's name day, 10 August, on the corner of the Rue du Marais and the Rue des Sables. It was also stipulated that if the Guild failed to do so, the privilege would pass to the Peetermannen. Every year the Peetermannen waited for an opportunity to stop the planting of the May Tree and finally succeeded in 1939, when they drove off with it after creating a diversion. The following year the Germans were in control of Brussels, so there was no chance for the Guild of St. Lawrence to gain its revenge. The people of Leuven now plant their own May Tree earlier in the day as they allege that the Guild of St. Lawrence lost its right to plant the real tree. Unfortunately, the St. Lawrence quarter was virtually obliterated by building works during the last century and is one of the least attractive in Brussels. The planting of the Meiboom is nevertheless still a significant event for anyone with connections to this area.

Leuven is home to the oldest university in Belgium, established here in 1425 after the Dukes of Brabant denied permission to start a university in Brussels for fear that it would corrupt young women. The Katholieke Universiteit van Leuven (Catholic University of Leuven), as it is properly called, was officially founded by the Pope and remains the largest Catholic university in Europe. Erasmus taught here in 1504 and visited in 1521 when he was staying in Anderlecht near Brussels; he is remembered by a statue on the Mechelse Straat in Leuven. In the nearby Busleidengang is the Collegium Trilingue founded by Hieronymus Busleyden with the encouragement of Erasmus for the study of Latin, Greek and Hebrew. The religious troubles of the late sixteenth century had their effect on the university, and professors and students alike had to take great care not to fall foul of the Inquisition. Leuven became a haven for English and Irish Catholics escaping persecution at home. There remains a strong affinity between the Flemish and Irish.

On the Monseigneur Ladeuzeplein stands a startling work of art by the Antwerper Jan Fabre, an upside-down beetle impaled on a giant

needle—possibly the most modern, and certainly the most incongruous object one is likely to see in Leuven. Fabre is particularly noted for using body fluids in his work. In 2000 he wrapped pieces of the local Ganda ham around the columns in the entrance of the University of Ghent as part of the art project "Over the Edges". Although the ham was under 24-hour guard, a drunken student still managed to eat some of it.

The other main universities in Flanders, the Universiteit Gent (UGent) and the Universiteit van Antwerpen (UA), were started by freemasons or liberals in the nineteenth century. There is also a small Katholieke Universiteit van Brussel (KUB). The much larger Université Libre de Bruxelles (ULB), started by freemasons, has a Dutch-speaking offshoot, the Vrije Universiteit Brussel (VUB). To become a professor at the University of Leuven it is necessary to be a Catholic. On the other hand, it is difficult to become a professor at a liberal university if you are not a member of the freemasons.

Leuven Vlaams: The Ideology of Language

The Katholieke Universiteit van Leuven was the focus of the final battle in the Flemish struggle against domination by French-speakers and priests. Little thought was given to the use of Dutch in the university until the end of the nineteenth century. Yet the upheavals at the University of Ghent during the First World War, when it was temporarily Dutchified under the German occupation, followed by its conversion to Dutch from 1930, meant that Leuven had to follow suit in some way. The first moves made were to offer courses in both Dutch and French, but French remained the dominant language. There was also the problem of finding space for courses in two languages and staff to teach in Dutch. The rise in the 1950s of the Flemish nationalist party, the Volksunie, and the first moves towards splitting national institutions between Dutch and French placed the top hierarchy, many of them Catholic priests, in a difficult situation. Many of the professors were incapable of giving courses in Dutch or had no knowledge of the Dutch language at all. In 1962 negotiations began in an attempt to find a solution. The Flemish students regularly took to the streets to demand the conversion to Dutch with the slogan, "Leuven Vlaams" (Leuven Flemish). Many students also wanted the university to be secularized— something they have not yet achieved—and the slowness of the Catholic hierarchy to react to their demands gave their protests an anti-clerical tone. The student unions had Marxist as well as Flemish nationalist backers, who were adept at stirring up unrest.

The Flemish could no longer tolerate a French-speaking university in Leuven, in as much as it breached the fundamental principle that all institutions on Flemish territory could only use Dutch. There were, and still are, French-medium schools on Flemish territory, but these do not receive any subsidies from the Flemish Region and are entirely private. French-speakers, for their part, claimed that they were being discriminated against during the Leuven crisis and even took their case to the Council of Europe in Strasbourg, but the reality was rather the opposite. In 1966, for example, the French-speaking students demonstrated against so-called "Flemish racism" with some of them wearing the Star of David. The protests became more intense, if not actually violent. A decision to remove the French-speakers to a new site in Wallonia was finally taken in July 1968 after the Belgian government had fallen over the question. This was a victory for the Flemish students over all the vested, conservative interests of the university and the Belgian establishment. The Belgian Cardinal Suenens and the priesthood were forced to back down, more or less spelling the end of Catholic control over Flemish society. The French-speaking university is now located in Louvain-la-Neuve, to the south of Brussels.

Mechelen

The world-weary Charles Baudelaire thought that "every day feels like Sunday in Mechelen." The French writer Eugène Fromentin (1820-76) was also uncomplimentary: "Only two things have survived from the splendid past of this metropolis, or rather necropolis: the extremely rich altars and the Rubens paintings." This city, it is true, is neglected in comparison with much-restored Bruges and badly signposted to boot, but it has over 300 listed monuments (more than Bruges) and is worth a visit. Unlike Bruges, the authorities had the money to fill in or cover over almost all the canals to stop flooding and disease, but in so doing removed an asset that later might have attracted tourists. The greater tragedy of Mechelen, however, is that it was bombed by both the Allies and the Germans in the Second World War, and the structures raised between historic buildings have a rather temporary appearance in which lack of funds or taste has created an unaesthetic muddle of styles.

But Mechelen was never a Bruges-la-Morte. In the sixteenth century it was a thriving centre of luxury industries including the manufacture of gilded leather wall coverings, gold, silver, pewter, woodcarvings and brass. In the seventeenth and eighteenth centuries the city was reputed for its lace. The first train on the European continent ran from Brussels to Mechelen in 1835, and the town is still home to Belgium's largest railway workshops. Tobias Smollett and other eighteenth-century English writers refer to it as Mechlin; the name is used now in tourist guides. There is a small remnant of the old canal system in the quarter known as 't Groenwaterke, and Mechelen also retains its old harbour front along the River Dijle, with some unusual buildings near the Kraanburg that once belonged to retired sea captains.

Mechelen's glory years were from 1467 to 1530 when it was the capital of the Low Countries and enjoyed the favour of the Habsburgs. Although now a quiet city, it has had a tumultuous past, most of all in the sixteenth century. Philip the Good's reckless son, Charles the Bold, disliked Brussels and moved his court to Mechelen in 1467, attracted in part by the absence of a local count or duke with whom to share taxes. After his death in 1477 his widow, Margaret of York, had the former palace of the bishops of Cambrai, along with seven neighbouring houses, converted into a suitable residence. She then sold it to the city, which handed it on to Maximilian of Austria and Philip the Fair in the hope that they would keep their court in Mechelen. Charles V (1500-55) did not want to remain in the city although he spent much of his early youth there and appointed his aunt, Margaret of Austria, as Regent of the Low Countries. Margaret of York's palace, a large white building on the Keizerstraat, is now the city's theatre (Stadsschouwburg), while on the other side of the street Margaret of Austria's residence—a red and white brick building—houses the law courts. Margaret of Austria decided to move back to Brussels in 1530, to be closer to the hunting forest of Soignes, from which time Mechelen went into decline.

Op-Signoorke: Aerial Doll

The Hof van Busleyden, on the F. de Merodestraat, was once the property of the priest and statesman Hieronymus van Busleyden, who played host to Erasmus and Sir Thomas More. In 1620 it became a charitable institution, the Berg van Barmhartigheid, and continued as such until it was burned down during the First World War. After repairs the city museum was opened here in 1935, becoming at the same time home to an important symbol of the city, "Op-Signoorke". This is a wooden doll or *smijtpop*, which is thrown up in the air using a large cloth during the annual Mechelse Ommegang or city parade held in September. The doll was first made in 1647 and was called Vuile Bruid or Vuile Bruidegom (unfaithful bride or bridegroom) or Sotscop (fool) until 4 July 1775, when he was thrown into the air and landed on the head of a certain Jacobus de Leeuw from Antwerp. The crowd assumed that de Leeuw was trying to steal the doll and thrashed him within an inch of his life. He then took the city to court and this led to a long-standing rivalry between Mechelen and Antwerp. The doll was locked away in a wooden chest, but in 1949 some Antwerp students kidnapped Op-Signoorke and kept him prisoner for a month. (These days he is kept in a glass case.)

At one time it was customary to throw petty criminals in the air from a blanket. If they were unlucky, the blanket was pulled away and they landed on the road. The doll thus serves as a substitute victim for the people of Mechelen. There is a metal statue of Op-Signoorke and his blanket on the Grote Markt in front of the Town Hall near the tourist office. The Brussels playwright Michel de Ghelderode took an unrelated story about a certain Margaret Harstein, who was burned at the stake in Berchem (near Antwerp) in 1555, and created a play, *Hop-Signor* (1936), with the figure of Op-Signoorke in a background role.

Lunatic City

The most visible building in the city is the Sint-Rombouts Cathedral, with a 300-foot tower visible from miles around. The architect, Rombout Keldermans, was commissioned by Margaret of Austria, regent of the Netherlands and sister of Emperor Charles V. The tower was originally intended to be over 500 feet tall, but even so the French military architect Vauban called the shorter tower the Eighth Wonder of the World because of its shallow foundations. The funds to build it were raised by selling indulgences or *aflaeten* to sinners from all around. Work was interrupted by the religious troubles of the sixteenth century, and so the unfeasibly large tower was never completed. The tower has 514 steps and one can see as far as Antwerp and Brussels on a clear day. The church was particularly badly damaged by Iconoclasts in 1567 as it was the seat of the archbishops of the Low Countries.

A nickname for the Mechelaars—*maneblussers* or "moon extinguishers"—refers to an incident in 1687 when a drunkard looked up at the tower silhouetted against the moon and, believing it was on fire, called on the fire brigade to climb the tower to put out the moon. The people of Mechelen duly became the butt of numerous jokes, while the rest of Flanders followed suit with an epidemic of imaginary fires. In 1712 the *maneblussers* tried to put out the sun when they saw a haze rising from a brewery. The people of Diest near Leuven became *zonneblussers* after one of them tried to extinguish the sun in 1728. (The same story is told about Hondschoote in French Flanders.) Clouds of mosquitoes were mistaken for fires in Bruges, Peer in the Kempen and the Abbey of St. Bernard on the Scheldt. The people of Tienen in Vlaams Brabant are also *maneblussers*.

Carillon School,
Mechelen

On the corner of the Grote Markt and the IJzerenleen is a museum of medieval art, the Schepenhuis, the earliest stone town hall in Flanders and the only medieval Flemish town council building left in the region. On the second floor is a large hall that served as the Parliament of Mechelen during 1473-7, the highest court in the Low Countries, with some remnants of the original wall paintings showing the Last Judgment and other hellish scenes as if to remind the judges to do their duty. The building opposite, De Beyaert, became the town hall in the fifteenth century. The present town hall is an amalgamation of the cloth hall (Lakenhalle) the belfry (Belfort) and the Paleis van de Grote Raad, the latter the building where the supreme council of the Netherlands held its meetings during the sixteenth century. It was also designed by Rombout Keldermans between 1526 and 1547, but never completed.

Carillons and Tapestries
Mechelen promotes the ancient Flemish tradition of carillons with a training school for would-be carillon players, the Internationale

Beiaardschool, on the corner of the Sint-Jansstraat and the F. de Merodestraat. The building dates from 1772 and has a keyboard in the front room. Students can be heard practising sophisticated melodies in the nearby octagonal tower all day long, sometimes in competition with nearby churches. Carillon concerts are held every Monday evening between June and September from the Sint-Rombouts tower and the Onze Lieve Vrouw tower.

Mechelen also houses the only privately owned tapestry restoration workshop in Belgium, the Koninklijke Manufactuur De Wit, on the Schoutetstraat. The workshop has developed highly sophisticated techniques for conserving and restoring antique tapestries and also manufactures new ones. Tapestries were important in the past as a way of keeping out drafts in big buildings, and King Philip II of Spain was particularly proud of his collection of Flemish tapestries, carrying 500 of them around with him when he went travelling.

Beethoven and the Physic Garden
Connoisseurs of the great composer (1770-1827) will be aware that Ludwig was called van Beethoven and not von Beethoven; this was a tribute to his Flemish ancestry on his father's side. His name rather prosaically means "turnip patch" in Flemish and his ancestors were peasants from Leuven. His great-great-grandfather was a wine merchant in Leuven, his great-grandfather a tailor in Antwerp and his grandfather, also born in Antwerp, became a *kapellmeister* in Bonn after training as a bass in Leuven, Mechelen and Antwerp. He is registered under the name Lodewijk van Beethoven in 1717 in the Schola Cantorum of Sint-Rombout, Mechelen. The Beethovens were serious drinkers: his great-uncle, the burgomaster of Mechelen, drank himself to death, as did his mother and grandfather. The Steenstraat, where Beethoven's grandfather once lived, fittingly runs past the Lamot brewery. It was renamed the Beethovenstraat in 1936.

The main street that runs past the Botanical Gardens in Mechelen, the Bruul, is familiar to all Belgians as the only Mechelen street to figure in the Belgian version of Monopoly. The Kruidtuin (gardens) is partly a memorial to the Mechelen botanist Rembert Dodoens (1517-85), author of the herbal *Het Cruyteboeck* (1554), the standard work on the subject for 200 years in Europe and the most translated book of its time after the Bible. (Dodoens made a point of writing his book in Flemish, so that it would have to be translated into Latin.) There is a statue of him in a corner of the Kruidtuin, surrounded by 250 kinds of herbs, organized by genus, species and colour. The physic garden of the Erasmushuis in Anderlecht, near Brussels, is also inspired by Dodoens.

Rik Wouters

The painter Rik Wouters (1882-1916) was born in Mechelen. After leaving school he worked as a carpenter in his father's furniture business while following sculpture courses at the academies of Mechelen and Brussels. He was self-taught as a painter. In 1905 he went to live in Watermaal near Brussels with his wife Nel Duerinckx, who was his preferred model. From 1907 the Wouters lived in Bosvoorde, Brussels, and he started to gain deserved artistic success. After escaping imprisonment in 1914, Wouters reached the Netherlands where he was interned in a camp for Belgian deserters, but the following year he became gravely ill with cancer of the jaw and was allowed to go to live in Amsterdam. The many operations he endured did not prevent him from continuing to paint luminous pictures. The Museum of Fine Arts in Antwerp has a self-portrait of a miserable-looking Wouters with a patch over his eye, which has just been removed. He died the same year at the age of thirty-three.

A more cheerful side of Wouters can be seen in his exuberant sculpture *Crazy Girl* (which shows the influence of Rubens) in the open-air sculpture museum in Middelheim, near Antwerp. The largest collection of Wouter's considerable *œuvre* is in the Antwerp Museum of Fine Arts. He is classified as a Brabant Fauvist, the term *fauve*, meaning "wild animal", having been originally applied to Derain and other French artists who used vivid unmixed colours. The thinly applied flecks of paint and bare patches of white canvas create an intense impression of bright sunlight, entirely at odds with the painter's own tragic and painful life. Wouters practised painting on cardboard with thin layers of paint in order to save money, but his technique had more in common with Cézanne's than real Fauvism.

Chapter Eleven
The Kempen and Limburg

"Know: I live with my soul in the light of my blessed dreamland
my pious Kempen has been for centuries.
May she always bloom with deeds and virtues of yore
here in the heart of the poet, faithful in days of deceit."

Lambrecht Lambrechts, 1909

East of Antwerp is an area of some 4,000 square miles of heathland known as the Kempen (or Campine in French). Most of the Belgian provinces of Antwerp and Limburg, as well as North Brabant in the Netherlands, belong to this region. It is bounded to the west by the Scheldt, to the east by the Maas and to the south by the Demer, Dijle and Rupel. The Kempen is generally very flat, primarily covered by heather and small bushes and reeds, overgrazing in the first millennium AD having destroyed the original forests. The underlying sandy soil was deposited by the north wind after the last Ice Age, and recent attempts at reforestation have not always taken account of the fact that much of the soil is not suitable for trees. The name Kempen apparently derives from the Latin Campania, meaning a flat plain. The Romans called this area Taxandria, after a local tribe; the only reminder of this period is the name of the town Tessenderlo. The Ostend animator Raoul Servais made use of the name for his alternative reality film, *Taxandria* (1994), which drew heavily on the Surrealist Paul Delvaux's paintings for its settings.

The Kempen and Limburg have always been peripheral areas as far as the rest of Belgium or the Netherlands are concerned. The ground became infertile by the twelfth century and could not support a large population. The present border artificially cuts the old Limburg in half, although the Belgian half more or less corresponds to the medieval County of Loon. Communities of monks in the early Middle Ages settled here to escape from the rest of the world and tried to improve the soil, but with little success. In the twentieth century Limburg did well

"All is dead quiet in the Beguinage after noon. A crow sits on the copper weathervane while sparrows dance on the cobblestones."
Felix Timmermans, *Begijnhofsproken*, 1917

from coalmining and the car factories around Genk, but mining has now ended, at least temporarily, and the automobile industry has downsized. The post-industrial age may be less kind, but many small firms are relocating here, attracted by Limburg's open spaces. The tourist office makes the justifiable claim that Limburg has eighty square miles of unspoiled countryside, a paradise for walkers and cyclists.

Kempenaars are known as *zandboeren* or "sand farmers". They have had to work hard to make something from the arid soil, more so than their counterparts from the more fertile Haspengouw closer to Liège in southern Limburg. Limburgers, for their part, have more of a reputation for Latin joviality and *joie de vivre*, even if the region is traditionally conservative and Catholic. Despite this, Limburg has had fewer difficulties assimilating immigrants than other parts of Flanders. Before the Second World War many Poles came to work in the mines, and later it was mainly poor Italians who moved to find employment in factories. The immigrants inspired local writers, notably Jos Vandeloo and his *Een mannetje uit Polen* (A Little Boy from Poland, 1965).

Limburg has its own language, a branch of the small Middle German family spoken in the area between Leuven, Maastricht, Aachen and Luxembourg. Speaking a sort of hybrid between Dutch and High German, Limburgers use more German words than other Flemings such as *ich* for "I" and *mich* for "me". Other Flemish tend to think that Limburgers speak with a distinctive singsong accent. Their first great writer, Hendrik van Veldeke, started his translation of the *Aeneid* (which he called the *Eneit*) around 1184 into a language that is neither German nor Dutch but Old Limburgish, and he finished it in Old German after he was appointed court poet to the Pfalzgraf Hermann of Thuringia. Until the nineteenth century it was thought that van Veldeke was German. All that is known about him is that he was born into a noble family in Spalbeek near Hasselt in 1128 and that he died around 1210. There is a statue of van Veldeke in Hasselt, a fairly unremarkable city and the centre of the Belgian gin industry.

Lier and the Sheepheads

Lier is situated close to Antwerp on the edge of the Kempen, described by local writer Felix Timmermans in purple prose: "Where the meandering Nete Rivers tie a silver knot; where the pot-bellied

cornucopia of Brabant divides from the day-dreamy, arid Kempenland."
Romantically inclined etymologists believe that Lier is named after the
Celtic god Lir, but it is more likely that the name merely means "clay".
Lier was once an important textile town, and although it was sacked by
Spanish troops in 1582 and 1595 and later damaged in the First World
War, it has retained much of its original charm. As a tourist destination
it has as much to offer as Leuven and Mechelen, but without the great
historical associations of these two much larger cities. Lier's patron St.
Gummarus built a hut at the confluence of the two rivers in the eighth
century and is regarded the founder of the city. He is supposed to have
married a hideously ugly woman and has since then been invoked in
solving marital disputes.

Lier has a tradition of folkloric processions, giants and societies. Its
inhabitants are rather unflatteringly known as *schapekoppen*
(sheepheads), allegedly because the citizens were offered the chance to
house a university in 1425 but preferred a sheep market. (Another story
has it that they were rewarded for their bravery at the Battle of Neuss in
1475 with a cattle market, but they forgot to ask for a sheep market.)
In any event, the people of Lier take their nickname in good heart and
there is even a Schapekoppenstraat (Sheep Head Street). Lier has some
fine Gothic buildings, the most noteworthy being the Brabant High
Gothic church of St. Gummarus, although the interior is in a rather
overblown Baroque style. The tower is a sort of self-contained history of
Flemish architecture: the square base is Gothic from 1455; the eight-
sided section on top is High Gothic; above this is a late Baroque
eight-sided section; and the whole is topped off in Rococo. The altar
painting is ascribed to Goswin van der Weyden, grandson of Rogier van
der Weyden. St. Gummarus also has a 52-bell carillon weighing thirty
tons, the heaviest eighteenth-century carillon in Europe. Next to St.
Gummarus is the Romanesque chapel of St. Peter dating from around
1225 and restored in 1922, a reminder of a less complicated era of
Christian devotion. The eighteenth-century town hall was built up
against a Gothic belfry, which itself carries four small towers at the
corners. Other Gothic buildings are the Butchers' Hall (Vleeshuis) from
1412, and the chapel of St. Jacob from 1383. The Dominican
Kluizekerk from 1413 has a fine early fifteenth-century statue of St.
Cornelis.

Lier is well known for its Zimmertoren, a tower that was originally part of the city's fourteenth-century defences, when it was called the St. Cornelistoren. After various vicissitudes it was decorated with astronomical symbols and renamed after the local astronomer Louis Zimmer (1888-1970) in 1930. The four quarterboys who strike the hours represent the four phases of the life of man.

Felix Timmermans and Pallieter

Lier has a remarkable complex of beguinages, a cobbled town within a town, with a statue of the beguines' fictitious patron St. Begga over the entrance. This is perhaps the oldest beguinage in the Low Countries, dating from the thirteenth century. Felix Timmermans (1886-1947) drew a great deal on the lives of beguines, and one of his most charming works deals with a beguine who falls in love with a postulant monk, *De zeer schone uren van juffrouw Symforosa* (The Fine Hours of Miss Symforosa, 1918). The Ghent horror writer Jean Ray also situates one of his stories here: *La maison des cigognes* (House of Storks).

Timmermans is Lier's most famous son and the town's greatest promoter. He left school at fourteen and became one of Belgium's most successful writers and illustrators, best known for the character Pallieter, a sort of Flemish Falstaff with a liking for excess, who first appeared in 1916. The adventures of the rambunctious Pallieter inevitably upset the Catholic clergy, but Timmermans had his own view of religion, which started from his love of nature and his native town. He transposed the story of the Nativity to Lier in *Het kindeken Jezus* (The Little Child Jesus, 1917):

> ... and in those days, when Joseph and Mary heard the glad news that the evil King Herod was dead, they quickly left the tidy village in Zeeland by the Scheldt, where they had lived quietly, in peace and unknown to anyone, and they came through the Kempen to put up their tents at the spot called Nazareth, situated on the dear River Nete.

Timmermans represents a style of literature that is termed *heimatliteratuur*, an unsophisticated type of folkloric literature popular before the Second World War. He has remained more popular than the other great exponent of this genre, Stijn Streuvels, mainly because he is easier to read and uses a more standard Dutch than Streuvels. Timmermans came under suspicion as an alleged collaborator after the war, and the extreme right-wing magazine, *'t Pallieterke*, has appropriated the name of his immortal character, Pallieter. There is a museum dedicated to Timmermans on the banks of the Kleine Nete, the Timmermans-Opsomer Huis. The only work by Timmermans available in English is a hagiography: *The Perfect Joy of St. Francis* (1998).

Haspengouw

The Haspengouw is an area of undulating hills and valleys, forming the eastern end of a low clay plateau, with elevations from 250 feet in the north to 700 feet in the south. Its historical origins lie in the *Pagus Hasbaniae*, part of the central swathe of Charlemagne's empire which became Lotharingia, and finally came under the control of the Holy Roman Empire. The name means "jurisdiction of the Hessians". Split by the language frontier (in Wallonia it is known as La Hesbaye), it is bounded on the south and east by the Meuse as far as Namur, in the west by the watershed of the Dijle and Grote Gete rivers, and in the north by a line running from Tienen through St. Truiden to Veldwezelt. Haspengouw is known for fruit-growing these days, in particular apples and cherries around Borgloon, Sint Truiden and Tongeren.

Hasselt is now the provincial capital of Limburg, but Tongeren is far older and more attractive to visitors. In the pre-Roman era the town was known as Atuatuca, but after the local Celtic leader Ambiorix defeated Julius Caesar by a ruse in 54 BC, his people, the Eburones, were exterminated in reprisal, to be replaced by the more peaceful Tungri. The Romans then named the city Atuatuca Tungrorum. Ambiorix's statue, with an Asterix-style winged helmet, now looks up at the Basilica of Our Lady (see p.2). Some Roman remains can be seen outside the cathedral; part of the city wall dates back to the second century AD. Nearby is Belgium's main Gallo-Roman Museum. Tongeren has retained a backwater charm as it has not expanded outside its medieval walls.

The Basilica of Our Lady was the first church to be dedicated to the Virgin Mary north of the Alps. St. Maternus, who was responsible for converting the local population to Christianity, dedicated a small wooden church here in 315 AD. The first bishop of Tongeren, St. Servaas (or Servatius), appointed in 343, erected a cathedral—the

Autumn in the Haspengouw

"Flanders, our lavish home, where we are guests at rich tables,
who can know you and not rejoice at heart;
not be thankful for days, beautiful as triumphant young gods,
like a beggar is thankful for warm wheat loaves."

Karel van de Woestijne, *The Orchard of Birds and Fruit*, 1905 foundations are visible in the crypt of the current church and are soon to form part of a new tourist attraction. A Romanesque chapterhouse, apparently made from local flint, burned down in 1213. For a while it was not replaced, but then in 1240 the city decided to put up a much more ambitious structure in marl sandstone in the latest Gothic style, reflecting Tongeren's prosperity. Yet as with many other cities in Flanders, the plans had to be changed as work went on because funding became restricted, and it took until 1541 to complete the work. The church is striking because of its position on a hill, where it can be seen from far away, and also because of its oddly trapezoidal shape, with a broad base and narrow top. There are differences in style between the lower and upper layers of the church, as also between the older east and the newer west side of the nave. The tower was meant to have a tall spire, but only a part was ever built, a thirty-foot extension that was meant to take the spire. A rumour started in 1990 that the tower was in danger of falling down and, thanks to widespread media coverage, the city had no difficulty in assembling funds for repair work.

At the back of the church are the original Romanesque cloisters or *claustrum*, dating back to the twelfth century. The cloisters have three sides (where they originally had four) and are unusual in having survived to the present day. Another attraction is the church's treasury, the most significant piece being a highly decorated sixth-century Frankish brooch, along with other pre-Reformation masterpieces. Ten side-chapels were added on at the request of the guilds and other societies, and it is hard to miss the many recent statues of saints with their typical attributes who stand around the walls. The cult of the Virgin has been central to the church for most of its history. In the ninth century an image is supposed to have appeared spontaneously in the new Carolingian church. Another Madonna was installed in 1479 and credited with a miracle. Two men from Tongeren were captured by the Turks while taking part in the Seventh Crusade. They directed their prayers to the Virgin Mary at home in Tongeren and were understandably surprised to find themselves transported back to the altar in Tongeren, with their chains still attached. The miraculous statue is now in the north transept. Tongeren became a place of pilgrimage, and the tradition still continues. In 1890 the Bishop of Liège instituted the custom of crowning the Virgin, who is then taken around the town in a procession. The ceremony only takes place once every seven years, and attracts up to 300,000 people. The next procession is due in 2009.

The Maas and Georges Simenon

The River Maas, or Meuse in French, the largest river in Holland after the Rhine, starts out in France at Pouilly-en-Bassigny in the Haute Marne, flows through Wallonia, the gorge at Dinant, the city of Liège and under the bridges of Maastricht, and then forms the border with Holland until it leaves Belgium north of Maaseik (the birthplace of the painters of the *Mystic Lamb*, Hubert and Jan Van Eyck). The river is prone to flooding; the most recent major floods were in 1995. It is supposed that the name Maas comes from a Finnish word for rolling river, which seems to point to a prehistoric population of Finns in Wallonia.

The Liège-born writer Georges Simenon (1903-89) rarely set his novels in Belgium because he wanted to be accepted as a French writer (he wrote exclusively in French). One rare exception is *La maison du canal* (The House by the Canal, 1932) situated in an isolated house a few hundred yards from the Zuid Willemsvaart to the west of the Maas. Simenon calls the house *De Wateringen*, meaning drainage ditches, as the area around it was once marshland but was drained to become hayfields. The first supervisor of the drainage ditches was Simenon's maternal grandfather, a certain Wilhelm Brüll, a German who had moved to Belgium in 1854. The house that came with his job evidently remained in Simenon's family, and the young Georges came to stay in 1915 or 1916, when he was twelve or thirteen. Now called Watering 1, the house stands in the commune of Elen, now part of Dilsen-Stokkem. The family living there at the time provided Simenon with the characters for his later novel, including the murderer Fred, named after a boy called Alfred, who was only four years older than Simenon himself. The rest of the characters have greatly exaggerated personality traits, based on real people Simenon remembered from his stay. The house, at least as it exists today, is not the desolate place that Simenon makes it out to be, nor does it rain all the time.

Simenon's ancestors on his father's side lived for many years in Vlijtingen, near the Dutch border, only settling down in Liège in 1874. Simenon was hostile towards the Flemish, largely because his mother was

Flemish, and the violent and distasteful characters in *La maison du canal* seem to represent a rejection of Simenon's Flemish roots. Still Simenon was more Flemish than anything else, not least in his enormous output and drive suggestive of a Flemish work ethic.

Sint Truiden and Aldous Huxley

Sint Truiden (or Saint Trond in French) is in the south-west of Belgian Limburg. A small market town in the fruit-growing area of the Haspengouw, it was founded by the Frankish St. Trudo in 650 AD and was one of the 23 cities that made up the Prince-Bishopric of Liège until 1792. St. Truiden would have attracted little notice from the English literary world had it not been for the stay of Aldous Huxley in 1919. Huxley was brought to Sint Truiden by a young Flemish woman, Maria Nys (1898-1958), whom he had met when she was a guest of Ottoline Morrell at Garsington Manor near Oxford in 1916. Maria Nys had left for England in 1914 and became the mascot of the Bloomsbury set. Huxley was mesmerized by her beauty. He wrote to his brother Julian: "I have finally met an amusing Belgian. Wonders will never cease." All the glitterati of the time were at Garsington, but Nys was penniless and had to beg for favours. She was more interested in women than men and first fell in love with Lady Ottoline Morrell and then with Virginia Woolf, both of whom rejected her advances. She was thrown out of Garsington after she tried to kill herself by drinking bleach.

In April 1919 Huxley went to Sint Truiden and stayed with relatives of Maria. By all accounts he worked on his first novel, *Crome Yellow*, in the Astoria restaurant, now renamed Het Theater; there is a plaque to this effect on the wall. Huxley talks of his time in Sint Truiden in his short story *Uncle Spencer* in the collection called *Little Mexican* (1924). Parts of *Point Counter Point* (1928) were also written here. Huxley writes in a letter from the "Grand' Place, St. Trond" soon after he arrived:

> Here I am, settled down in this rather oddly un-English life. A quite Balzacian Ville de Province, where nothing happen and where everybody who is anybody is everybody else's relation... I think they are fairly reassured by my appearance. They had, I fancy, rather anticipated a roaring lion: they are relieved to find a sheep. We are just going on a trip to the Nys' destroyed home in East Flanders,

"Few are cultured, the rest not at all."
The Huxleys in 1932

sightseeing in Brussels, Ghent and Bruges by the way. I wonder if you could send me five pounds' worth of Belgian money in a registered envelope.

Huxley was astounded by the pig market in Sint Truiden but less impressed by the local middle classes: "Few are cultured, the rest not at all." The Huxleys were married in July 1919 at the town hall in Bellem, near Aalter in East Flanders, without much ceremony. Nys' father had a wool factory nearby. Both families were opposed to the marriage; the witness was a local butcher. On their return to Sint Truiden they moved into a rented house at 29 Stationstraat. Their time here was short, and they left for London soon after. Maria Huxley had a son, Matthew, whom she called Tcheunke—a local dialect nickname for Mathieu—and a character in Huxley's short story *Uncle Spencer*.

Huxley's interest proved to be rather superficial—intimate relationships were not his strong point—and the marriage went sour quite quickly. Maria Nys Huxley's real love was an Italian woman by the name of Costanza Fasola, and Nys became one of the twentieth century's great *femmes fatales*, living at the heart of the literary and artistic movements of her time. She was by D. H. Lawrence's bedside when he died. (It was said that she had altered *Lady Chatterley's Lover*.) In Hollywood she had affairs with Greta Garbo, Marlene Dietrich and Audrey Hepburn (Hepburn was born in Brussels). She was a close friend of Charlie Chaplin and Igor Stravinsky, held séances, dabbled in palmistry and astrology, experimented with mescaline and other hallucinogenic drugs along with her husband, and was psychoanalysed by the anti-guru Jiddu Krishnamurti. The Antwerp thriller writer Stan Lauryssens compiled Maria Nys' biography on the basis of the letters she sent to her family in Belgium, which he found in the Bibliothèque Royale in Brussels. *Mijn heerlijke nieuwe wereld* (Welcome to My Brave New World, 2001) may soon become a major motion picture.

Chapter Twelve

New Landscapes and Dutch Flanders

"Between the sugar beet fields and the flax
Like the Pope in his sedan chair
The top half of a coaster sometimes glides along."
Martien J. G. de Jong, *Zeeuwsch-Vlaanderen*, 1979

Zeeuws Vlaanderen, or Dutch Flanders, forms part of the province of Zeeland, a collection of islands and peninsulas joined by giant bridges and tunnels. Zeeuws Vlaanderen is not itself an island, but rather the southern side of the Scheldt estuary, connected to the rest of the Netherlands by a tunnel. Here people tend to feel more connected to Belgian Flanders than to the provincial capital of Middelburg on the island of Walcheren. On Mercator and Ortelius' maps of the sixteenth century the western end of the Scheldt estuary is shown as Den Dullaert and the eastern end as De Honte. The name Honte is still remembered in the village of Hontenisse. With the Eighty Years' War between the Dutch and Spanish, the area became a frontier battleground. In 1583 the Count of Parma took Hulst before it was retaken by the Dutch Prince Maurits in 1591, and then recaptured by the Spanish in 1596. The English poet Sir Philip Sidney (1554-86), who later died fighting for the Protestant cause at the Battle of Zutphen, was instrumental in ensuring that the town of Axel near Terneuzen was permanently freed from the Spanish in 1586. From this time onwards the part of Flanders in Dutch hands was called Staats Vlaanderen, the Staten being the Dutch federal parliament.

The area's economy was ruined by natural floods, as well as by tactical flooding in 1583-4. The Spanish intended Hulst to be an impregnable fortress, but the Dutch Prince Frederik Hendrik still managed to take it in 1645. Between 1794 and 1814 Zeeuws Vlaanderen

Cadzand beach huts

was part of the French province of L'Escaut (Scheldt). With the defeat of Napoleon, the south bank of the Scheldt became part of the Dutch province of Zeeland, that is Zeeuws Vlaanderen. To the rest of the Dutch, Zeeuws Vlaanderen signifies heavy industry and holiday resorts. Linguistically, Zeeuws Vlaanderen can be divided into two. The western half is linked with West Flemish and the eastern half, logically enough, with East Flemish. The language is more standardized here than in Belgium, dialect being only spoken at home and not used with outsiders. The houses are in the Dutch style, small and often surrounded by trees to keep out the freezing winds.

Changing Landscapes
The Romans built fortresses at Aardenburg and Oostburg. Count Baldwin IV of Flanders was given Zeeuws Vlaanderen as a fief from the Holy Roman Emperor in 1014. Sint-Anna-ter-Muiden was a Hanseatic port, and Sluis a natural entrance to Flanders from England. In the Middle Ages the port of Sluis was an island, as was Cadzand, with two

smaller islands near them, Wulpen and Koezand. The German *Gudrunsage* from the ninth century mentions battles against the Vikings on Wulpen, which is often called the "legendary island of Wulpen". Willem Brakman refers to it in *Een winterreis* (A Winter Journey, 1961):

> An island at that time right before the very stormy coast, "three hours long", with farms, wheatfields and a church founded by St. Willibrord. Between the island and the land there was the so-called "horse market", a white-maned piece of sea that had taken centuries to eat up the island.

Brakman is one of the most prolific and popular Dutch authors of recent times, born in The Hague but with parents originally from the Terneuzen region. *Een winterreis*, his first novel, charts his return to Terneuzen in search of his roots. The novel mixes real and fictitious streets in the area; the story starts in a café in Hulst, Het Bonte Hert. Akijn (the main character, but clearly Brakman himself) travels around Hulst, Terneuzen and Duindorp, describes meeting an uncle who has drawn up a family tree and explores his relationship with his father, who happened to have a large nose, or *neuze* in the local dialect. (Terneuzen was once on a spit of land shaped like a nose.)

Cadzand and Groede

Cadzand is the first seaside resort northwards after the Belgian border. The contrast with its Belgian equivalents is striking; there are few restaurants or hotels on the beach itself, but a plethora of houses and caravans discreetly hidden away behind dunes and walls. From here towards Belgium it is a short distance to the beauty of Het Zwin, a nature reserve where rare birds breed, again with houses well concealed. This was where the River Zwin came to meet the sea in Bruges' heyday; now there is only the Zwingeul or ditch, which floods at high tide. Cadzand was an island until the creation of polders in the seventeenth century attached it to the mainland. In 1613 large numbers of French Huguenots landed at Cadzand and some of them settled in the area. There was another wave of immigration in 1733 of Lutherans from Salzburg in Austria, who had their own church in Groede, today a small tourist village between Cadzand and Breskens.

Lodovico Guicciardini, *Descrittione di Tutti i Paesi Bassi*, Antwerp, 1561.

The Dutch writer Frans Erens (1857-1942) suggests in *Stille steden* (Silent Cities, 1906) that immigration made the locals less inclined to joking:

> Especially in the land of Cadzand, where the population consists of descendants of exiles and immigrant Salzburgers and Huguenots, the inhabitants are subdued in heart and soul. As a result, their character has suffered and there is perhaps no region in all of the Netherlands which is less susceptible to pure humour than this one. The people are not naïve, and when a people are not naïve, then they are lacking a very creative spiritual characteristic.

The village of Groede has its own unusual identity. The old brick church is in need of restoration; outside is a statue of Jacob Cats (1577-1660), a writer of classical Dutch poetry who gave up his law practice in Middelburg and came here to reclaim twelve polders in the area during the Twelve Years Truce between the Dutch and the Spanish from 1609 to 1621. His efforts were mostly wasted, as his polders were flooded to frustrate the Spanish. Cats' verse is Dutch Miltonian, in the "nymphs and shepherds come away" vein. The Molenstraat and Slijkstraat have been turned into a row of tourist shops and museums known as Het Vlaemsche Erfgoed (Flemish Heritage). The Slijkstraat (Mud Street) has a mysterious bench, with "Lie Bench" written on it in English—in other words, a traditional Dutch Leugenbank where old people tell each other tall stories. Near Groede are sandy beaches, a constant procession of ships to and from Terneuzen and Antwerp and a view across to the port of Vlissingen or Flushing.

Balzac's short morality tale *Jésus-Christ en Flandre* (1831) opens in Cadzand at some imaginary time in the early Middle Ages.

> At some time in the far distant past wealthy Ostend was an unknown harbour, flanked by a citadel timidly populated by some fishermen, poor traders and unpunished pirates. Nevertheless the stronghold of Ostend made up of some 20 houses and 300 huts, cottages and slums made of the debris of wrecked ships had a governor, a militia, gallows, a convent, a mayor and indeed all the parts of an advanced civilization.

The bark which was to take the travellers from the Island of Cadzand to Ostend was about to cast off. Before detaching the iron chain that fixed the sloop to a stone on the little jetty where you embarked, the captain blew several times on his horn to call the laggards, because this was the last voyage. Night was approaching, the last embers of the setting sun made it barely possible to make out the Flemish coast or to make out the latecomers, wandering either along the earth walls surrounding the fields, or between the tall reeds.

A stranger in plain dress with an authoritative air is last to board. A storm rises and the passengers start to panic. A merchant, kneeling on sacks of gold, prays to the Virgin Mary: "Our Lady Saviouress who art in Antwerp, I promise you 1,000 pounds of wax and a statue if you get me out of this." A bishop blesses the waves and orders them to calm but without success—as he is too busy thinking of his girlfriend. Then the Saviour, the stranger, guides the boat until they are fifty paces from the shore at Ostend. He tells those who have faith in him to follow and he walks on the water to dry land. All the sinners sink to the bottom of the sea, while those with faith reach dry land. The bishop, who falls into the former category, has too much faith in graven images and too little understanding of real religion. In Balzac's version, the Convent of Thanks was built for sailors at a place where the imprint of Christ's feet in the sand could be seen. In 1793, when the French entered Belgium, the monks took away this precious relic, evidence of Jesus' last visit to this earth. (Balzac's tale has been translated into English as *Jesus Christ in Flanders*.)

Sluis

When Bruges was in its heyday Sluis (which means "lock") stood on the same River Zwin that brought goods to the port of Damme. Sluis is now connected by reclaimed land to Cadzand and Oostburg. In 1340 King Edward III of England won a great victory against the French here and destroyed 200 of their ships. This was also the preserve of the *watergeuzen* or "sea beggars", Protestant rebels who fought the Spanish from fast, shallow boats. From here Emperor Charles V and Philip II of Spain set out to punish the recalcitrant Dutch and came back with a bloody nose. Prince Maurice captured the area from the Spanish in 1604.

The people of Sluis also owed much to a bell-ringer by the name of Jantje who neglected to ring the bell after drinking too much at a fair. The Spanish were waiting for the bell to ring to start their attack, but the signal never came. The hero Jantje van Sluis is now remembered in the form of a *jacquemart* or quarterboy who rings the bell—on time of course—from the tower of the Belfort. There is also a beer named after him, made in Ertvelde near Ghent.

Sluis was completely destroyed in the Second World War, but has been sympathetically restored. It is now a holiday town, much favoured by tourists from Germany. The city was home to the first great Dutch dictionary-maker, Johan Hendrik Van Dale (1828-1872), the headmaster and archivist of the town. He started his dictionary a few years before he died from smallpox and never saw it published, but he became a national figure posthumously. The name Van Dale is equivalent to the Oxford English Dictionary in the Netherlands and in Belgium, which does not have its own separate standard dictionary (because of reluctance to recognize Belgian Dutch as an official language). Only Dutch publishers have the resources to produce a large dictionary, it seems, and Van Dale covers both types of Dutch. Even so, Van Dale's dictionary work does not enjoy universal approval; a spoof website, Schandale (Scandal), lists all his mistakes.

The largest hotel in town is called "De Dikke Van Dale", the "Big Van Dale", as the dictionary's creator was apparently of small stature. There is a statue of the great man by the tourist office, which has been sandblasted and painted bright gold. Van Dale owed much of his success to the fact that he came from a border area near Belgium on the fringes of the Netherlands. His parents were from Eeklo in Flanders, and his statue looks south to where his roots lay. He certainly spoke West Flemish dialect; his impartial approach towards Belgian Dutch—Van Dale lists "Zuidnederlands" or southern Dutch words—made him acceptable to the Belgians. The term Zuidnederlands is applied to all dialects south of the great rivers, the Rhine, IJssel and Maas, thus the southern Netherlands, but this no longer holds much water, as the language of the southern Netherlands is more or less standard Dutch. The Dutch refer to the southern Netherlands as "onder de Moerdijk" (beneath the Moerdijk, or great rivers), where the people resemble the Belgians (an unflattering reference to their supposed lack of intelligence).

Sluis and its surrounding area along the Belgian border have another more sinister reputation as the haunt of smugglers bringing drugs from Holland through Belgium to France. In the 1960s Belgians came to Holland to buy butter, pornography and Bols (a kind of Dutch gin) to take home and were shot at by Belgian police for their trouble. The local tourist offices have made this into an attraction by signposting a "Smokkelroute"—smugglers' route—through the polder landscape.

Hulst and Reinaert the Fox

Towards the eastern end of Zeeuws Vlaanderen, close to Sint Niklaas, is the small town of Hulst. The name means "holly" and the town's shield is surrounded by holly leaves. Hulst prides itself on being the "fortress city", its star-shaped walls still visible from the air; on the ground are eighteenth-century city gates and battlements. In 1315 Hulst was linked to Ghent by a canal, while the Hulsterhaven, a tributary of the Scheldt, linked it with the sea. The eastern half of Zeeuws Vlaanderen at one time consisted of the Vier Ambachten, or Four Guilds, of Hulst, Axel,

Assenede and Boekhoute. The name Four Guilds refers to the organization of four *waterschappen* or water boards, formed to build and maintain dikes. South and west of Hulst were *moeren*, peat bogs which provided fuel. The peat absorbed seawater from flooding; after burning the peat the ash was heated with seawater, giving salt. There was once a substantial linen industry here, and the Museum De Vier Ambachten in Hulst has an exhibition of linen making. Zeeuws Vlaanderen produced flax similar to that of the Belgian Waasland, with blue flowers, less valuable than that of the Lys Valley in West Flanders. The flax was processed in people's houses, and rather than being rotted in a river, as in West Flanders, it was laid out on the fields for the dew to soften it. A local riddle tells us:

When I was young and pretty
I had a blue crown.
When I became old and stiff
They bound a rope around my body.
Then I was broken
Bruised and beaten,
And later worn by princes and counts.

Hulst also had a railway and factories. The Dutch writer Ferdinand Bordewijk writes of a couple of immigrants coming to Hulst to search for work and their reaction to the noise from the shipyard, in *Hulst I. Werf* (Hulst I Wharf, 1950).

Next to the Gentpoort or Ghent Gate stands the statue of Reinaert the Fox, the cunning tormentor of other animals in the twelfth-century saga, *Van den Vos Reynaerde* (see p.100), with his pilgrim's staff and bag made from a piece of Bruin the Bear's fur. Rainaert's connection with Hulst rests on a few verses where he narrowly escapes being hanged by deceiving King Noble the Lion into believing that he has hidden a treasure next to a birch tree in a peat bog:

At the eastern end of Flanders lies
A forest called Hulsterlo.
Not far from there, to the southwest
Is the meandering creek called the Kriekeputte.

This is one of the biggest wildernesses
That you could find in any kingdom.
I tell you, truthfully
That sometimes in half a year
Comes neither man nor woman
To this place.

In his final gesture of defiance, Reinaert sends the severed head of Cuwart the Hare back to King Noble in the pilgrim's bag the king had made for him to take to the Holy Land. For Hulst, Reinaert is a symbol of independence and resourcefulness, even if few have read the original story. This is not bedtime reading for children, but rather a darkly medieval tale of human baseness.

Chapter Thirteen
French Flanders

"When the Flemish between Wissant and Bruges
In fear of the waves washing against their shores
Build dikes to drive away the sea…"

Dante, *Inferno*, Canto XV, 1312

The coast of French Flanders is nowadays very different from how it must have been in Dante's time. The coastline first emerged in 2000 BC, and was then flooded again on three occasions by the Dunkirk Transgressions (see p.xv). Today's coast was an expanse of islands and estuaries when Pliny the Elder wrote his account (77 AD) of people living on artificial hills in the middle of the sea, which certainly refers to this area. The first maps show the sea penetrating as far as Saint-Omer. At the time of the Roman invasion the present region of the Nord-Pas-de-Calais was inhabited by the Celtic Menapii tribe and by the Morini in the south-west between Boulogne and the River Aa. Virgil speaks of "the Morini at the end of the world" in his *Aeneid*.

From the fourth century more Germanic peoples, Angles, Saxons, Frisians and Jutes, settled along the coast, encouraged by the Romans to defend the coastline against invaders (the so-called *litus Saxonicum*). Hence the existence of Anglo-Saxon place names around the coast, such as Fréthun (Freetown), a stop on the Eurostar railway line near Calais. The Salian Franks then arrived here in the seventh century. Arnulf I, Count of Flanders, expanded his territory as far as he could to the south in the face of the French king, and by 962 he had taken over an area as far south as Artois. French Flanders remained a stable part of Flanders under subsequent foreign rulers, namely the Burgundians, Habsburgs and Spanish. King Louis XIV of France aimed to expand his kingdom and successfully incorporated an area between Douai and Dunkirk between 1659 and 1679. The plan was to annex all of Belgium, but this was all he could conquer.

"No dawn whitened the dead sky, only the blast
furnaces flamed the darkness with blood, giving
no light to the stranger."
Emile Zola, *Germinal*, 1885

Smugglers and Heretics

From the thirteenth century the area of Hondschoote, near Dunkirk, became the centre of a textile industry based on cheap woollen cloth known as *sayes* or serge. A more egalitarian and independent culture developed here than in the main textile cities of Bruges, Ghent and Ypres, and the weavers were easily won over to the ideas of the Reformation.

The Protestant Iconoclast movement began in French Flanders in August 1566 with a *hagepreek* (hedge sermon) held at the Cloostervelt near Hondschoote during a traditional pilgrimage to the Chapel of St. Lawrence in Steenvoorde, which ended with the destruction of the chapel. (To atone for this misdeed the Catholic Church built a Geuzenkapel or "Protestant Chapel" at the Cloostervelt in 1888, located by the side of the D66 to Killem.) The Iconoclasts burned or smashed religious images and brought animals allegedly used by witches into churches as a sign of their rejection of the corruption of the Catholic Church. Roving bands of armed Calvinists, whose leaders were trained in England, attacked remote churches and murdered priests wherever there was no one to guard them. From French Flanders the violence spread north to the rest of Flanders.

The Spanish authorities quickly restored order and within months the Catholic rites were being celebrated again, while the heretics were tortured and executed. Those who were guilty of less serious crimes were either banished for life or had to pay fines to the Church. Just across the border from Belle (Bailleul) at Nieuwkerke one can see three stained glass windows in the neo-Gothic Onze Lieve Vrouwkerk of Catholic priests being murdered by Protestant weavers at nearby Reningelst on 12 January 1568. This event is known as Verlorenmaandag (Lost Monday), but the stained glass only dates from 1924.

For those who still speak Flemish in this region, the border is known as *de schreve* (meaning something like "drawn line") and the Flemish spoken is *Vlamsch over de schreve* (from over the border). As with all borderlands there are ample opportunities to make money by smuggling cheaper goods from the other side of the frontier—in this case cigarettes. As tobacco is now less expensive in Belgium than in France, there are now dozens of cigarette warehouses all along the border, which are hugely popular with British smugglers. The frontier still has something *louche* about it, with truckers' cafés and Union Jacks flying over the cheap tobacco stores. The French-Belgian border is also a crossing point for drugs from the Netherlands, but in the past the locals mainly smuggled tobacco into France while taking rabbit skins back into Belgium. The local poet, Jean-Noël Ternynck, born in Steenvoorde in 1946, writes in his Flemish dialect about smuggling brown sugar by bicycle on the muddy backroads from Watou in Belgian Flanders in the 1950s in his collection *Van de Leie toet de zee* (From the Leie to the Sea, 1998).

Smuggling was known locally as *blauwe*—"to blue"—and the archetypal smuggler was Jan de Blauwer (even if his real name was Jan Van de Velde). The *blauwers* carried on a remorseless battle against the *kommiezen* or police, who stayed out at night in sleeping bags with their guns at the ready. A favourite trick was to carry a false gasoline tank on a motorcycle in which to hide contraband. With the inauguration of the European Economic Community in 1956, goods no longer had to be smuggled, and many a smuggler published his or her memoirs, most notably Albert Capoen and his *Confessions d'un fraudeur Flamand* (1996). The local tourist office has seen an opportunity here as well: around the Mont des Cats are signs leading to "Estaminet-Fraude", a smuggler's café and a Musée de la Vie Frontalière (Museum of Frontier Life) at Rue des Calicannes in Godewaersvelde. The local nerve centre of the Flemish cultural movement, 't Blauwershof in Godewaersvelde, keeps a well-stocked library of such confessions as well as an extensive collection of traditional Flemish café games.

Flemish in France

The Flemish language was brought here by invading Salic Franks from the fifth century AD; the evidence is apparent from all the place names ending in –hem, -voorde, -becque, -brouck and so on, while the original population mainly have Flemish surnames. By the sixth century proto-Dutch was spoken as far south as Etaples on the coast, but by the fourteenth the language border had retreated to Wissant (or Witsant in Flemish). Until the Second World War, Dunkirk was part of the Flemish area, but the coastal region has very few Flemish-speakers now. The Dutch language, or rather the local dialect, is now only spoken by a dwindling number of elderly people and a few younger enthusiasts. The area around Steenvoorde and Hazebrouck is the most Flemish of all, known as *Cœur de Flandre* (Heart of Flanders). Further to the east,

Flemish was first replaced by the French dialect, Picard, and then by standard French. The Flemish nationalist organization, Michiel de Swaen Kring, estimates that there are 100,000 people who speak some Flemish in the French *département* of the Nord, a very optimistic assessment. Perhaps only 20,000 actually use the language on a daily basis. Those who were actually brought up speaking Flemish are now mostly over sixty and are dying out. Almost no one under the age of twenty knows a word of Dutch, unless they have studied it in school.

The future of Flemish in France hangs by a thread. Unlike other minority languages such as Breton, Corsican, Occitan, Alsatian and Basque, Flemish (and its neighbour, Picard) has no official status and, therefore little support, something that Flemish nationalists see as nothing other than anti-Germanic prejudice. A start was made in the 1980s to allow the teaching of Dutch in some schools, in particular in Bailleul and Wervik, but there was no funding to support such an initiative and little coordination with local academics and experts. These days children in Bailleul learn Dutch at school after a difficult choice was made between the local dialect of Flemish and standard Dutch. Quite reasonably, standard Dutch was chosen, but there is still confusion among non-Dutch speakers as to which language is being taught. The local "South" Flemish does not have a standard written form, which more or less excludes it from contention. Because it has been isolated from standard Dutch for so long, South Flemish is more archaic than that north of the border; it is a variant of the south-western dialect of the Westhoek, itself a form of West Flemish. There are many local French-speaking people who want to retain the language along with their Flemish culture, but for most it is not practical to master standard Dutch when only tourists are likely to speak it. There is also the fact that the Flemish nationalist movement and its far-right fellow travellers put off many French people from taking an interest in their Flemish heritage. Yet knowledge of Dutch could have real benefits in this area of very high unemployment. About 25,000 French commute to work across the border to West Flanders every day.

Paris against Flanders

In 1922 Georges Blachon wrote in *Pourquoi j'aime la Flandre* (Why I Love Flanders):

There is in France a hostility against Flanders and the Flemish which
does not diminish in the face of any disapproval and which I cannot
give its real name, because it is too ugly. Everything that touches
them, everything that comes from them, is placed on the list of
banned publications and has to constantly change its name to be
accepted. To such a degree that you only have to react against this
appalling phobia to appear to fall into the opposite camp. In any case,
what harm would there be if Flanders received more bouquets than
brickbats for once?

Like French-speakers in Belgium, the French state does not fully grasp
the grievances of the Flemish. A measure of folklore and the odd local
festival are quite acceptable but any demands for greater recognition are
not. The Flemish nationalists, among other things, wish to see the name
of their French region, Nord-Pas-de-Calais changed to Les Pays Bas
Français (French Low Countries). The French *départements* were created
by the Jacobins in 1792 in order to break down the sense of local identity
and the regions created in the 1960s continue the same tradition. As it
is, the inhabitants are now called *nordistes*, a recently invented name that
infuriates Flemish nationalists.
    Blachon continues:

> When detractors state in principle that the Fleming is a stupid
> Boeotian, an inferior being, brutalized by work and trading, then
> they are referring to the ordinary Flemish in France. The Flemish
> in France have been relegated to the lowest ranks of humanity by
> the anti-North administration, while the Flemish of old Flanders
> have retained their universal esteem.

To be Germanic is an offence against French culture:

> The South—Le Midi—is the centre of Latin culture, while the
> North is relegated to a lower rank, thus the Flemish are forced
> to look towards the Germans for support. The French in the
> North did not wish to learn Flemish (after 1918) at the
> universities; the Flemish in France have had to give up their
> language to be accepted as French. The Bretons do not suffer

that kind of discrimination. The Nord is useful because it produces a lot, but it doesn't get any special status from the central government.

The geographical boundary of Flanders was always the River Aa. North of here the Flemish plain stretches to the Scheldt, and traditional culture is much the same as in Flanders (if one defines Flemishness by the visible symbols of windmills, cock fighting, beer, archery and carnival giants). French Flanders also once had many Belforts—the towers intended to express civic pride. The finest Belfort in Flanders at St. Winoksbergen (French: Bergues) was blown up by the Germans in 1944 and rebuilt in 1961. The Belfort in Lille is a concrete replica. More pertinently, the poverty of the Nord makes it more Flemish in a way than Belgian Flanders, which is dominated by large-scale agribusiness and industry. The chain of hills running from Dunkirk through Cassel and north to Ypres is another feature that gives the landscape more variety than to the north. Charles Dickens wrote of the region in *The Uncommercial Traveller* (1868):

> It is neither a bold nor a diversified country, said I to myself, this country which is three-quarters Flemish and a quarter French; yet it has its attractions too. Though great lines of railways traverse it, the trains leave it behind, and go puffing off to Paris and the South, to Belgium and Germany, to the Northern Sea-Coast of France, and to England, and rarely smoke it a little in passing.

The Coalfields and *Germinal*

The old *bassin minier* or coal-mining area is mainly concentrated in a band south of Lille, between St.-Paul-en-Ternoise in the west and Valenciennes in the east, in the old county of Artois. Coal was first mined around 1660 near Boulogne. After the 1713 Treaty of Utrecht cut France off from its coal supplies in Belgium, new coalfields had to be developed in the Nord, until the area finally became the main source of coal and the most industrialized in France by the time of the industrial revolution. The coalmines have now all closed, along with much of the textile industry that was once the second pillar of the economy in the north-west. The authorities are now confronted with the problem of decontaminating old spoil tips (*terrils*) and mine workings and trying to turn them into something attractive to tourists.

Understandably, the area of Lille has become a centre for industrial archaeology and for a new kind of tourism: visiting disused factories. There are some 240 *terrils* in the Nord-Pas de Calais: some are now covered with bushes or trees (they have unusual flora and fauna), but they are still a scar on the landscape. A *terril* at Nœux-les-Mines has been turned into a ski slope. The temperature at the heart of the largest *terril* can reach 1000°C, and 50°C on the surface, an ideal environment for tropical flowers.

The mines of Anzin close to the city of Valenciennes and alongside the Scheldt, or Escaut as it is called in France, provided the background for Emile Zola's novel *Germinal* (1885) in which he revealed to the world the desperate lives of the miners in their settlements or *corons*. In February 1884 Zola arrived at Anzin at the start of a violent strike against the Compagnie d'Anzin that lasted for 56 days. He was accompanied by a socialist member of parliament, went underground and saw for himself what was happening. He also researched records of earlier court cases involving trade unions and workers and visited miners' houses. Zola had already planned his novel before he went, but incorporated his own impressions of Anzin. It is still a shocking novel, but it had little political impact at the time. The word Germinal became a rallying cry for the workers as well as the name adopted by several Belgian football teams.

Dunkirk and the Pirates

Dunkirk or Duinkerken (meaning "church in the dunes") started out as a fishing village, a creek protected by dunes. In 1170 it received its first charter from the Count of Flanders, Baldwin III, who built fortifications. The town stands on a branch of the River Aa, the natural frontier between Flanders and France and is well protected by the dunes and the dikes built by man. The port of Gravelines, or Grevelingen in Dutch, was founded by Thierry of Alsace, Count of Flanders in 1160, but when the Aa silted up, Dunkirk became the main port of the region. Dunkirk now lies just outside the Flemish area and has its own patois, a mixture of Flemish and Picard French.

Louis XIV bought Dunkirk from Charles II of England 1662, even though the town theoretically already belonged to him. He then had it made into an impregnable fortress by the legendary military engineer Vauban (1633-1707). It became the base for the state-sponsored pirate, Jan Baert (Jean Bart in French) and others corsairs, who used their knowledge of the local sandbanks and shallow-draft vessels to capture English and Spanish shipping, with the protection of the French navy. The pirates were national heroes to the French, much as was Sir Francis Drake to the English. This golden age only lasted until 1713, when the British demanded that the fortifications be dismantled under the terms of the Treaty of Utrecht, which ended the War of the Spanish Succession, and Dunkirk had to go back to fishing and smuggling. Towards the end of the nineteenth century it became a major port again, but after surviving the First World War almost unscathed, it was completely destroyed in the Second World War—with the exception of the Town Hall and Belfry, and the statue of Jean Bart.

Dunkirk became a legend, thanks to the successful evacuation of 330,000 British and other Allied soldiers, but the town did not survive. From 26 May to 4 June 1940 an event took place that was described as a miracle of deliverance. The Allied expeditionary forces were sitting ducks waiting to be wiped out by the advancing Germans, but most of them escaped. Winston Churchill had warned the British that only 20,000 to 30,000 troops could be saved and yet over 330,000 were evacuated. All kinds of available British craft, some manned by civilians, were involved in a rescue mission launched across the Channel from British ports. Poet laureate John Masefield said of the evacuation: "Hope and Help are stronger things than death. Hope and Help came together in their power into the minds of thousands of simple men, and plucked them from ruin."

The Allies may have been spared by Hitler's tactics, since he inexplicably stopped his Panzers and armoured divisions from pressing home the attack and rather left it to the Luftwaffe to finish the job. In any case, the Allies were spread out along the beaches all the way from Nieuwpoort in Belgium to Gravelines. The Germans, for their part, lost as many casualties as the Allies in the battle for Dunkirk. Dunkirk is now a heavily industrialized city, with only a remnant of the charm that it surely once had. There is a fine maritime museum. Carnivals and even cross-dressing on Mardi Gras also have their enthusiastic supporters. The female impersonators of Dunkirk wear more respectable costumes than their counterparts in Aalst in Belgium and their giants are rather more *soigné* than the Belgian equivalents.

The great playwright, Michiel de Swaen, was born in Dunkirk in 1654 and died there in 1707. He was both a surgeon and the leading writer of French Flanders of his age, producing much of his work in his local Flemish dialect. He wrote some half-dozen dramas on the model of the classical French theatre, but the subject matter was taken from Flemish themes. His last and most important play, *L'abdication de Charles-Quint* deals with the abdication of Charles V, who was more popular in French than in Belgian Flanders. De Swaen's comic play, *La botte couronnée* (translated as *The Boot beneath the Crown* in 1960), develops a popular Flemish story about Charles V and is the best comedy in Flemish literature from the seventeenth century, remaining popular for many years in Flanders, Holland and South Africa. De Swaen represents the end of an era in Flemish literature, which remained somnolent until Belgium gained its independence in 1830. There has never been another Flemish writer in France of his stature since.

Inland from Dunkirk are the Moëres (Dutch: Moeren), an area originally full of peat. After the peat had been extracted in the twelfth century, the resulting depression flooded and had to be reclaimed by digging canals and building a ring of earth around it. The area is much the same as the polders of Belgian Flanders. The defences are organized by a committee known as Wateringues, similar to those over the border in Belgium; the ditches are known as *watergangs*.

Monts de Flandre

The three hills along the border with Flanders, Mont des Cats, Mont Noir and Mont de Cassel, as well as the Kemmelberg in Flanders itself, mark a natural line that is clearly visible as one travels on the Eurostar from Calais towards Lille. The hills are known locally as Houtland or Woodlands. The tallest, the Mont de Cassel or Kasselberg at 580 feet, is a natural military strongpoint that has often been fought over since prehistoric times. The hill takes its name from the Roman Castellum Menapiorum, meaning the "fortress of the Menapii" after the Celtic tribe who occupied it at the time. Local legend has it that there was once a giant who was carrying a pile of earth and dropped it here at Cassel.

The Cassel carnival on Easter Monday gives pride of place to Reuze Papa (Father Giant), born in 1827 and Reuze Maman (Mother Giant), born in 1860. With its elevated position, old town gates and a fine square, Cassel is one of the most attractive places in the region. The highest point is decorated with an ancient windmill, whose steps are granite boulders from the sea. The Café aux Trois Moulins and 't Kasteelhof, two traditional *estaminets* or local cafés, preserve a real Flemish atmosphere.

Cassel has seen three major battles. The first, in 1071, saw Robert the Frisian defeat the Count of Flanders, Arnulf III, who had the support of the French. In 1323 the West Flemish revolted against the Count of Flanders, Louis of Nevers, and the French over excessive taxation and were finally defeated at Cassel in 1328, after they rashly charged down the hill to attack the French army. The leader of the Flemish army, Nicolaas Zannekin, took on the status of a legendary Flemish patriot after he died in battle here. The third battle of Cassel, in 1677, saw Louis XIV defeat a combined army of Dutch, Austrian, Spanish, German and Danish troops, and resulted in the annexation of a large part of Flemish territory by France. From October 1914 to June 1915, the French commander, Maréchal Foch had his headquarters in Cassel, and "spent the most anxious days of my life" here. Many of Cassel's historic buildings are still pockmarked by bullet holes and are in need of renovation. The Renaissance Hôtel de la Noble Cour or 't Landshuys contains the main historical museum for French Flanders. Also on the Grand'Place is the Gothic Church of the Virgin, which was built between the eleventh and sixteenth centuries.

The West Flemish poet, Guido Gezelle, took a keen interest in the language of French Flanders. He dedicated one of his poems, "Casselkoeien", to the cows of Mont de Cassel:

> in their brown splendour, the cows of Cassel
> bloom like so many flowers,
> in the grass and in sun which, as it drowns,
> pours red sparks all over the red field.

Marguerite Yourcenar

The first woman to be elected a member of the prestigious Académie Française had her roots in Flanders. Her real name was Marguerite Cleenewerck de Crayencour (Yourcenar is an anagram of Crayencour). She was born in Brussels of a Belgian mother and a French father, who had a château in Saint-Jans-Cappel on top of the Mont Noir, a stone's throw from the Belgian border. Yourcenar (1903-87) writes of her happy childhood, her pet donkey and a goat with gold-painted horns. Her father had to sell the house in 1912 to pay off debts and it was completely destroyed in the First World War. There is now a centre for writers in the rebuilt Villa Mont-Noir and offices belonging to the Conseil Régional as well as a park. Visitors are allowed to walk around the park but there is no access to the building itself. There is, however, a small museum in Saint-Jans-Cappel with items relating to Yourcenar.

The Mont Noir is French on one side and Belgian on the other, but the origins of its name, "the black hill", are not immediately apparent. The hill, it seems, was originally covered with pine trees, but these were all blown away in the First World War and replaced by lighter coloured species, hence its rather un-black appearance. The hills are covered with wild purple hyacinths or *jacinthes* in spring.

Marguerite Yourcenar returned to Flanders, figuratively speaking, during the last ten years of her life. In books such as *Souvenirs pieux* (1974), *Archives du Nord* (1977) and *Quoi? L'Eternité* (1988), which are essentially about her father, she creates her own mystical version of the region, revealing that this was where she learned to appreciate the beauty of the natural world. During this latter period of her life she wanted to buy the Mont Noir to turn it into a nature reserve.

The third main hill is the Mont des Cats or Katsberg, with a vast Cistercian abbey on its peak where Paeterskaes (Monks' Cheese) is made. This is a major pilgrimage site in the summer and is surrounded by a nature reserve planted with trees. This area fell within the Canadian sector in the First World War and there are many monuments to the French-speaking Canadian troops who had their headquarters here. The hill has nothing feline about it, but is named after a Germanic tribe called Katts.

Lille and Tourcoing

The Dutch name for Lille is "Rijsel", which derives from the Dutch *ter IJsel*, meaning "on the island"—more or less the same as the French *l'Isle* or Lille. The first known settlement was a castle built on an island in the middle of the River Deûle by Count Baldwin V of Flanders around 1050 and the name L'Isle first appears in a charter given in 1066. Lille shared the same history as the rest of Flanders until it was captured from the Spanish by Louis XIV in 1668. The Lillois were not Flemish-speakers but rather spoke the French dialect of Picardie. Lille became a major textile city with the industrial revolution from the 1840s and suffered all the social ills of industrialization. This was the hometown of Charles de Gaulle, the French President and leader during the Second World War. He was born in 1890 at 9 Rue Princesse and spent much of his youth in the city. At the age of 16 he won a literary competition for a short play, *Une mauvaise rencontre* (Unfortunate Meeting) and retained his interest in writing all his life, while following his career of professional soldier and politician.

The area of Lille is the largest urbanized region of France and has the highest unemployment in the country. It has also become a large student centre. The city had the idea of bidding for the Olympic Games in 2004, but was instead made European City of Culture that year. The formerly grim inner-city districts were cleaned up and beautified.

The northern Lille suburb of Tourcoing borders onto Belgium. This was the home town of one of France's most respected comedians, Raymond Devos (1922-2006), who was born in Moeskroen, just inside Belgium at his parents' holiday home but rapidly returned to Tourcoing. A multi-talented musician and mime artist, he was highly regarded for his mastery of French wordplay, which was so fast that few foreigners would understand it. He typically invented absurd situations on the basis of ambiguities in French: thus a *sac à main*, or handbag, became a bag full of hands, *un sac à mains*. He also acted in films, including Jean-Luc Godard's film *Pierrot le Fou* (1965).

People from Tourcoing are known as *broutteux*, referring to the wheelbarrows (*brouettes*) that were formerly used in the wool industry (wool still survives as a major economic activity). They were also once renowned for their role as smugglers, and since the French-Belgian border runs right through the streets, before 1956 and the creation of the European Community one had only to buy something from the other side of the street to be a smuggler. Raymond Devos (the name is Flemish) called himself a *ch'timi*—a term for miners from the north who have their particular language, *le ch'ti*—a type of patois based on Picard, a northern French language that derived from Vulgar Latin at the end of the first millennium AD. The word *ch'ti* or *ch'timi* was invented during the First World War by French troops who were not from the North and who called their comrades from the Nord-Pas-de-Calais *ch'ti* or *ch'timi* after the Picard expression *ch'est ti, ch'est mi* (in French: *c'est toi, c'est moi*, "it's you, it's me").

Picard has also been spoken in parts of southern Belgium, although it is dying out rapidly. The adventures of the ageless boy detective Tintin, however, are translated into Picard, presumably because the publishers of the Tintin series, Casterman, are based in the Picard-speaking town of Tournai in Belgium. The term *ch'ti* has strong connotations of solidarity among traditional mining communities, and it is perhaps no coincidence that the people of Nord-Pas-de-Calais are reputed for their friendliness and lack of pretension.

Further Reading

Abicht, Ludo *et al, Hoe Vlaams zijn de Vlamingen?* Leuven: Davidsfonds, 2000.

Alphabet des lettres belges de langue française. Brussels: Association pour la Promotion des Lettres belges de langue française, 1982.

Arot, Dominique, *Sur les pas des écrivains à Lille.* Louvain-la-Neuve: Octogone, 2005.

Barnard, Benno *et al, How Can One Not Be Interested in Belgian History?: Language and Consensus in Belgium since 1830.* Ghent: Academia Press, 2005.

Beaufils, Thomas, *La Flandre: Anvers, Gand, Bruges.* Paris: Editions Autrement, 2003.

Beaussant, Philippe, *Marguerite Yourcenar, une enfance en Flandre.* Paris: Desclée de Brouwer, 2002.

Becks-Malorny, Ulrike, *James Ensor.* London: Taschen, 1999.

Berten, Jo, *Brugge en de franstalige letterkunde.* Brugge: Centrum voor culturele vorming, 1998.

Blyth, Derek, *Belgium: Blue Guide.* New York: WW Norton, 2000.

Blyth, Derek, *Brussels for Pleasure.* London: Pallas Athene, 2003.

Blyth, Derek, *Flemish Cities Explored.* 4th ed. London: Pallas Athene, 1999.

Bodart, Roger; Galle, Marc; Stuiveling, Garmt, *Guide littéraire de la Belgique, de la Hollande, et du Luxembourg.* Paris: Hachette, 1972.

Bollen, André et al. (ed.), *Flanders: A Well-kept Secret.* Antwerp: Pandora, 2000.

Bonneure, Fernand, *Literaire gids voor West-Vlaanderen.* Schoten: Hadewijch, 1985.

Borré, Jos & Van Hoof, Guy, *Literaire gids voor provincie en stad Antwerpen.* Schoten: Hadewijch, 1985.

Bourgeois, Pierre & Fernand Verhesen (ed.), *A Quarter Century of Poetry from Belgium.* Brussels: A. Manteau, 1970.

Brown, Carol (ed.), *James Ensor 1860-1949: Theatre of Masks.* London: Barbican Art Gallery, 1997.

Bruges and Europe. Antwerp: Mercator Fonds, 1992.

Burema, Alma, *Pioniers van het Vlaams expressionisme.* Groningen: Groninger Museum, 2004.

Carson, Patricia, *The Fair Face of Flanders.* Tielt: Lannoo, 1995.

Carson, Patricia, *Fascinating Flanders.* Tielt: Lannoo, 2003.

Carson, Patricia, *Flanders in Creative Contrasts.* rev.ed. Tielt: Lannoo, 1991.

Carson, Patricia & Danhieux, Gaby, *Ghent: A Town For All Seasons.* Ghent: Story-Scientia, 1972.

Carson, Patricia, *James Van Artevelde: The Man from Ghent.* Ghent: Story-Scientia, 1980.

Clough, S. B., *A History of the Flemish Movement.* New York: Richard R. Smith, 1930.

Conway, Martin, *Collaboration in Belgium: Léon Degrelle and the Rexist Movement.* New Haven & London: Yale University Press, 1993.

Conway, Martin and Buchanan, Tom, *Political Catholicism in Europe.* Oxford: Clarendon Press, 1996.

Cox, Marina *et al, Baraques à frites = Fritkot.* Louvain-la-Neuve: Octogone, 2002.

Crane, Nicholas, *Mercator: The Man who Mapped the Planet.* London: Weidenfeld & Nicolson, 2002.

Cuypers, Peter, *Flanders.* Tielt: Lannoo, 1988.

Daane, Marco & Wieneke 't Hoen, *U schijnt de stad niet goed te kennen?* Amsterdam: Bas Lubberhuizen, 2002.

de Coster, Charles, *Flemish Legends.* Whitefish, Montana: Kessinger Publishing, 2003.

De Coster, Marc, *Le parc naturel Campine et pays de Meuse.* Louvain-la-Neuve: Octogone, 2003.

De Lattin, Amand, *Sinjorenstad.* Hasselt: Heideland, 1961.

Delmelle, Joseph, *Abbayes et béguinages de Belgique.* Brussels: Rossel Edition, 1973.

Delmelle, Joseph, *Guide du folklore permanent en Belgique.* Brussels: Rossel Edition, 1974.

de Sainte-Hilaire, Paul, *Brugge: De tempel en de graal.* Brussels: Sympomed-Edimed, 1993.

De Vos, Luc, *Le guide des champs de bataille de Belgique et du Grand-Duché de Luxembourg.* Louvain-la-Neuve: Octogone, 1994.

de Vries, André, *Brussels: A Cultural and Literary History.* Oxford: Signal Books, 2003.

Deprez, Ada, *Literaire gids voor Oost-Vlaanderen.* Schoten: Hadewijch, 1987.

Deprez, Kas, *Language and Intergroup Relations in Flanders and the Netherlands.*

Dordrecht, Providence: Foris Publications, 1989.

Deprez, Kas, *Nationalism in Belgium: Shifting Identities, 1780-1995.* London: Macmillan, 1998.

Dewilde, Bart, *Flax in Flanders throughout the Centuries.* Tielt: Lannoo, 1987.

Dictionnaire de la peinture flamande et hollandaise. Larousse: Paris, 1989.

Dieckhoff, Alain (ed.), *Belgique: la force de la désunion.* Brussels: Editions Complexe, 1996.

Dobbelaere, Karel, *Belge toujours: fidélité, stabilité, tolérance: les valeurs des Belges en l'an 2000.* Brussels: De Boeck université, 2001.

Donaldson, Bruce, *Dutch: A Linguistic History of Holland & Belgium.* Leiden: Martinus Nijhoff, 1983.

Dumont, Georges-Henri, *Belgique, des maisons et des hommes.* Brussels: Nouvelles Editions Vokaer, 1980.

Dumont, Georges-Henri, *Histoire de la Belgique.* Brussels: Le Cri, 1999.

Dusausoit, Yvan, *James Ensor à la lumière d'Ostende.* Brussels: Bernard Gilson, 1999.

Dusausoit, Yvan, *La mer du Nord du Zoute à la Panne.* Brussels: Bernard Gilson, 1997.

Dusausoit, Yvan, *Sur les pas des écrivains de la Mer du Nord.* Louvain-la-Neuve: Octogone, 2000.

Eskens, Erno, *Filosofische reisgids voor Nederland en Vlaanderen.* Amsterdam: Uitgeverij Contact, 2000.

Etienne, Stéphan, *Le guide des pélérinages de Belgique.* Louvain-la-Neuve: Octogone, 1994.

Fairclough, Oliver *et al, Art in Exile: Flanders, Wales and the First World War.* Cardiff: National Museums & Galleries of Wales, 2002.

Fitzmaurice, John, *The Politics of Belgium.* London: Hurst, 1995.

Friedman, Donald, *The Symbolist Dead City: A Landscape of Poesis.* New York: Garland, 1990.

Goddard, Stephen H., *An Eye on Flanders : the Graphic Art of Jules de Bruycker.* Lawrence, KS: University of Kansas, Spencer Museum of Art, 1996.

Goffin, Joël, *Sur les pas des écrivains à Bruxelles.* Louvain-la-Neuve: Octogone, 1998.

Goffin, Joël, *Sur les pas des écrivains de Bruges à Damme.* Louvain-la-Neuve: Octogone, 1999.

Goffin, Joël & Lacroix, Jean, *Sur les pas des écrivains de Brabant.* Louvain-la-Neuve: Octogone, 2000.

Goris, Jan A., *Belgian Letters*. 3rd Ed. New York: Belgian Government Information Center, 1950.

Gruyaert, Harry and Claus, Hugo, *Made in Belgium*. Paris: Delpire, 2000.

Guicciardini, Lodovico, *Description of the Low Countreys*. [1593] Norwood NJ: Walter J. Johnson, 1975.

Haesaerts, Paul, *James Ensor*. London: Thames & Hudson, 1959.

Haesaerts, Paul, *Laethem-Saint-Martin: Le village élu de l'art flamand*. Brussels: Arcade, 1965.

Harline, Craig, *Miracles at the Jesus Oak*. New York: Doubleday, 2003.

Hayton, Susan, *Flanders: An Industrial Archaeology Site Guide*. Orpington: Daniel H. W. Hayton, 1998.

Hill, Richard, *The Art of Being Belgian*. Brussels: Europublications, 2005.

Holt, Tonie, *Major & Mrs Holt's Battlefield Guide to the Ypres Salient*. London: Leo Cooper, 1997.

Hooghe, Liesbet, *A Leap in the Dark: Nationalist Conflict and Federal Reform in Belgium*. Ithaca NY: Cornell University Press, 1991.

Hoozee, Robert *et al*, *Impressionism to Symbolism: the Belgian Avant-Garde 1880-1900*. London: Royal Academy of Arts, 1994.

Hoozee, Robert (ed.), *Moderne kunst in België, 1900-1945*. Antwerp: Mercatorfonds, 1992.

Ilegems, Paul, *De Frietkotcultuur*. Antwerp: Loempia, 1993.

Ilegems, Paul, *Frietgeheimen*. Antwerp: Artus, 2005.

Ilegems, Paul, *Het volkomen frietboek, een Belgische cultuurgeschiedenis*. Antwerp, Amsterdam: Nijgh & Van Ditmar, 2002.

Keegan, John, *The First World War*. London: Pimlico, 2002.

Keyes, Roger, *Outrageous Fortune: The Tragedy of Leopold III of the Belgians*. London: Secker & Warburg, 1984.

Kossmann, E. H., *The Low Countries*. Oxford: Clarendon Press, 1986.

Labio, Catherine (ed.), *Belgian Memories*. New Haven: Yale University Press, 2002.

Lauryssens, Stan, *Mijn heerlijke nieuwe wereld: leven en liefdes van Maria Nys Huxley*. Leuven: Uitgeverij Van Halewyck, 2001.

Lee, Phil, *Bruges Directions*. London: Rough Guide, 2005.

Les Flandres dans les mouvements romantiques et symbolistes. Paris: Didier, 1958.

Liebaers, Herman *et al*, *Flemish Art from the Beginning till Now*. Antwerp: Mercatorfonds, 1985.

Lilar, Suzanne, *Belgian Theater since 1890*. New York: Belgian Government Information Center, 1950.

Lissens, R. F., *De Vlaamse letterkunde*. Brussels: Elsevier, 1967.

Macdonald, Lyn, *They Called it Passchendaele*. London: Penguin, 1993.

McDonnell, Ernest W., *The Beguines and Beghards in Medieval Culture with Special Emphasis on the Belgian Scene*. New York: Octagon Books, 1969.

Maes, Paul, *De laatste restjes groen*. Zellik: Globe, 1995.

Mallinson, Vernon, *Modern Belgian Literature: 1830 to 1960*. London: Heinemann, 1966.

Mallinson, Vernon, *Power and Politics in Belgian Education, 1815 to 1961*. London: Heinemann, 1963.

Mason, Antony, *Brussels, Bruges, Ghent, Antwerp*. London: Cadogan Guides, 1995.

Messiant, Jacques, *La cuisine flamande traditionnelle*. Morbecque: SA Presse Flamande, 1998.

Mierlo, J. van, *Beknopte geschiedenis van de oud- en middel-nederlandsche letterkunde*. Antwerp: N.V. Standaard-Boekhandel, 1946.

Mommaers, Paul, *Hadewijch: Writer, Beguine, Love Mystic*. Leuven: Peeters, 2004.

Morelli, Anne (ed.), *Les grands mythes de l'histoire de Belgique, de Flandre et de Wallonie*. Brussels: Editions Vie Ouvrière, 1995.

Muylaert, Willy, *Guido Gezelle en Brugge*. Brugge: Koninklijke Gidsenbond, 1980.

Naegels, Tom, *Wandelgids Antwerpen boekenstad*. Tielt: Lannoo, 2004.

Neirinckx, Hugo, *Literaire gids voor Brabant en Brussel*. Schoten: Hadewijch, 1986.

Nieuwe Encyclopedie van de Vlaamse Beweging. Tielt: Lannoo, 1998.

Pavy, Didier, *Les Belges*. Paris: Grasset, 1999.

Pearson, Harry, *A Tall Man in a Low Country: Some Time among the Belgians*. London: Abacus, 1999.

Peeters, Frank, "The 'Flemish Wave': Cultural Auto-affirmation in the Low Countries", in C. Schumacher (ed.), *Small is Beautiful: Small Countries Theatre Conference*. Glasgow: Theatre Studies Publications, 1991.

Pickels, Antoine and Sjocher, Jacques (eds.), *Belgique toujours grande et belle*. Brussels: Editions Complexe, 1998.

Pradt, Abbé Dominique de, *De la Belgique de 1784 à 1794*. Brussels: Chez Lecharlier, 1820.

Puttemans, Pierre and Hervé, Lucien, *Modern Architecture in Belgium*. Brussels: Vokaer, 1976.

Quaghebeur, Marc, *Balises pour l'histoire des lettres belges.* Brussels: Labor, 1998.

Quaghebeur, Marc, *Lettres belges entre absence et magie.* Brussels: Labor, 1990.

Rajotte, Pierre, *Belgian Ale.* Boulder CO: Brewers Publications, 1992.

Reynebeau, Marc, *Het klauwen van de leeuw. De Vlaamse identiteit van de 12de tot de 21ste eeuw.* Leuven: Uitgeverij Van Halewijck, 1995.

Ruys, Manu, *De Vlamingen.* Tielt: Lannoo, 1972.

Scholliers, Peter, *Arm en rijk aan tafel: twee honderd jaar eetcultuur in België.* Berchem: EPO, 1993.

Septentrion (series). Rekkem: Stichting Ons Erfdeel, 1972- .

Slosse, Peter, *Wegwijs in Ieper.* Bruges: Uitgeverij Marc Van de Wiele, 1987.

Smeyers, Maurits and Van der Stock, Jan (eds.), *Flemish Illuminated Manuscripts 1475-1550.* Ghent: Ludion, 1996.

Stabel, Peter, *Dwarfs among Giants: the Flemish Urban Network in the Late Middle Ages.* Leuven: Garant, 1997.

Stechow, Wolfgang, *Pieter Bruegel the Elder.* London: Thames & Hudson, 1970.

Strikwerda, Carl, *A House Divided: Catholics, Socialists and Flemish Nationalists in Nineteenth-Century Belgium.* Oxford: Rowman & Littlefield, 1977.

The Low Countries (series). Rekkem: Stichting Ons Erfdeel, 1993-.

Uyttendaele, Marc (ed.), *De la Belgique unitaire à l'Etat fédéral.* Brussels: Bruylant, 1996.

Uytterhoeven, Michel (ed.), *Pigment: Current Trends in the Performing Arts in Flanders.* Ghent-Amsterdam: Ludion, 2003.

Vanacker, Daniël, *Het aktivistisch avontuur.* Ghent: Stichting Mens en Kultuur, 1991.

Vandeputte, O., Vincent, P. and Hermans, T., *Dutch, the Language of Twenty Million Dutch and Flemish people.* [1981] Rekkem: Flemish-Netherlands Foundation, 2005.

Vandorselaer, Thibaut, *Bruges and Damme through Comic Strips.* Louvain-la-Neuve: Versant Sud, 2005.

Vandorselaer, Thibaut, *Brussels through Comic Strips.* Louvain-la-Neuve: Versant Sud, 2004.

Vanhecke, Leo, *Landschappen in Vlaanderen vroeger en nu.* Brussels: Nationale Plantentuin van België, 1981.

Van Istendael, Geert, *Het Belgisch labyrint: wakker worden in een ander land.* Amsterdam, Antwerpen: Arbeiderspers, 2001.

Vanheste, Bert, *De baan op met Boon.* Antwerp & Amsterdam: De

Arbeiderspers, 2004.

Vanheste, Bart, *De stad is woord geworden*. Amsterdam: Meulenhoff, 2002.

van Nuis, Hermine, *Guido Gezelle: Flemish Poet-Priest*. New York: Greenwood Press, 1986.

Van Waerebeek, Ruth, *Everybody Eats Well in Belgium Cookbook*. Workman Publishing Company: New York: 1996.

Verhoeyen, Etienne, *La Belgique occupée*. Brussels: De Boeck Université, 1994.

Verhulst, Adriaan, *Histoire du paysage rural en Flandre de l'époque romaine au XVIIIe siècle*. Brussels: La Renaissance du Livre, 1966.

Verhulst, Adriaan and Stappaerts, Dirk, *Landschap en Landbouw in Middeleeuws Vlaanderen*. Brussels: Gemeentekrediet, 1995.

VIZIT, *A Bent for Ghent*. Tielt: Lannoo, 2003.

Voiturier, Michel, *L'Escaut: fleuve sans frontières*. Tournai: La Renaissance du Livre, 2001.

Voiturier, Michel, *Sur les pas des écrivains de l'Escaut*. Louvain-la-Neuve: Octogone, 1998.

Vroede, Maurits de, *The Flemish Movement*. Antwerp: Kultuurraad voor Vlaanderen, 1975.

Weisgerber, Jean, *Formes et domaines du roman flamand, 1927-1960*. Brussels: La Renaissance du Livre, 1963.

Winch, Michael, *Introducing Belgium*. London: Methuen, 1964.

Winkler Prins Encyclopedie van Vlaanderen. Sint-Stevens-Woluwe: Elsevier Sequoia, 1972-4.

Witte, Els and Van Velthoven, Harry (eds.), *Language and Politics: The Belgian Case Study in a Historical Perspective*. Brussels: VUB Press, 1999.

Witte, Els; Craeybeekx, Jan; Meynen, Alain (eds.), *The Political History of Belgium from 1830 Onwards*. Brussels: VUB Press, 2000.

Wulms, Guido, *Literaire gids voor Limburg*. Schoten: Hadewijch, 1985.

d'Ydewalle, Charles d'Outryve, *A Belgian Manor in Two Wars*. London: Macmillan, 1949.

d'Ydewalle, Charles d'Outryve, *Confession d'un Flamand*. Paris: De Meyere, 1967.

d'Ydewalle, Charles d'Outryve, *Enfances en Flandre*. Brussels: Nouvelle Société d'Éditions, 1934.

d'Ydewalle, Charles d'Outryve, *Psychologie de la Belgique*. Liège: Les Petites Etudes de Belgique, 1938.

d'Ydewalle, Charles d'Outryve, *Ma Flandre que voici*. Ostend: Erel, 1974.

Zuckerman, Larry, *The Rape of Belgium*. New York: New York University Press, 2004.

Fiction, Poetry and Drama

Boon, Louis-Paul, *Chapel Road*. Normal, Illinois: Dalkey Archive Press, 2003.

Claus, Hugo, *Desire*. Harmondsworth: Penguin, 1997.

Claus, Hugo, *Four Works for the Theater*. New York: CASTA, 1990.

Claus, Hugo, *Friday*. Amsterdam: Uitgeverij International Theatre & Film Books, 1993.

Claus, Hugo, *Greetings: Selected poems*. New York: Harcourt Inc., 2005.

Claus, Hugo, *Selected Poems 1953-1973*. Portree: Aquila Poetry, 1986.

Claus, Hugo, *The Sign of the Hamster*. Leuven: Leuvenseschrijversaktie, 1983.

Claus, Hugo, *The Sorrow of Belgium*. Woodstock NY: Overlook TP, 2003.

Claus, Hugo, *The Swordfish*. New York: Peter Owen Publishers, 1997.

de Coster, Charles, *The Legend of Ulenspiegel and Lamme Goedzak*. Whitefish, Montana: Kessinger Publishing, 2003.

De Ghelderode, Michel, *La Flandre est un songe*. Brussels: Les Editions Durendal, 1953.

De Ghelderode, Michel, *The Siege of Ostend*. Austin TX: Host Publications, 1990.

De Ghelderode, Michel, *Voyage autour de ma Flandre*. Brussels: Les éperonniers, 1988.

Elsschot, Willem, *Cheese*. London: Granta Books, 2002.

Elsschot, Willem, *Three Novels*. New York: House & Maxwell, 1965.

Friedman, Donald, *An Anthology of Belgian Symbolist Poets*. New York: Garland, 1992.

Gevers, Marie, *La comtesse des digues*. Brussels: Labor, 1983.

Gezelle, Guido, *The Evening and the Rose*. Antwerp: Guido Gezellegenootschap, 1989.

Gezelle, Guido, *That Limpid Singer*. Hull: Association for Low Countries Studies, 1999.

Gilliam, Maurice, *Elias, or the Struggle with the Nightingales*. Los Angeles: Sun and Moon Press, 1995.

Hollinghurst, Alan, *The Folding Star*. London: Chatto & Windus, 1994.

Holmes, James S. & William Jay Smith (eds.), *Dutch Interior: Postwar Poetry of the Netherlands and Flanders*. New York: Columbia University Press, 1984.

Lampo, Hubert, *The Coming of Joachim Stiller*. New York: Twayne Publishers, 1974.

Longfellow, Samuel Wadsworth, *The Belfry of Bruges and Other Poems.* Cambridge MA: J. Owen, 1846.

Lovelock, Yann, *The Line Forward: A Survey of Modern Dutch Poetry in English Translation.* n.p.: Riverrun Pr, 1984.

Moeyaert, Bart, *Bare Hands.* Asheville NC: Front Street Press, 1998.

Moeyaert, Bart, *Hornet's Nest.* Asheville NC: Front Street Press, 2000.

Moeyaert, Bart, *It's Love that We Don't Understand.* Asheville NC: Front Street Press, 2002.

Mortier, Erwin, *Marcel.* London: The Harvill Press, 2001.

Mortier, Erwin, *My Second Skin.* London: The Harvill Press, 2003.

Mortier, Erwin, *Shutter Speed.* London: The Harvill Press, 2007.

Nijmeijer, Peter. *Four Flemish Poets.* Deal: Transgravity Press, 1976.

Ray, Jean, *Ghouls in my Grave.* New York: Berkley Pub. Co., 1965.

Ray, Jean, *Malpertuis.* London: Atlas, 1998.

Rodenbach, Georges, *Bruges-la-morte.* Sawtry: Dedalus, 2005.

Roggeman, Willem M., *The Revolution Begins in Bruges.* Windsor, Ontario: Netherlandic Press, 1983.

Royle, Nicholas, *Antwerp.* London: Serpent's Tail, 2004.

Ruusbroec, John, *The Spiritual Espousals and other Works.* New York: Paulist Press, 1985.

Streuvels, Stijn, *The Flaxfield.* Los Angeles: Sun and Moon Press, 1988.

Streuvels, Stijn, *The Long Road.* Boston: Twayne Publishers, 1976.

Van Bastelaere, Dirk, *The Last to Leave.* Exeter: Shearsman Books, 2005.

Willems, Paul, *The Drowned Land.* New York: Peter Lang, 1994.

Willems, Paul, *Four Plays of Paul Willems: Dreams and Reflections.* New York: Garland, 1992.

Willinger, David, *An Anthology of Contemporary Belgian Plays, 1970-1982.* Troy NY: Whitston Publishing Company, 1984.

Willinger, David, *Theatrical Gestures from the Belgian Avant-Garde.* New York: New York Literary Forum, 1987.

Willinger, David, *Theatrical Gestures of Belgian Modernism.* New York: Peter Lang, 2002.

Yourcenar, Marguerite, *The Abyss.* London: Weidenfeld & Nicolson, 1976.

Yourcenar, Marguerite, *How Many Years.* Henley: Aidan Ellis, 1995.

Index of Literary and Historical Names

Index of Places & Landmarks